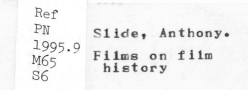

Films on Film History

by

Anthony Slide

**The Scarecrow Press, Inc.
Metuchen, N.J., & London 1979**

Also by Anthony Slide

Early American Cinema (1970)
The Griffith Actresses (1973)
The Idols of Silence (1976)
The Big V: A History of the Vitagraph Company (1976)
Early Women Directors (1977)
Aspects of American Film History Prior to 1920 (1978)

With Edward Wagenknecht

The Films of D. W. Griffith (1975)
Milestones of the Silent Film: 1912-1920 (1980)

Library of Congress Cataloging in Publication Data

Slide, Anthony.
Films on film history.

Includes index.
1. Moving-picture industry in motion pictures.
2. Moving-pictures--Catalogs. 3. Moving-pictures--Plots, themes, etc. I. Title.
PN1995.9.M65S6 016.79143'0909'3 79-17662
ISBN 0-8108-1238-X

Manufactured in the United States of America

CONTENTS

INTRODUCTION

The title of this book is self-explanatory. Films on Film History offers a complete listing of all films--features and shorts, documentaries and compilations--on the history of the cinema. This book is not intended to provide information on films on film-making, and readers are warned that they will look in vain for material on productions such as How They Filmed the Grand Prix (1971) or Plimpton! Shootout at Rio Lobo (1970). Also excluded are contemporary shorts or featurettes on the production of a specific film, even though a short such as Happy Days Are Here Again, shot by M-G-M to promote its 1934 production of The Merry Widow, may now have historical interest.

Films dealing with the history of a particular film personality, studio or genre have been included, but films in which a personality discusses a specific contemporary film, such as Polanski Meets Macbeth (1971), do not meet the criteria set down by this compiler for inclusion. Fictional film biographies--The Buster Keaton Story, W. C. Fields and Me, etc.--are included, as are features dealing with a particular period in film history, such as James Ivory's The Wild Party or The Day of the Locust.

Specifically excluded from this filmography are productions made for television and which have never been made available on 16mm. It is obvious that productions such as the recently syndicated "That's Hollywood" series from 20th Century-Fox Television, which was produced on videotape, will never find its way to the 16mm distribution field, if for no other reason than the cost of transferring videotape to film.

Films are arranged alphabetically by title, and a subject index at the back of this volume is intended to direct the reader to a film on a specific subject or period in the history of the cinema. Following the title of the film is information as to its length and the gauge in which it was produced; the gauge refers to the compilation or documentary itself, not to the films with which it deals. Detailed credits are given, wherever possible, for each production as well as a description of the content of the film, plus an occasional critical comment. Information as to the availability of the film at the time of writing completes the entry. It must, of course, be pointed out that distributors for specific films do frequently change, and, in the case of a feature-length production, readers are strongly urged to consult James Limbacher's Feature Films on 8mm and 16mm (published annually by R. R. Bowker) for the latest information on a film's availability. A list of distributors with their addresses may be found at the back of the volume.

In an effort to make this book as complete as possible, many films are listed for which there are no distributors in the United States. It is hoped that interest may be sparked in some of the more worthwhile productions currently unavailable--such as Highlight: The Singing Cinema, The House That Shadows Built or It Happened in Brighton--and that they will once again become accessible.

Aside from the films themselves, I have included entries on two men whose contributions to the field of films on film history have been tremendous: Paul Killiam and Robert Youngson.

There are, quite obviously, deficiencies in this index. I have no doubt that I have omitted some titles, and in many cases it was impossible to find adequate information as to a film's credits or content. Every effort has been made to check the titles and dates of films extracted in the various compilations, but in some instances I have had to rely on information provided in a particular distributor's catalogue, and cannot guarantee that such information was correct. This applies especially to compilations of films from the 1890s and early 1900s.

In preparing this volume, I have used many resources, and must acknowledge in particular the files of The Monthly Film Bulletin (published by the British Film Institute), James Limbacher's Feature Films on 8mm and 16mm (published by R. R. Bowker), Denis Gifford's The British Film Catalogue: 1895-1970 (published by McGraw-Hill, 1973), Leonard Maltin's The Great Movie Shorts (published by Crown, 1972), the catalogues of the various 16mm film distributors including Twyman, Swank, Macmillan, Kit Parker Films, Budget, Blackhawk, Em Gee, Reel Images, Films Incorporated, the University of Southern California Film Library, and the University of California Extension Media Center, the Margaret Herrick Library of the Academy of Motion Picture Arts and Sciences, Geoffrey Bell, John Canemaker, Murray Glass, Vernon Harbin, John Hall of RKO Radio Pictures, David Smith of the Walt Disney Studio Archives, Leonard Maltin, Robert Gitt, Emily Sieger of the Museum of Modern Art, Patricia Coward of the British Film Institute, Maryann Chach of the Educational Film Library Association, Ken Murray, William K. Everson, Patrick Montgomery and Paul Killiam of Killiam Shows, Marty Kearns of Reel Images, and John Belton.

For those interested in films covering the entire spectrum of film-making, I would refer them to two excellent checklists: Judith Trojan's "Films on Film," published in Take One (March, 1977), page 30 and Take One (May, 1977), pages 52 and 61; and John Canemaker's "Informational Films about Animation and Animators," published in Millimeter (February, 1978), pages 88-90 and 94. Although generally out-dated, Robert W. Wagner's and David L. Parker's "Films about Films and Film Making," published in Film News (February, 1965), pages 11-13 and Film News (April, 1965), pages 19-21, is still useful.

My interest in this project goes back many years. In 1966, as the honorary secretary of the long-defunct Society for Film History Research, I organized a program on "Films on Film History" at the Crescent Theatre in Birmingham, England. The day-long event included films from Britain, France and Sweden, together with two lecture-presentations by John Huntley and Liam O'Leary, both of whom were then with the British Film Institute. This present volume is far removed from the eight-page brochure which I edited for that occasion, and I hope it will prove a useful tool for film educators, librarians and all those who are interested in how the film industry has attempted to record its own history.

Anthony Slide

Los Angeles, July 1978

ALPHABETICAL LISTING OF FILMS

ABBOTT AND COSTELLO MEET THE KEYSTONE KOPS
(7,083 ft./79 mins/35mm)

U.S. Universal-International. 1954. Producer: Howard Christie. Director: Charles Lamont. Screenplay: John Grant. Based on a Story by Lee Loeb. Photography: Reggie Lanning. Art Directors: Alexander Golitzen and Bill Newberry. Film Editor: Edward Curtiss. Music Director: Joseph Gershenson. Sound: Leslie I. Carey and William Hedgecock.

With Bud Abbott (Harry Pierce), Lou Costello (Willie Piper), Fred Clark (Joseph Gorman), Lynn Bari (Leota Van Cleef), Maxie Rosenbloom (Hinds), Frank Wilcox (Mr. Snevely), Harold Goodwin (Cameraman), Mack Sennett (Himself), Roscoe Ates (Old Wagon Driver), Paul Dubov (Jason), Joe Besser (The Hunter), Harry Tyler (Piano Player), Henry Kulky (Second Brakeman), Joe Devlin (Policeman), William Haade (First Tramp), Jack Daly (Burglar), Byron Keith (First Officer), Houseley Stevens (Pilot), Murray Leonard (Studio Cop), Sam Flint (Conductor), Colin Campbell (Elderly Guard), Billy Varga (Passerby), Bob Jellison (Man), Marjorie Bennett (Stout Woman), Carl Christian (Dining Car Waiter), Charles Dorety (Watermelon Peddler), Donald Kerr (Projectionist), Heinie Conklin (Cop), Carole Costello (Cashier in Theatre), Frank Hagney (Usher), Allan Ray (Assistant Director), Forrest Burns (First Motorcycle Cop), Don House (Second Motorcycle Cop), Jack Stoney (First Brakeman), Hank Mann (Ad Lib).

A typical Abbott and Costello comedy, which might never have warranted inclusion in this volume had it been released under its original title of Abbott and Costello as the Stunt Men. The final chase sequence is in the true tradition of silent screen slapstick comedy. The opening gag of Fred Clark selling Abbott and Costello the Edison Studio is amusing, and it is a delight, albeit a brief one, to see Mack Sennett, Heinie Conklin and Hank Mann.

Availability (16mm): Universal 16/Twyman/Swank

ABEL GANCE, HIER ET DEMAIN see ABEL GANCE, YESTERDAY AND TODAY

ABEL GANCE--THE CHARM OF DYNAMITE (1,782 ft./50 mins/16mm)

G.B. Rath Films for BBC Television. 1968. Producer: Barrie Gavin. Production Manager: Johanna Suschitzky. Screenplay and Film Editor: Kevin Brownlow. Photography: Chris Menges. Narrator: Lindsay Anderson.

Kevin Brownlow's loving tribute to the great French director Abel Gance, which includes an interview with the director, rare footage of him at work, and clips from J'accuse, La Roue and Napoléon. The highspot of the production is the snowball fight from Napoléon. For more information, see The Monthly Film Bulletin (November, 1968), page 185.
Availability: Images

ABEL GANCE, YESTERDAY AND TODAY / ABEL GANCE, HIER ET DEMAIN (972 ft./27 mins/16mm)

France. Office de Documentation par le Film. 1963. Producer: Jean Ruault. Director, Screenplay and Film Editor: Nelly Kaplan. Photography: D. Harispé, Nelly Kaplan and Raymond Picon-Borel. Music: Michel Magne.

An introduction to the work of the great French pioneer director Abel Gance, with film of him at work on Napoléon, and film clips from Austerlitz, Cyrano et d'Artagnan, La Folie du Docteur Tube, J'Accuse! and La Roue, among others. For more information, see The Monthly Film Bulletin (July, 1967), page 111.
Availability: Indiana University Audio-Visual Center

ACRE OF SEATS IN A GARDEN OF DREAMS, AN (2,016 ft./ 56 mins/16mm)

G.B. 1973. Producers: Ray Ball and David Furnham. Screenplay: David Furnham. Photography: Peter C. Amsden. Film Editor: David Furnham. Sound: Ray Ball.

"This is a worthy and entertaining attempt to trace the history of the cinema building from its fairground origins to the present day," wrote David Atwell in The Monthly Film Bulletin (April, 1974). Cinema exteriors in the following English cities are shown: Leeds, Manchester, Sheffield, London, Worthing, and Brighton. The film features the following London cinemas: Astoria, Brixton; New Victoria; State, Kilburn; Grange, Kilburn; and State, Grays. Also included are interviews with Roy Hudd, Ena Baga, Don Dansie, Nat Matthews, Douglas Reeve, and John Stewart.

Availability: None

ACTRESS, THE

A 1953 fictionalized account of the life and career of Ruth Gordon, which does not deal with her film career.

ADVENTURE TO REMEMBER, AN (950 ft./11 mins/35mm)

U.S. Warner Bros. 1955. Producer and Screenplay: Robert Youngson. Film Editor: Albert Helmes. Narrator: Dwight Weist.

This short features a highly truncated version of Irvin Willat's Isle of Lost Ships (1929).

Availability: None

ALL IN GOOD FUN (4,251 ft./47 mins/35 mm)

G.B. Butcher's. 1956. Producer: Henry E. Fisher. Director and Screenplay: James M. Anderson. Music: De Wolfe. Illuminations: James M. Anderson. Lighting Cameraman: H. M. Glendining. Camera Operator: Cyril Gray. Sound: Alan Vetter. Make-Up: Gerry Fairbank.

A compilation of early film clips, all shown for their laugh value. Among silent personalities included are Max Linder, Tontolini, John Bunny, Ford Sterling, Mabel Normand, Marie Dressler, Fred Mace, Mack Sennett, the Keystone Kops, Charles Chaplin, Ruth Roland, Pearl White, and Helen Holmes. Rarer items in this compilation include scenes from Vitagraph's A Tale of Two Cities and a Lieutenant Daring drama from the early 'teens.

Availability: None

ALL-STAR CAST, AN (1 reel/11 mins/16mm)

A 1978 Blackhawk Films compilation, taken from issues of Fox Movietone News, and showing Buddy Rogers and Mary Pickford's courtship and wedding, one of Marie Dressler's birthday parties, Charles Chaplin and Paulette Goddard returning from the Orient, Ginger Rogers, Will Rogers, and Carl Laemmle.

Availability (16mm and Super 8mm): Blackhawk (sale only)

AMERICA AT THE MOVIES (166 mins/35mm)

U. S. The American Film Institute. 1976. Producer: George Stevens, Jr. Film Design: James R. Silke. Narration Written by Theodore Strauss. Associate Producer: Harrison Engle. Film Editor: David Saxon. Title Music Arranged and Conducted by Nelson Riddle. Historical Consultant: Arthur Schlesinger, Jr. Design Consultant: Ivan Chermayeff. Associate Film Editors: Joseph Parker and Ana Luisa Corley Perez. Production Assistants: Judith C. Scott, Dency Nelson and Sandra Feller Zank. Titles: Chermayeff and Geismar Associates and Wayne Fitzgerald. Narrator: Charlton Heston.

America at the Movies is described as "a feature length compilation motion picture consisting of scenes from eighty-three films which illustrate how the American character and spirit have been portrayed on the screen." Sponsored by the American Revolution Bicentennial Administration, America at the Movies contains ninety-two scenes, divided into five thematic segments: The Land, The Cities, The Families, The Wars, and The Spirit.

Availability: Cinema 5

AMERICAN FILM, THE (37 mins/16mm)

Charlton Heston narrates this 1967 documentary in which clips from High Noon, North by Northwest, Shane, Friendly Persuasion, and On the Waterfront are shown to illustrate the distinctive styles of their various directors.

Availability: Indiana University Audio-Visual Center

AMERICAN MUSICALS OF THE 1930s (38 mins/16mm)

A package of extracts from five early musicals, compiled by the Museum of Modern Art: Forty-Second Street (1933), Gold Diggers of 1933 (1933), Gold Diggers of 1935 (1935), Flying Down to Rio (1933), and Sunnyside Up (1929).

Availability: The Museum of Modern Art

AMERICAN WEST OF JOHN FORD, THE (54 mins/35mm)

U. S. Bob Banner Associates/Group One Productions. 1971. Executive Producer: Bob Banner. Producers: Tom Megan, Dan Ford and Britt Lomond. Director: Denis Sanders. Screenplay: David H. Vowell.

The Westerns of John Ford are discussed by John Wayne, James Stewart and Henry Fonda, with asides from Ford himself and clips from a number of the films, including The Iron Horse, My Darling Clementine and Stagecoach. Variety's Tone (December 6, 1971) described the production as "an informative, informal study of a man's life work." The American West of John Ford was first televised on the CBS network on December 5, 1971.

Availability: None

AMERICA'S SWEETHEART, THE MARY PICKFORD STORY (78 mins/35mm)

U.S./G.B. The Mary Pickford Company and Polytel Film Ltd. 1978. Producers: Matty Kemp and Michael Small. Director and Screenplay: John Edwards. Story and Research: Matty Kemp. Music Composed and Arranged by David Fanshawe. Conductor: Owain Arwel Hughes. Vocals: Nick Curtis. Film Editor: Al Gell. Assistant Film Editor: Michael Bateman. Title Design: Nick Sop. Sound Mixer: Ted Ryan. Music Editor: Peter Oliff. Photography: Irv Goodnuff. Assistant Photography: Jacques Haitkin. Producer Manager: Jim Gates. Narrator: Henry Fonda. Commentary Highlights by Mary Pickford. Special Commentary by Gene Kelly, Charles "Buddy" Rogers, Lord Lewis Mountbatten, Yvonne Vallée (the former Mrs. Maurice Chevalier), and Galina Kravtchenko (recorded in the U.S.S.R.)

A feature-length documentary on the life and career of Mary Pickford, including commentary by her friends and occasionally by the actress herself. The film contains clips from a number of Pickford features, including Rebecca of Sunnybrook Farm, Tess of the Storm Country, Little Lord Fauntleroy, and Daddy-Long-Legs, together with newsreel footage, and shots of Pickfair. "This is a work of adulation with little social awareness," commented Morna Murphy in The Hollywood Reporter (March 24, 1978).

Availability: Mary Pickford Company

ANATOMY OF A MOVIE see HOLLYWOOD AND THE STARS

THE ANGRY SCREEN see HOLLYWOOD AND THE STARS

ANIMATED CARTOONS: THE TOY THAT GREW UP (17 mins/16mm)

The first part, with English commentary, of the fine French documentary on pre- and early cinema, Naissance du Cinema (q. v.). This particular short concentrates on the development of the animated film in general and Emile Reynaud's Praxinoscope in particular. For more information, see Film News (September-October, 1947), page 9.

Availability: Radim (rental)/Thunderbird (sale)/Em Gee (rental)

ANIMATION # 1 (1 reel/16mm)

A compilation of examples of the works of three lesser-known animators: Marius Rossilon's Evils of Alcohol (1912), Willie Hopkin's Swat the Fly (circa 1925) and Willis O'Brien's Morpheus Mike (1916)

Availability: Em Gee

ANIMATION # 2 (1 reel/16mm)

A compilation of four early animated shorts, including a Bray cartoon and J. Stuart Blackton's The Enchanted Drawing.

Availability: Em Gee

ANIMATION: THE BEGINNING

A fifty-minute compilation of American and European animated shorts, produced between 1908 and 1922, and including subjects by Emile Cohl, Winsor McCay's Gertie the Dinosaur, Starevich's Revenge of the Kinematograph Cameraman, various Krazy Kat subjects, Winsor McCay's The Sinking of the Lusitania, Max Fleischer's Modeling, and Disney's Puss in Boots.

Availability (16mm): Budget/Cinema Eight (sale only)

ANNEES LUMIERE, LES--1895-1900 see LUMIERE YEARS, THE

ANTHOLOGY OF ITALIAN CINEMA, 1896-1943/ANTOLOGIA DEL CINEMA ITALIANO (Part One: 152 mins and Part Two: 189 mins/16mm)

Italy. Il Centro Sperimentale di Cinematografia. Produced in Collaboration with the Cineteca Nazionale and the Cineteca Italiana. Compiler: Domenico de Gregorio.

A survey of the Italian cinema, illustrating all the important milestones in the history of film-making in Italy. Part One, devoted to the silent era, includes extracts from Cabiria (1913) and Messalina (1923), among others. Sound films from 1929 to 1943 are covered by Part Two, which includes sequences from Nerone (1930), 1860 (1933), Cavalleria (1936), Luciano Serra, pilota (1938), and Teresa Venerdi (1941). The extracts are not subtitled, and there are apparently errors in the narration, which is in English.

Availability: The Museum of Modern Art (The British Film Institute distributes a four-part version of this anthology in England)

ANTOLOGIA DEL CINEMA ITALIANO see ANTHOLOGY OF ITALIAN CINEMA, 1896-1943

ARCHAEOLOGY OF THE CINEMA (30 mins/16mm)

A 1963 production which begins with the Javanese "Shadow Plays," and traces the pre-history of the cinema and the work of the early film pioneers, such as Muybridge,

Méliès, Edison, Porter, and D. W. Griffith. It closes with clips from the films of Charlie Chaplin and William S. Hart.

Availability: Cinema Eight (16mm and 8mm sale)/Radim/Em Gee/Reel Images (sale)

ART DIRECTOR, THE see LET'S GO TO THE MOVIES

ART OF LOTTE REINIGER, THE (16 mins/16mm)

G.B. Primrose Productions. 1970. Producer: Louis Hagen. Director: John Isaacs.

A study of Lotte Reiniger at work on the production of her silhouette films, using a technique she has utilized since 1919. The Art of Lotte Reiniger also includes stills from various of her shorts, together with film clips from Papageno, The Star of Bethlehem and The Adventures of Prince Achmed.

Availability: Macmillan

ART OF THE FILM, THE (Each Part: 22 mins/16mm)

U.S. A William Becker-Saul J. Turell Presentation for Janus Films. 1977. Producers, Directors and Screenplay: Saul J. Turell and Jeff Lieberman. Film Editor: Wendy Greene Bricmont. Technical Director: Robert Schmidt. Research: Steven Greenberg, Peter Cowie and Frances Morris. Graphic Background from Jordan Belson's Allures. Study Guide Materials Prepared and Written by Steven Greenberg. Narrator: Rod Serling.

A series on the various aspects of film-making, with each part featuring a selection of film clips as follows: Volume One: Screenwriting (Oliver Twist, Metropolis, The 400 Blows, Pygmalion, and Caesar and Cleopatra). Volume Two: The Camera (Beauty and the Beast, Two English Girls, The Rocking Horse Winner, The Lady Vanishes, The Most Dangerous Game, The Silence, and Shadows of Forgotten Ancestors). Volume Three: Performance (Richard III, Summertime, The Gold Rush, and La Strada). Volume Four: Music and Sound (Wild Strawberries, Alexander Nevsky, Dodes'ka-den, M, Dead of Night, and Valerie). Volume Five: The Edited Image (Battleship Potemkin, Saraband, Olympia, Le Bonheur, Metropolis, Evergreen, and Citizen Kane). Vol-

ume Six: The Director (*The Lady Vanishes*, *The 39 Steps*, *Two English Girls*, *Jules and Jim*, *Shoot the Piano Player*, *Rashomon*, *Dodes'ka-den*, *Winter Light*, *The Seventh Seal*, *The Magician*, and *All These Women*). For teaching purposes a study guide is also available with each unit.
Availability: Janus (rental)/Perspective (sale)

ARTHUR AND LILLIE (1,055 ft./29 mins/16mm)

U.S. Stanford University, Department of Communication. 1975. Producers: Jon Else, Steven Kovacs and Kristine Samuelson. Supervisor: Henry Breitrose. Production Supported by the National Endowment for the Arts.

Produced by three former students of Arthur Mayer, this affectionate documentary recounts the life of a pioneer distributor, exhibitor and publicist who has now become one of this country's most popular film professors. Mr. and Mrs. Mayer are seen at home, in the classroom, and talking with film critic Pauline Kael. Arthur Knight wrote, in *The Hollywood Reporter* (November 14, 1975), "What one gets from the film is the sense of two lives that have remained marvellously open--open to fresh ideas, open to new experiences, reaching out to new friends, and the younger the better. Above all, there is the realization that while the body may age, the mind need not stagnate along with it." *Arthur and Lillie* was nominated for the 49th Academy Award for Best Documentary Short Subject.
Availability: Pyramid Films (rental and sale)

ARTHUR PENN (1922-): THEMES AND VARIANTS (86 mins/35mm)

U.S. A Robert P.S.B. Hughes Production. Sponsored by National Educational Television, Canadian Broadcasting System and British Broadcasting Corporation. 1970. Producer and Director: Robert P.S.B. Hughes. Associate Producers: Bernard Stone and Jeffrey Eger. Photography: Paul Goldsmith and Robert Fiore. Film Editor: Bernard Stone. Sound: Peter Hildal and Bruce Rubin.

A study of director Arthur Penn at work and at home with his family. Penn's career is also dealt with through the medium of interviews with various of his actors, including Warren Beatty, Dustin Hoffman, Paul Newman, Anne Bancroft, and Patty Duke, and with film clips from six of his features: The Left-Handed Gun, The Chase, The Miracle Worker, Bonnie and Clyde, Alice's Restaurant, and Little Big Man. William Tusher, in The Hollywood Reporter (May 29, 1970), wrote: "The Penn portrait is a masterful blending of interviews, excerpts from a procession of pictures, and off-camera eavesdropping on his unique way of empathizing with his performers and aiding them in his ceaseless pursuit of spontaneity and revelation of character." The production was shown with success at the Cannes Film Festival--its premiere screening on May 15, 1970--and also received an Emmy. For more information, see Richard Coombs' review in The Monthly Film Bulletin (May, 1971), page 91.

Availability (16mm): Twyman/University of California Extension Media Center/Select/Macmillan

BARBED WIT: THE CINEMA OF BILLY WILDER, A (45 mins/16mm)

Germany. Zweites Deutsches Fernsehen (ZDF). 1976. Director, Screenplay and Narrator: Hans C. Blumenberg.

A documentary in which Billy Wilder talks about his career, with asides from I. A. L. Diamond, Jack Lemmon and Joseph LaShelle.

Availability: None

BEFORE HOLLYWOOD THERE WAS FORT LEE, NEW JERSEY (4 reels/16mm)

U.S. A Thomas Hanlon Production. Date unknown. Producer: Thomas Hanlon. Screenplay: Jake Moon and Thomas Hanlon. Film Editor: Robert Matthews. Music: Jack Shaindlin. Piano for Griffith Section: Paul Norman. Recording Engineer for Griffith Section and Assistant to Producer: Robert E. Lee. Narrator: Phil Tonken.

Produced for the tercentenary of New Jersey. A documentary on the development of the American silent film industry in Fort Lee, New Jersey, during the 'teen years, told chiefly through the use of stills. An interesting and informative production, which would have been a lot more valuable had more film footage been utilized.

Availability: None

BEGINNINGS OF BRITISH CINEMA, THE (36 mins/16mm)

A package of four early British films, compiled by the Museum of Modern Art: R.W. Paul's The Funeral of Queen Victoria (1901), Cecil Hepworth's Rescued by Rover (1905), Arthur Melbourne-Cooper's The Airship Destroyer (1909), and A. E. Coleby's Tatters: A Tale of the Slums.

Availability: The Museum of Modern Art

BEGINNINGS OF THE CINEMA (1 reel/14 mins/35mm)

A representative sampling of films produced between 1895 and 1903, compiled, with musical accompaniment, by the British Film Institute: Train Entering a Station (1895), The Derby: On the Road to Epsom (1896), The Derby (1896), The Brighton Fire: Arrival of the Brigade (1899), Panorama of Calcutta (1899), The Vanishing Lady (1897), Peintre à l'envers (circa 1898), Will Evans, the Musical Eccentric (1899), A Chess Dispute (1903), and The Miller and the Sweep (1898).

Availability (35mm and 16mm): British Film Institute, London (no American distributor)

BEGINNINGS OF THE CINEMA (16mm)

A 23-part compilation of films from the Paper Print Collection of the Library of Congress, illustrating the development of the cinema from 1898 through 1912. Part One (35 mins) includes the following Edison productions: Elopement on Horseback (1898), Strange Adventure of New York Drummer (1899), Uncle Josh's Nightmare (1900), Terrible Teddy, the Grizzly King (1901), Love by the Light of the Moon (1901), Circular Panorama of Electric Tower (1901), Panorama of Esplanade by Night (1901), Martyred Presidents (1901), Uncle Josh at the Moving Picture Show (1902), The Twentieth Century Tramp (1902), Fun in a Bakery Shop (1902), Jack and the Beanstalk (1902), and Life of an American Fireman (1903). Part Two (43 mins) includes Edison productions directed by Edwin S. Porter: Uncle Tom's Cabin (1903), The Gay Shoe Clerk (1903), A Romance on the Rail (1903), and Rounding Up the "Yeggmen" (1904). Part Three (42 mins) also includes Edwin S. Porter productions for the Edison Company: European Rest Cure (1904), The Ex-Convict (1904) and The Kleptomaniac (1905). Part Four (24 mins) includes further Edwin S. Porter productions for the Edison Company from 1905: The Seven Ages, How Jones Lost His Roll and The Whole Dam Family and the Dam Dog. Part Five (37 mins) includes American Mutoscope and Biograph productions: The Dude and the Burglars (1903), The Story the Biograph Told (1904), Personal (1904), The Widow and the Only Man (1904), and The Lost Child (1904). Part Six (37 mins) also includes American Mutoscope and Biograph productions: The Suburbanite (1904), Tom, Tom, the Piper's Son (1905) and An Acadian Elopement (1907). Part Seven (35 mins) includes further American Mutoscope and Biograph productions: Grandpa's Reading Glass (1902), Mr. Hurry-Up of New York (1907), The Tired Tailor's Dream (1907), and The Sculptor's Nightmare (1908). Part Eight (42 mins) includes further American Mutoscope and Biograph productions: A Search for Evidence (1903), The Moonshiner (1904) and The Hero of Liao Yang (1904). Part Nine (37 mins) includes further American Mutoscope and Biograph productions from 1905: The Nihilists, Mystery of the Missing Jewel Casket and A Kentucky Feud. Part Ten (34 mins) includes American Mutoscope and Biograph productions from 1906: The Silver Wedding, The Black Hand and The Paymaster. Part Eleven (12 mins) includes American Mutoscope and Biograph productions from 1906: The Tunnel Workers and The Skyscrapers. Part Twelve (42 mins) includes American Mutoscope and Biograph productions from 1908: The Boy Detective, Her First Adventure, Caught by Wireless, and At the French Ball. Part Thirteen (40 mins) includes American Mutoscope and Biograph productions directed by D.W. Griffith: Balked at the Altar (1908), Faithful (1910) and A Dash through the Clouds (1912). Part Fourteen (45 mins) includes American Mutoscope and Biograph productions directed by D.W. Griffith: A Calamitous Elopement (1908), Where Breakers Roar (1908), An Awful Moment (1908), and The Cord of Life (1909). Part Fifteen (14 mins) consists of the edited and unedited version of D.W. Griffith's 1909 production of The Girls and Daddy. Part Sixteen (38 mins) includes three D.W. Griffith productions from 1909: Golden Louis, At the Altar and Fools of Fate. Part Seventeen (33 mins) includes two D.W. Griffith productions from 1911: His Trust and His Trust Fulfilled. Part Eighteen (39 mins) includes two D.W. Griffith productions from 1912: The Girl and Her Trust and A Temporary Truce. Part Nineteen (43 mins) includes four Lubin productions: Bold Bank Robbery (1904), She Would Be an Actress (1909), Drunkard's Child (1909), and An Unexpected Guest (1909). Part Twenty (36 mins) includes films by various producers: Love and War (1899, James H. White), The Girl from Montana (1907,

Selig), His First Ride (1907, Selig), The Bandit King (1907, Selig), and The Bank Robbery (1908, Oklahoma Mutoscene Company). Part Twenty-One (42 mins) includes productions by Georges Méliès: The Inn Where No Man Rests (1903), A Spiritualist Photographer (1903), The Kingdom of the Fairies (1903), The Magic Lantern (1903), The Clock Maker's Dream (1904), The Cook in Trouble (1904), and The Mermaid (1904). Part Twenty-Two A (42 mins) includes British productions: How the Old Woman Caught the Omnibus (1903), The Eviction (1904), The Bewitched Traveller (1904), An Englishman's Trip from Paris to London (1904), The Lover's Ruse (1904), Automobile Parade on the Coney Island Boulevard (1901), The Other Side of the Hedge (1904), and Fine Feathers Make Fine Birds (1905). Part Twenty-Two B (38 mins) also includes British productions: The Pickpocket (1903), The Child Stealers (1904), Raid on a Corner's Den (1904), Revenge! (1904), A Railway Tragedy (1904), Decoyed (1904), and Rescued by Rover (1905). Part Twenty-Three (73 mins) includes two Nordisk Film Company productions of 1912: The Aviator's Generosity and Love and Friendship.

Availability: Indiana University Audio-Visual Center

BEHIND THE SCENES (17 mins/16mm)

"Shows how the Films Division--of the Indian Government--has been recording history through newsreels and participating in national progress through production of documentaries on the Indian scene."

Availability: Information Service of India

BELOVED INFIDEL (11, 061 ft. /123 mins/35mm)

U.S. The Company of Artists and Twentieth Century-Fox. 1959. Producer: Jerry Wald. Director: Henry King. Screenplay: Sy Bartlett. Based on the book by Sheilah Graham and Gerold Frank. Photography: Leon Shamroy. Music: Franz Waxman. Song, "Beloved Infidel," by Paul Francis Webster. Art Directors: Lyle R. Wheeler and Maurice Ransford. Set Decorators: Walter M. Scott and Eli Benneche. Film Editor: William Reynolds. Costumes: Bill Thomas. Makeup: Ben Nye. Hair Styles: Helen Turpin. Assistant Director: Stanley Hough. Sound: E. Clayton Ward and Harry M. Leonard. Orchestrations: Edward B. Powell and Leonard Raab. Color Consultant: Leonard Doss.

With Gregory Peck (F. Scott Fitzgerald), Deborah Kerr (Sheilah Graham), Eddie Albert (Carter), Philip Ober (John Wheeler), Herbert Rudley (Stan Harris), John Sutton (Lord Donegall), Karin Booth (Janet Pierce), Ken Scott (Robinson), Buck Glass (Dion), A. Cameron Grant (Johnson), and Cindy Ames (Miss Bull).

Film based on Sheilah Graham's account of her Hollywood romance with F. Scott Fitzgerald, when she was starting her career as a columnist and he was ending his as a screenwriter. The Eddie Albert character--Robert Carter--is based on the couple's neighbor at the Garden of Allah apartments, Robert Benchley.

Availability (16mm): Films Incorporated

BEST OF BOGART, THE (13 mins/35mm)

"Produced for exclusive use by those colleges and universities actively enrolled as participants in the Warner Bros.-NEC Film Project.... Few stars have blazed their way across the screen with such versatility as Humphrey Bogart. Here are historic highlights from some of his greatest films. Narrated by Edward G. Robinson."--description in Warner Bros. catalogue.

Availability (16mm): Warner Bros.

BEST THINGS IN LIFE ARE FREE, THE (9,386 ft./104 mins/35mm)

U.S. Twentieth Century-Fox. 1956. Producer: Henry Ephron. Director: Michael Curtiz. Screenplay: William Bowers and Phoebe Ephron. Based on a Story by John O'Hara. Photography: Leon Shamroy. Music Supervisor and Conductor: Lionel Newman. Vocal Supervisor: Charles Henderson. Orchestration: Herbert Spencer, Earle Hagen and Bernard Mayers. Musical Numbers Staged by Rod Alexander. Musical Settings: John De Cuir. Art Directors: Lyle R. Wheeler and Maurice Ransford. Set Decorators: Walter M. Scott and Paul S. Fox. Special Photographic Effects: Ray Kellogg. Film Editor: Dorothy Spencer. Executive Wardrobe Designer: Charles LeMaire. Additional Choreography: Bill Foster. Assistant Director: David Silver. Makeup: Ben Nye. Hair Styles: Helen Turpin. Sound: E. Clayton Ward and Harry M. Leonard. Color Consultant: Leonard Doss.

With Gordon MacRae (De Sylva), Dan Dailey (Henderson), Ernest Borgnine (Brown), Sheree North (Kitty), Tommy Noonan (Carl), Murvyn Vye (Manny), Phyllis Avery (Maggie Henderson), Larry Keating (Sheehan), Tony Galento (Fingers), Norman Brooks (Al Jolson), Jacques d'Amboise (Specialty Dancer), Roxanne Arlen (Perky Nichols), Byron Palmer (Hollywood Star), Linda Brace (Jeannie Henderson), Patty Lou Hudson (Susie Henderson), Julie Van Zandt (Miss Van Seckland), Eugene Borden (Louis), Harold Miller (Percy), Emily Belser (Photographer), Paul Glass (Piano Player), and Bill Foster (Dance Director).

A surprisingly pleasant and entertaining film biography of the song writing team of De Sylva, Brown and Henderson, who, from 1926 through 1931, produced a host of great numbers and were particularly active in Fox productions

Availability (16mm): Films Incorporated

BETTY BOOP FOLLIES, THE (3,348 ft./93 mins/16mm)

U.S. Ivy Films. 1972. Electronically Colored under the Supervision of J. H. Song.

A package of fourteen Max and Dave Fleischer Betty Boop cartoons from the Thirties: Mask-a-Raid (1931), Betty Boop's Bamboo Isle (1932), Boop-Oop-a-Doop (1932), Betty Boop's Ups and Downs (1932), Stopping the Show (1932), Betty Boop's Penthouse (1933), Betty Boop's Crazy Inventions (1933), Morning Noon and Night (1933), Ha Ha Ha (1934), Betty Boop's Prize Show (1934), Betty Boop's Trial (1934), Stop That Noise (1935), More Pep (1936), and Riding the Rails (1938).

Availability: Ivy Films

BIG PARADE OF COMEDY, THE / M-G-M's BIG PARADE OF COMEDY (90 mins/35mm)

U.S. Metro-Goldwyn-Mayer. 1964. Producer, Screenplay and Titles and Effects Design: Robert Youngson. Narrator: Les Tremayne. Associate Producer: Alfred Dahlem. Production Manager: I. Hill Youngson. Research Supervisor: Jeanne Keyes. Music: Bernie Green. Song, "The Big Parade of Comedy": Music by Bernie Green and Lyrics by Robert Youngson.

A flawed but nonetheless entertaining compilation by Robert Youngson, utilizing the product of one studio, M-G-M. As well as such obvious choices as comedies by Pete Smith and the Three Stooges, the feature includes clips from a number of lesser known M-G-M productions, including *The Boob* with Joan Crawford and George K. Arthur; *The Red Mill* with Marion Davies; *Hollywood Party* with Laurel and Hardy; *What, No Beer* with Buster Keaton; *Reducing* with Marie Dressler, Polly Moran and Anita Paige; *The Gay Bride* with ZaSu Pitts and Carole Lombard; *The Cameraman* with Buster Keaton; *Rio Rita* with Abbott and Costello; and *Meet the People* with Bert Lahr and Lucille Ball. There are also classic comedy clips from *Dinner at Eight*, *Ninotchka*, *David Copperfield*, *The Philadelphia Story*, and a number of Jean Harlow vehicles. Nothing later than 1947 is included. As *Variety* (August 26, 1964) noted, "Feature is slickly handled with know-how technique."

Availability (16mm): Films Incorporated

BIOGRAPH PROGRAM No. 1 (25 mins/16mm)

A package of five films produced during 1903 and 1904 by the American Biograph Company: *The Dude and the Burglars* (1903), *The Story the Biograph Told* (1904), *Personal* (1904), *The Widow and the Only Man* (1904), and *The Lost Child* (1904).

Availability: Macmillan

BIOGRAPH PROGRAM No. 2 (24 mins/16mm)

A package of three films produced between 1904 and 1907 by the American Biograph Company: *The Suburbanite* (1904), *Tom, Tom, the Piper's Son* (1905) and *An Acadian Elopement* (1907).

Availability: Macmillan

BIOGRAPH PROGRAM No. 3 (23 mins/16mm)

A package of four films produced between 1902 and 1908 by the American Biograph Company: *Grandpa's Reading Glass* (1902), *Mr. Hurry-Up of New York* (1907), *The Tired Tailor's Dream* (1907), and *The Sculptor's Nightmare* (1908).

Availability: Macmillan

BIOGRAPH PROGRAM No. 4 (28 mins/16mm)

A package of three films produced during 1903 and 1904 by the American Biograph Company: A Search for Evidence (1903), The Moonshiner (1904) and The Hero of Liao Yang (1904).
Availability: Macmillan

BIOGRAPH PROGRAM No. 5 (25 mins/16mm)

A package of three films produced during 1905 by the American Biograph Company: The Nihilists, The Great Jewel Mystery and A Kentucky Feud.
Availability: Macmillan

BIOGRAPH PROGRAM No. 6 (23 mins/16mm)

A package of three films produced during 1906 by the American Biograph Company: The Silver Wedding, The Black Hand and The Paymaster.
Availability: Macmillan

BIOGRAPH PROGRAM No. 7 (17 mins/16mm)

A package of two films produced during 1906 by the American Biograph Company: The Tunnel Workers and The Skyscrapers.
Availability: Macmillan

BIOGRAPH PROGRAM No. 8 (28 mins/16mm)

A package of four films produced during 1908 by the American Biograph Company: The Boy Detective, Her First Adventure, Caught by Wireless, and At the French Ball.
Availability: Macmillan

BIOGRAPHY

A 1962/1963 television series, produced by David Wolper, dealing with leading figures of the 19th and 20th centuries, from Adolph Hitler to Eleanor Roosevelt and from Eamon de Valera to Queen Elizabeth II. The following episodes (q. v.) dealt with film history: Grace Kelly, John Barrymore, Thomas Edison, and Will Rogers.

BIOGRAPHY OF THE MOTION PICTURE CAMERA (20 mins/16mm)

The second part, with English commentary, of the fine French documentary on pre- and early cinema, Naissance du Cinema (q. v.). For more information see Film News (September-October, 1947), page 9.
Availability: Radim/U. S. C. Film Library

BIRTH OF A LEGEND, THE (2, 340 ft. /26 mins/35mm)

U. S. Mary Pickford Company. 1966. Producer, Director and Screenplay: Matty Kemp. Film Editor: Mario Mora. Music Editor: Ed Norton. Narrator: Leslie Gargan.

A brief tribute to Mary Pickford, utilizing newsreel footage, photographic stills, and clips from Little Lord Fauntleroy, Suds, Sparrows, and Secrets.
Availability: Mary Pickford Company

BIRTH OF A STAR see HOLLYWOOD AND THE STARS

BIRTH OF A STAR, THE (4 reels/35mm)

U. S. Astor Pictures. 1944. Director: Bud Pollard.
A director discusses Danny Kaye's film career and screens lengthy extracts from three of Kaye's Educational comedies: Dime a Dance (1937), Cupid Takes a Holiday (1938) and Money or Your Life (1938).
Availability: None

BIRTH OF SOVIET CINEMA, THE (49 mins/16mm)

U. S. S. R. Mosfilm Studios. 1972. English Version by Harold Mantell. Screenplay and Narrator: Richard Schickel.

An examination of Soviet cinema in the Twenties, including a study of the work of Eisenstein, Pudovkin and Dovzhenko. Included are clips from Strike, Earth, October, Battleship Potemkin, Mother, The End of St. Petersburg, and Storm over Asia. The narration by Richard Schickel is played over the original Russian commentary.

Availability: Films for the Humanities

BIT OF THE BEST, A (975 ft. /11 mins/35mm)

U.S. Warner Bros. 1955. Producer and Screenplay: Robert Youngson. Film Editor: Albert Helmes. Narrator: Dwight Weist

This short features a highly truncated version of the 1927 Rin-Tin-Tin vehicle, Tracked by the Police.

Availability: None

BLACK SHADOWS ON THE SILVER SCREEN (60 mins/16mm)

U.S. Post-Newsweek Television. 1975. Executive Producer: Ray Hubbard. Producers: Bill Bowman and Stephan Henriques. Director: Steven York, Screenplay: Thomas Cripps. Organ Music: Ray Brubaker.

"The film is a one-hour development of the idea that Blacks were not passive witnesses to their own victimization by Hollywood depictions of their character. Their counter-strategies are seen in three forms: active, political protest against the racial content of The Birth of a Nation, the development of a small but active 'race movie' industry which made movies for predominantly Black audiences, and the making of overseas films by expatriates such as Josephine Baker and Paul Robeson. Of the race moviemakers the two who are given most prominence are Oscar Micheaux and the Lincoln Motion Picture Company, while the film that is given the closest analysis is The Scar of Shame, a production of the Colored Players Company of Philadelphia. With accentuated irony the movement toward this independent Black cinema is seen as the unintended victim of the liberalism that emerged from World War II that opened up Hollywood to Negroes but thereby helped squelch Black moviemaking." --Tom Cripps. Black Shadows on the Silver Screen won a Golden Gate at the San Francisco Film Festival, and was also screened at the London and Cannes Festivals.

Availability: Lucerne

BOGART (54 mins/16mm)

U.S. Flaum-Grinberg Productions. 1967. Executive Producer: Sherman Grinberg. Producer, Director and Screenplay: Marshall Flaum. Music: Nelson Riddle. Narrator: Joseph Campanella.

An in-depth documentary on the life and career of Humphrey Bogart, including interviews with Ida Lupino, George Raft, Ingrid Bergman, Joseph L. Mankiewicz, Stanley Kramer, and Joan Blondell, and clips from many of the actor's films including Casablanca, To Have and Have Not, The Petrified Forest, Treasure of Sierra Madre, The Barefoot Contessa, The Maltese Falcon, and Key Largo.

Availability (Super 8mm): Niles

BROTHER, CAN YOU SPARE A DIME?

A 1975 British feature which deals with the Depression years of the Thirties through film clips, contemporary recordings, etc. However, it does not concern itself with film history, and as the film clips are not identified it has little value as a film on film history.

BUGS BUNNY AND HIS AUTEURS: THREE CLASSICS FROM THE FORTIES (3 reels/16mm)

A compilation of three Warner Bros.-Bugs Bunny cartoons: Unruly Hare (1944), Bugs Bunny and the Three Bears (1944) and Stage Door Cartoon (1945). A study guide is also available.

Availability: United Artists 16 (rental and lease)

BUGS BUNNY SUPERSTAR (100 mins/35mm)

U.S. Hare Raising Films. 1973. Producer and Director: Larry Jackson. Associate Producers: Terrence Corey, Rob McMicking and Martha Pinson. Production Supervisor: Richard Waltzer. Photography: Gary Graver. Camera Assistants: Michael Ferris, Michael Stringer, Jim Gille, and David Donnelly. Additional Photography and Film Editor: Brian King. Sound: Darcy Vebber. Graphic Designer: Candance Clemens. Production Coordinator: Sody Clampett. Production Assistant: Lyn Radeloff. Carrot Coordinator: Dal LaMagna. Associate Film Editor: J. Keith Robinson.

An anthology of classic Warner Bros. cartoons from the Forties, together with comments by three of their creators: Bob Clampett, Tex Avery and Friz Freleng. The following cartoons are included: What's Cookin', Doc? (1944), A Wild Hare (1940), I Taw a Putty Tat (1948), Walky Talky Hawky (1946), The Corny Concerto (1943), Rhapsody Rabbit (1946), My Favorite Duck (1943), A Slick Hare (1946), Hair-Raising Hare (1946), and The Old Grey Hare (1944).

Availability: United Artists 16

BUSBY BERKELEY AND THE GOLDDIGGERS (13 mins/35mm)

Produced for exclusive use by those colleges and universities actively enrolled as participants in the Warner Bros.-NEC Film Project.... Busby Berkeley--the name's synonymous with lavish musical numbers that never have been surpassed for spectacle, music and eye-filling opulence. With legions of beautiful Busby Berkeley girls weaving their way through intricate and imaginative dance drills, here are historic highlights from famous Berkeley classics. Narrated by William Conrad."--description in Warner Bros. catalogue.

Availability (16mm): Warner Bros.

BUSTER KEATON (The History of the Motion Picture/Silents Please series)

A study of the work of the great silent comedian, with clips from Daydreams, College and Steamboat Bill Jr., co-produced by Paul Killiam and Saul J. Turell and written by Paul Killiam. For more information see The History of the Motion Picture series.

Availability (16mm): Blackhawk (sale)/Killiam Shows (rental)

BUSTER KEATON RIDES AGAIN (56 mins/35mm)

Canada. National Film Board of Canada. 1965. Producer: Julian Biggs. Director and Photography: John Spotton. Narrator: Donald Brittain.

Buster Keaton Rides Again was shot while Keaton was working on The Railrodder for the National Film Board of Canada. It illustrates how Keaton works on his sight gags and how he relaxes with his friends and family. The comedian talks about his career, and excerpts from a number of his classic motion pictures are shown. A beautifully produced film, both informative and entertaining.

Availability (16mm): National Film Board of Canada (sale)/University of California Extension Media Center

BUSTER KEATON STORY, THE (8,210 ft. /91 mins/35mm)

U.S. Paramount. 1957. Producers and Screenplay: Robert Smith and Sidney Sheldon. Director: Sidney Sheldon. Photography: Loyal Griggs. Art Directors: Hal Pereira and Carl Anderson. Set Decorators: Sam Comer and Ray Moyer. Special Photographic Effects: John P. Fulton. Costumes: Edith Head. Film Editor: Archie Marshek. Make-up: Wally Westmore. Hair Styles: Nellie Manley. Sound Recording: Gene Merritt and Winston Leverett. Music: Victor Young. Technical Advisor: Buster Keaton. Assistant Director: Francisco Day.

With Donald O'Connor (Buster Keaton), Ann Blyth (Gloria), Rhonda Fleming (Peggy Courtney), Peter Lorre (Kurt Bergner), Larry Keating (Larry Winters), Richard Anderson (Tom McAfee), Dave Willock (Joe Keaton), Claire Carleton (Myra Keaton), Larry White (Buster Keaton, age 7), Jackie Coogan (Elmer Case) Dan Seymour (South American Indian Chief), Mike Ross (Assistant South American Indian Chief), Nan Martin (Edna), Robert Christopher (Nick), Richard Aherne (Franklin), and Minta Durfee (Boarder).

A fictionalized account of the life of the great screen comedian. Life (May 6, 1957) commented, "As a movie, The Buster Keaton Story is sadly lacking. Most importantly, it lacks Keaton."

Availability (16mm): Films Incorporated

CALLING ALL GIRLS (2 reels/20 mins/35mm)

U.S. Warner Bros. Released January 24, 1942. "Broadway Brevities" series.

A selection of Busby Berkeley musical numbers from the Thirties, including "Lullaby of Broadway," "Shanghai Lil," "Shadow Waltz," and "By a Waterfall." Some of the numbers are slightly truncated.

Availability (16mm): Macmillan/United Artists 16

CAMEOS OF COMEDY (20 mins/16mm)

A compilation of comedy highlights from the following silent films: Mr. Flip (1909), Goodness Gracious (1914), Tillie Wakes Up (1917), The Butcher Boy (1917), and The Counter Jumper (1922).
Availability: Roa's Films

CAMERA GOES ALONG, THE / DIE KAMERA FÄHRT (12 mins/16mm)

Two sequences, photographed by Werner Brandes, from a survey of German newsreel production compiled in 1936. Featured are the 1934 Nuremberg Rally and preparations for the 1936 Olympic Games in Berlin.
Availability: The Museum of Modern Art

CAMERA REFLECTIONS (3, 450 ft. /35mm)

G.B. An Ariston Film released by Ambassador Film Productions. 1945. Producer: A. Fried. Screenplay: Yvonne Thomas. Film Editor: Julia Woolf. Music: W. L. Trytel. Sound Recording: Imperial Sound Studios. Narrators: Frederick Allen and John Stuart.

Described as "a joyous recollection of past successes with the stars who made film history," and featuring Sarah Bernhardt, Marie Lloyd, Priscilla Dean, William S. Hart, Mildred Harris, Lon Chaney, Rudolph Valentino, Marie Dressler, Constance and Norma Talmadge, Charles Chaplin, Mary Pickford, Norma Shearer, and Greta Garbo. Also included was newsreel footage of Edwardian England.
Availability: None

CAMERAMEN AT WAR (17 mins/35mm)

G.B. Realist Film Unit for the British Ministry of Information. 1944. Compiler: Len Lye.

A brief survey of well-known cameramen on battle fronts all over the world, during 1943 and 1944, compiled from newsreel and combat footage.
Availability: None (formerly available for rental in 35mm from the Museum of Modern Art)

CARPETBAGGERS, THE (150 mins/70mm)

U.S. Paramount/Joseph E. Levine. 1964. Producer: Joseph E. Levine. Director: Edward Dmytryk. Screenplay: John Michael Hayes. Based on the Novel by Harold Robbins. Photography: Joseph MacDonald. Production Manager: Frank Caffey. Unit Production Manager: William Gray. Art Directors: Hal Pereira and Walter Tyler. Set Decorators: Sam Comer and Arthur Krams. Costumes: Edith Head. Film Editor: Frank Bracht. Sound: John Carter and Charles Grenzbach. Music: Elmer Bernstein. Makeup: Wally Westmore and Gary Morris. Hair Style Supervisor: Nellie Manley. Special Photographic Effects: Paul K. Lerpae. Process Photography: Farciot Edouart. Technicolor Consultant: Richard Mueller. Property: Gordon Cole and Robert McCrillis. Dialogue Coach: Frank London. Assistant Director: D. Michael Moore.

With Carroll Baker (Rina), George Peppard (Jonas Cord, Jr.), Alan Ladd (Nevada Smith), Bob Cummings (Dan Pierce), Martha Hyer (Jennie Denton), Elizabeth Ashley (Monica Winthrop), Lew Ayres (McAllister), Martin Balsam (Bernard B. Norman), Ralph Taeger (Buzz Dalton), Archie Moore (Jedediah), Leif Erickson (Jonas Cord, Sr.), Arthur Franz (Morrissey), Tom Tully (Amos Winthrop), Audrey Totter (The Prostitute), Anthony Warde (Moroni), Charles Lane (Denby), Tom Lowell (David Woolf), John Conte (Ellis), Vaughn Taylor (The Doctor), Francesca Bellini (Cynthia Randall), and Victoria Jean (Jo-Ann).

The Carpetbaggers is best described as *Peyton Place* transferred to the world of Hollywood film-making in the Twenties and Thirties. The similarity between the leading characters and Howard Hughes and Jean Harlow is more than obvious. Sadly, the film has no period feel to it at all.

Availability (16mm): Films Incorporated

CARTOON FILM, THE (60 mins/35mm)

Canada. 1967. Director: Colin Low.

A history of world animation, produced for the Expo. International Animation Festival.

Availability: None

CAVALCADE OF ACADEMY AWARDS (3 reels/30 mins/35 mm)

U.S. Warner Bros. 1940. Supervision: Frank Capra. Director: Ira Genet. Screenplay: Owen Crump. Photography: Charles Rosher. Narrator: Carey Wilson.

Walt in Variety (April 17, 1940) commented, "Providing a kaleidoscopic symposium of the outstanding pictures and personalities that have been recipients of Academy Awards since 1928, and finishing with extended footage of the recent affair for distribution of the 1939 Oscars, this three-reeler falls into the novelty class." Among the celebrities who participated were Janet Gaynor, Marie Dressler, Norma Shearer, Shirley Temple, Jackie Cooper, Paul Muni, and Bette Davis. Mickey Rooney is seen presenting an Academy Award to Judy Garland, who sings "Over the Rainbow," and there is also a brief Technicolor sequence from Gone with the Wind.

Availability: Reel Images

CAVALCADE OF THE FILMS OF CECIL B. DeMILLE (2 reels/20 mins/35mm)

U.S. Produced in Cooperation with Paramount Pictures, Cecilia DeMille Harper and the Cecil B. DeMille Foundation. 1959. Screenplay: Sidney Kaufman. Narrator: Henry Wilcoxon.

Produced as a special attraction to open the DeMille Theatre in New York, this compilation contained clips from twenty-four DeMille productions, from The Squaw Man (1913) through The Ten Commandments (1956). For more information, see The Hollywood Reporter (December 3, 1959).

Availability: None

CAVALCADE OF THE MOVIES see FILM PARADE, THE

CHAPLIN--A CHARACTER IS BORN (40 mins/16mm)

U.S. S-L Film Productions. 1976. Producer, Director, Screenplay, and Film Editor: Gerald Schiller.

The evolution of Charlie Chaplin's Tramp character

shown through clips from public domain films such as The Tramp, Easy Street and The Immigrant.
Availability: S-L

CHAPLIN FESTIVAL (31 mins/16mm)

A package of four 1914 Charlie Chaplin Keystone comedies, complete with music and sound effects: The Face on the Barroom Floor, Between Showers, The Rounders, and Laughing Gas.
Availability: Macmillan

CHAPLIN POTPOURRI, # 1, # 2, # 3 (Each Part 1 reel/16mm)

Compilations of clips from various Chaplin public domain comedies. # 1 concentrates on the Keystone comedies, # 2 on Essanay, and # 3 on Mutual.
Availability: Em Gee

CHAPLIN REVUE, THE / THE CHAPLIN REVIEW (10,526 ft. /119 mins/35mm)

U.S. Charles Chaplin. 1958. Director, Screenplay and Music: Charles Chaplin.

A compilation of three Chaplin comedies--A Dog's Life (1918), Shoulder Arms (1918) and The Pilgrim (1923)--together with a prologue showing activity at the Chaplin studios in the Twenties. For more information, see The Monthly Film Bulletin (July, 1960), page 90.
Availability (16mm): rbc films/Films Incorporated

CHAPLINIANA (1 reel/16mm)

A compilation by Murray Glass of home movies and newsreel footage of Charlie Chaplin, including footage of the four founders of United Artists, Chaplin with Winston Churchill, the dedication of Grauman's Chinese Theatre, and guests at San Simeon.
Availability: Em Gee

CHAPLIN'S ART OF COMEDY (64 mins/35mm)

U.S. Pizor-Sherman. 1966. Producers: Irwin Pizor and Samuel M. Sherman. Screenplay: Samuel M. Sherman. Music: Elias Breeskin. Narrator: Dave Anderson.

A compilation of extracts from various of Chaplin's 1915 Essanay releases, including The Tramp, The Bank, The Champion, His New Job, A Night at the Show, and A Woman.

Availability: None

CHAPLIN'S ESSANAY FILMS (104 mins/16mm)

A package of four Chaplin comedies, compiled by the Museum of Modern Art: The Tramp (1915), A Woman (1915), The Bank (1915), and Police (1916).

Availability: The Museum of Modern Art

CHAPLIN'S FIRST FILMS (2 reels/22 mins/35mm)

A package of extracts from Chaplin films, produced between 1914 and 1916, compiled by the British Film Institute: Making a Living, Mabel's Strange Predicament, Tillie's Punctured Romance, The Fatal Mallet, Laughing Gas, His Trysting Place, Mabel's Married Life, His Prehistoric Past, The Champion, The Tramp, and The Bank.

Availability (35mm and 16mm): British Film Institute, London (No American distributor)

CHAPLIN'S KEYSTONE FILMS (81 mins/16mm)

A package of five Chaplin comedies, compiled by the Museum of Modern Art: Making a Living (1914), The Knockout (1914), The Masquerader (1914), The Rounders (1914), Getting Acquainted (1914).

Availability: The Museum of Modern Art

CHARLIE CHAPLIN CARNIVAL (8 reels/16mm)

A package of four Chaplin comedies, with music and sound effects, compiled by Thunderbird Films: The Vagabond (1916), The Fireman (1916), The Count (1916), and Behind the Screen (1916).

Availability: Thunderbird Films (sale)

CHARLIE CHAPLIN CAVALCADE (8 reels/16mm)

A package of four Chaplin comedies, with music and sound effects, compiled by Thunderbird Films: One A.M. (1916), The Pawnshop (1916), The Floorwalker (1916), and The Rink (1916).
Availability: Thunderbird Films (sale)

CHARLIE CHAPLIN COMEDY THEATRE, THE

A series of twenty-four Chaplin two-reelers with orchestral scores and synchronized sound effects.
Availability (Super 8mm and videotape): Cinema Eight (sale only)

CHARLIE CHAPLIN FESTIVAL (8 reels/16mm)

A package of four Chaplin comedies, with music and sound effects, compiled by Thunderbird Films: The Immigrant (1917), The Adventurer (1917), The Cure (1917), and Easy Street (1917).
Availability: Thunderbird Films (sale)

CHASE ME CHARLIE (4,199 ft./46 mins/35mm)

G.B. Exclusive. 1951. Narrator: Michael Howard.

A series of film clips from Chaplin's 1915 Essanay productions. Reviewers at the time of this production's initial release complained about the poor photographic quality of the clips.
Availability: None

CINEMA DU DIABLE (90 mins/35mm)

France. Producer and Date Unknown. Director: Marcel L'Herbier. Narrator: Claude Dauphin.

A history of surrealism in the French cinema, utilizing clips from fifty films and with the participation of Nicole Courcel, Micheline Presle, France Roche, and Marie Dea.
Availability (16mm): F.A.C.S.E.A.

CINEMA 1900 (25 mins/16mm)

A compilation of films from the Library of Congress Paper Print Collection, with an added music track but no linking titles.
Availability: Kit Parker

CINEMATOGRAPH SOUVENIRS OF AMERICA (1 reel/16mm)

A compilation by Blackhawk Films of thirteen Lumière shorts from the mid-1890s, including President McKinley's inauguration, a Chicago police parade, and harbor scenes in Brooklyn and New York.
Availability (16mm and 8mm): Blackhawk (sale only)

THE CINEMATOGRAPHER see LET'S GO TO THE MOVIES

CLASSIC AMERICAN MUTOSCOPE (1902-1905), THE (1 reel/10 mins/16mm)

U.S. The Museum of Modern Art. 1966. Compiler: Douglass Crockwell.

A selection of nine films, each lasting approximately one minute, produced by the American Mutoscope and Biograph Company between 1900 and 1905, and originally intended for viewing as a wheel of photographic cards on the Mutoscope machine. The following subjects are included: Tramp and the Muscular Cook, (W)ringing Good Joke, Affair of Honor, Horse Thief, Old Maid and the Burglar, Waltzing Walker, Fight for a Bride, Jail Break, and Robbed of Her All.
Availability: The Museum of Modern Art

CLIFF-HANGING MOMENTS FROM THE SERIALS (1 reel/16mm)

A compilation by Blackhawk Films of extracts from the following serials: The Steel Trail (1923) with William Duncan, A Woman in Grey (1919) with Arline Pretty, and Captain Kidd (1922) with Eddie Polo.
Availability (16mm and 8mm): Blackhawk (sale only)

CLOSE-UP ON CARTOONS (55 mins/16mm)

A program of animated short subjects compiled by Leonard Maltin for Select, and including Winsor McCay's Gertie the Dinosaur, Disney's Puss in Boots and The Whoopee Party, a Bugs Bunny cartoon, a Road Runner cartoon, Gerald McBoing Boing, and Ernest Pintoff's The Critic. For teaching purposes a study guide, also compiled by Leonard Maltin, is available.

Availability: Select

CLOWN PRINCES, THE (The History of the Motion Picture/ Silents Please series)

A study of the comedy styles of Chaplin, Harold Lloyd, Charlie Chase, Laurel and Hardy, Billy West, Ben Turpin, and Larry Semon, co-produced by Paul Killiam and Saul J. Turell, and written by Paul Killiam. For more information see The History of the Motion Picture series

Availability (16mm): Blackhawk (sale)/Killiam Shows (rental)/Budget (rental)

COHL, FEUILLADE AND DURAND PROGRAM (20 mins/ 16mm)

A package of five films produced by the French film pioneers Emile Cohl, Louis Feuillade and Jean Durand, compiled by the Museum of Modern Art: Emile Cohl's The Pumpkin Race (1907), Emile Cohl's Joyeux microbes (1909), Emile Cohl's Le Peintre neo-impressioniste (1910), Feuillade's Une Dame vraiment bien (1908), and Durand's Onésime horloger (1910).

Availability: The Museum of Modern Art

COMEDY AND MAGIC OF MELIES, THE (1 reel/16mm)

A compilation by Blackhawk Films of two George Méliès productions of 1903: The Witch's Revenge and The Inn Where No Man Rests.

Availability: None (formerly available for sale on 8mm and 16mm from Blackhawk Films)

COMEDY COMBO # 3 (1 reel/16mm)

A collection of clips from three comedies of the Thirties: an unidentified Harry Langdon short, Buster Keaton in Blue Blazes (1936) and Danny Kaye and Imogene Coco in Dime a Dance (1937).
Availability: Em Gee

COMEDY LEARNS TO TALK (80 mins/16mm)

A program of comedy shorts compiled by Leonard Maltin for Select, and including Railroad Stowaways (adapted from the 1926 Mack Sennett two-reeler, Whispering Whiskers), Keystone Hotel (1935), a Charlie Chase sound comedy, and a Joe McDoakes short, Behind the Eight Ball. For teaching purposes a study guide, also compiled by Leonard Maltin, is available.
Availability: Select

COMING OF SOUND, THE (70 mins/16mm)

A package of three shorts and two feature film extracts illustrating the use and misuse of early sound, compiled by the Museum of Modern Art: Shaw Talks for Movietone News (1927), The Jazz Singer, extract (1927), The Lights of New York, extract (1928), Steamboat Willie (1928), and The Sex Life of the Polyp (1928).
Availability: The Museum of Modern Art

CONVERSATION WITH INGRID BERGMAN, A (59 mins/16mm)

U.S. KCET and National Educational Television. 1968. Producer and Director: Gregory Heimer.

Cecil Smith, drama critic of the Los Angeles Times, interviews Ingrid Bergman, who discusses her childhood ambition to be an actress and the consequences of the fulfillment of that ambition.
Availability: Indiana University Audio-Visual Center

COSTUME DESIGNER, THE see LET'S GO TO THE MOVIES

CRAZY DAYS (3,104 ft./34 mins/35mm)

G.B. A Doverton Films Production released by Planet. 1962. Producer: Henry E. Fisher. Written and Compiled by James M. Anderson. Music: De Wolfe. Piano: Rose Treacher. Recorded at Kay Carlton Hill Film Studios. Narrator: Hughie Green.

Described as "a saga of screen comedy," and concentrating on Mack Sennett and his Keystone Comedies. Among the comedians included are Mabel Normand, Ford Sterling, Jimmie Aubrey, Edgar Kennedy, Bobby Dunn, Roscoe "Fatty" Arbuckle, Al St. John, Buster Keaton, Charles Chaplin, Eddie Lyons and Lee Moran, and the British film comedian, "Pimple."

Availability: None

CYGNE IMMORTEL, LE see THE IMMORTAL SWAN

D. W. GRIFFITH, AN AMERICAN GENIUS (60 mins/16mm)

U.S. WAVE-TV. 1970. Producer: Walt Lowe. Screenplay: Walt and Elizabeth Lowe. Narrator: Richard Schickel.

Produced for a Louisville, Kentucky, television station, this documentary tribute to the great director was first broadcast on May 16, 1970. The film contains interviews with those who knew Griffith, together with clips from a number of his productions.

Availability: Killiam Shows (rental and sale)

D. W. GRIFFITH COMPILATION (43 mins/16mm)

A compilation of four American Biograph productions directed by D. W. Griffith: What Drink Did (1909), A Corner in Wheat (1909), The Lonedale Operator (1911), and The New York Hat (1912).

Availability: Images

DALTON TRUMBO (10 mins/16mm)

U.S. NET. 1971. Producer: Barbara Gordon. Film Editor: Nick Masci.

Screenwriter and novelist Dalton Trumbo discusses blacklisting and his decision to film his novel, Johnny Got His Gun.

Availability: University of California Extension Media Center

DAVID LEAN: A SELF PORTRAIT (55 mins/16mm)

U.S. Thomas Craven Film Corporation for NBC. 1971. Producer and Director: Thomas Craven.

A documentary study of the director produced while he was working on Ryan's Daughter. Lean analyzes his films and his career, and there are clips from a number of his features, including In Which We Serve, Brief Encounter, Oliver Twist, Great Expectations, Bridge on the River Kwai, Lawrence of Arabia, and Dr. Zhivago.

Availability: Twyman/University of California Extension Media Center/U.S.C. Film Library/Indiana University Audio-Visual Center

DAY OF THE LOCUST, THE (144 mins/35mm)

U.S. Paramount Pictures in Association with Ronald Shedlo. 1975. Producer: Jerome Hellman. Director: John Schlesinger. Screenplay: Waldo Salt. Based on the Novel by Nathanael West. Photography: Conrad Hall. Associate Producer: Sheldon Schrager. Music: John Barry. Film Editor: Jim Clark. Art Director: John Lloyd. Production Designer: Richard MacDonald. Costumes: Ann Roth. Set Decorator: George Hopkins. Special Effects: Tim Smyth. Special Photographic Effects: Albert Whitlock. Makeup: Del Armstrong and Lynn Del. Gaffer: Richard Martens. Best Boy: Danny Marzolo. Key Grip: Danny Jordan. Property Master: Allan Gordon. Stunt Coordinator: Phil Adams. Script Supervisor: Karen Wookey. Production Associate: Michael Childers. Dance Supervision: Marge Champion. Title Design: Dan Perri. Unit Production Manager: Shelden Schrager. Assistant Director: Tim Zinnemann.

With Donald Sutherland (Homer), Karen Black (Faye), Burgess Meredith (Harry), William Atherton (Tod), Geraldine Page (Big Sister), Richard A. Dysart (Claude Estee), Bo Hopkins (Earle Shoop), Pepe Serna (Miguel), Lelia Goldoni (Mary Dove), Billy Barty (Abe), Jackie Haley (Adore), Gloria Le

Roy (Mrs. Loomis), Jane Hoffman (Mrs. Odlesh), Norm Leavitt (Mr. Odlesh), Madge Kennedy (Mrs. Johnson), Ina Gould and Florence Lake (The Lee Sisters), Margaret Willey and John War Eagle (The Gingos), Natalie Schafer (Audrey), Gloria Stroock (Alice Estee), Nita Talbot (Joan), Nicholas Cortland (Projectionist), Alvin Childress (Butler), Byron Paul, Virginia Baker, Roger Price, Angela Greene, Roger O. Ragland, and Abbey Greshler (Guests), Ann Coleman and Gyl Roland (Girls), Paul Stewart (Helverston), John Hillerman (Ned Grote), William C. Castle (Director), Fred Scheiwiller (First Assistant Director), Wally Rose (Second Assistant Director), De Forest Covan (Shoe Shine Boy), Grainger Hines (French Lieutenant), Michael Quinn (Major Domo), Robert Pine, Jerry Fogel, Dennis Dugan, and David Ladd (Apprentices), Bob Holt (Tour Guide), Paul Jabara (Nightclub Entertainer), Queenie Smith (Palsied Lady), Margaret Jenkins (Choral Director), Jonathan Kidd (Undertaker), Kenny Solms (Boy in Chapel), Wally Berns (Theatre Manager), Bill Baldwin (Announcer at Premiere), and Dick Powell Jr. (Dick Powell).

A flawed film version of Nathanael West's classic novel of film-making and Hollywood in the Thirties.

Availability (16mm): Films Incorporated

DAYS OF THRILLS AND LAUGHTER (93 mins/35mm)

U.S. Twentieth Century-Fox. 1961. Producer and Screenplay: Robert Youngson. Assistant Producers: John E. Allen and Alfred Dahlem. Music: Jack Shaindlin. Sound: Albert Gramaglio. Sound Effects: Alfred Dahlem and Ralph R. Curtiss. Narrator: Jay Jackson.

Robert Youngson's third anthology of silent screen comedy, and as entertaining as his earlier efforts. In this feature, Youngson broadens his outlook and also takes in silent heroes and villains, including Douglas Fairbanks, Pearl White, Ruth Roland, Harry Houdini, Boris Karloff, and Warner Oland. Comedy players featured include Laurel and Hardy, Harry Langdon, Ben Turpin, Charlie Chase, Roscoe "Fatty" Arbuckle, Mabel Normand, Monty Banks, Al St. John, Ford Sterling, Snub Pollard, and Charlie Chaplin. As Los Angeles Times film critic Philip K. Scheuer noted at the time, "If Robert Youngson isn't the best producer 20th Century-Fox has, it is only because he is the best reproducer." For more information, see The Monthly Film Bulletin (June, 1961) page 86.

Availability (16mm): Kit Parker Films/Budget Films/ Macmillan/United Films/Swank/Twyman. (8mm, sale): Ivy Films/Cinema Eight

DEMENY PROGRAMME, THE (1 reel/12 mins/16mm)

A collection of films produced by French film pioneer Georges Demeny in 1896, compiled by Brian Coe of the Kodak Research Laboratories for the Kodak Museum and the British Film Institute.

Availability: British Film Institute, London (no American distributor)

DIRECTED BY JOHN FORD (99 mins/35mm)

U.S. California Arts Commission/The American Film Institute. 1971. Producers: George Stevens, Jr. and James R. Silke. Director and Screenplay: Peter Bogdanovich. Associate Producer: David Shepard. Photography: L. Kovacs. Film Editor: Richard Patterson. Narrator: Orson Welles. With the Participation of John Ford, Henry Fonda, James Stewart, and John Wayne.

Extracts from twenty-six of John Ford's features, interspersed with on-camera commentary by Henry Fonda, James Stewart, John Wayne, and Ford himself. Mosk in Variety (September 15, 1971) commented, "The docu may get pros and cons depending on what people see in his work and what pix they have seen, but it does add up to proving the tenet that his forte was in simple visual delineation of men in action and with strong moral outlooks, and his Westerns said more and were more personal than his more ambitious and expressionist pix such as The Informer and others." John Ford, himself, commented--in Newsweek (December 6, 1971)--"I thought it was long and the print was bad," but Bogdanovich did "a superb job on a dull subject."

Availability (16mm): Films Incorporated

DISNEY, WALT European Compilations

Many dozens of compilations of Walt Disney cartoons have been released through the years in Europe, some taken from the company's American television series, and others specially produced. The content of these compilations would often vary from country to country, and there is no practical way of listing them all in this volume. However, three such compilations--The Donald Duck Story, Donald Duck Goes West and The Mickey Mouse Anniversary Show--have been included as examples of these features.

DONALD DUCK GOES WEST (5,962 ft./66 mins/35mm)

U.S. Walt Disney. 1976.

A compilation for the European market of the following Donald Duck cartoons: Don Donald (1936), Good Scouts (1938), Donald's Gold Mine (1942), The Legend of Coyote Rock (1945), Californy 'er Bust (1945), Wide Open Spaces (1947), Pueblo Pluto (1948), Dude Duck (1950), Up a Tree (1955), and A Cowboy Needs a Horse (1956).
Availability: None.

DONALD DUCK STORY, THE (5,310 ft./59 mins/35mm)

U.S. Walt Disney. 1954.

Originally compiled for the Disneyland television series, and first aired on the ABC network on November 17, 1954, this feature was theatrically released in Europe. It includes the following cartoons with no linking commentary: The Orphans' Benefit (1934 and 1941 versions), On Ice (1935), Clock Cleaners (1937), Donald's Golf Game (1938), A Good Time for a Dime (1941), Donald's Snowfight (1942), No Sail (1945), and Rugged Bear (1953). The film opens with a group of animators trying to decide on Donald's voice, and listening to a recording of Clarence Nash. For more information, see Geoff Brown's review in The Monthly Film Bulletin (July, 1975), pages 153-154.
Availability: None

DONALD DUCK'S DILEMMAS (400 ft./8mm)

Excerpts from five Walt Disney/Donald Duck cartoons: Modern Inventions (1937), Donald's Golf Game (1938), The Riveter (1940), Donald's Garden (1941), and Dude Duck (1951).
Availability: Walt Disney 8mm

DOWN MEMORY LANE (73 mins/35mm)

Mack Sennett/Eagle Lion. 1949. Supervisor: Aubrey Schenck. Director: Phil Carlson. Screenplay and Narrator: Steve Allen. Photography: Walter Strenge. Music: Sol Kaplan. Musical Director: Irving Friedman. Film Editor: Fred Allen.

A selection of clips from silent films and early talkies produced by Mack Sennett. The films are shown within the framework of what is supposed to be a television program, hosted by Steve Allen, assisted by Mack Sennett and Franklin Pangborn. The idea does not work and it is sad to see Franklin Pangborn trying so hard to be funny to no effect, but the film clips themselves are still entertaining. Bing Crosby is seen in sequences from Sing Bing Sing and Blue of the Night, Donald Novis appears in The Singing Boxer and W. C. Fields is featured in The Dentist. From the silent era, there are clips of Gloria Swanson, Mabel Normand, Ben Turpin, Phyllis Haver, Charlie Murray, James Finlayson, Mack Swain, and The Keystone Kops. The modern sequence in a television studio also features Frank Nelson, Yvonne Peattie, Rennie McEvoy, Jo Ann Joyce, and Rowland Mc-Cracken. Variety (August 11, 1949) summed up Down Memory Lane when it described the film as "a boisterous mumble-jumble of nostalgia."

Availability: None

DRAWINGS THAT WALK AND TALK (3 reels/34 mins/35mm)

G.B. The National Film Archive. 1938. Compilers: Marie Seton and K. H. Frank. Music for Silent Films Arranged by Barbara Banner. Narrator: Norman Shelley.

A compilation of films from England's National Film Archive, illustrating the development of the black-and-white cartoon from the early 1900s through 1933. Cartoon characters represented include Mutt and Jeff, Popeye, Felix the Cat, Bonzo, Krazy Kat, and Mickey Mouse.

Availability: None

DREAMLAND (87 mins/16mm)

Canada. National Film Board of Canada, CBC and

Canadian Film Institute. 1974. Producer: Kirwan Cox. Director and Screenplay: Donald Brittain. Music: Charles Hoffman. Film Editor: John Kramer.

A history of motion picture production in Canada from 1895 through 1939, and including rare clips from many films.
Availability: National Film Board of Canada

DU BIST DIE WELT FUR MICH see YOU ARE THE WORLD FOR ME

EADWEARD MUYBRIDGE, ZOOPRAXAOGRAPHER (60 mins/35mm)

U.S. A Film by Thom Andersen, with Fay Andersen and Morgan Fisher. 1975. Film Editor: Morgan Fisher. Music: Michael Cohen. Animation Photography: Thom Andersen, Don Baker, Bill Coffen, Morgan Fisher, Alan Harding, and Marlyn O'Conner. Narrator: Dean Stockwell.

A documentary on the life and work of the pioneer scientist and photographer, Eadweard Muybridge. Muybridge's sequences of still photographs are painstakingly re-animated. "The film is as rigorous and restrictive as Muybridge's work," wrote Linda Gross in the Los Angeles Times (May 26, 1976). "By faithfully embracing the photographer's experience, Andersen has also illuminated his own existential statement: What you see is what you get and if you need lyricism or universal significance, you are out of luck and way behind the prophetic Eadweard Muybridge."
Availability: New Yorker Films (rental and sale)

EALING COMEDIES, THE (75 mins/16mm)

G.B. BBC. 1970. Director: Harry Hastings.

A tribute to the famous comedy productions of Sir Michael Balcon from the Forties and Fifties.
Availability: None

EARLY ACTUALITIES (1 reel/12 mins/35mm)

A package of British newsreel films, produced between 1899 and 1905, compiled by the British Film Institute, Gordon Highlanders Leaving Aberdeen for the Boer War (1899), Return of Lord Roberts from the Boer War (1901), Funeral of Queen Victoria (1901), Turn-Out of the Leeds Fire Brigade (1902), Street Scenes in Leeds (1903-1905), and Some Early Fashions (1905).

Availability (35mm and 16mm): British Film Institute, London (no American distributor)

EARLY BRITISH COMEDIES (23 mins/16mm)

A package of eight British films produced between 1903 and 1905 from the Paper Print Collection of the Library of Congress: How the Old Woman Caught the Omnibus (1903), The Eviction (1904), The Bewitched Traveller (1904), An Englishman's Trip to Paris from London (1904), The Lover's Ruse (1904), A Race for a Kiss (1904), The Other Side of the Hedge (1904), and Fine Feathers Make Fine Birds (1905).

Availability: Macmillan

EARLY BRITISH DRAMAS (29 mins/16mm)

A package of seven British films produced between 1903 and 1905 from the Paper Print Collection of the Library of Congress: The Pickpocket (1903), The Child Stealers (1904), Raid on a Coiner's Den (1904), Revenge! (1904), Decoyed (1904), and Rescued by Rover (1905).

Availability: Macmillan

EARLY EDISON SHORTS (2 reels/28 mins/35mm)

A series of Edison films, produced between 1893 and 1901, chiefly from the collection of the Museum of Modern Art, compiled by the British Film Institute: Washing the Baby (1893), Fatima's Dance (1893), Fun in a Chinese Laundry (1896), A (W)ringing Good Joke (1896), Feeding the Chickens (1897), The Black Diamond Express (1897), The New York Steam Elevated Railway (1897), Easter Parade on Fifth Avenue (1898), Aboard the Olympia in Manila Bay (1898), Dewar's--It's Scotch (1898), etc. For more information, see The Monthly Film Bulletin (December, 1955), page 185.

Availability (35mm and 16mm): British Film Institute, London (no American distributor, but see Films of the 1890s, distributed by the Museum of Modern Art)

EARLY FILMS OF INTEREST (22 mins/16mm)

A package of early French and American factual productions, compiled by the Museum of Modern Art: *Excursion of the French Photographic Society to Neuville* (1895), *Gold Rush Scenes in the Klondike* (1898), *The Funeral of Queen Victoria* (1901), *McGovern-Corbett Fight* (1903), *San Francisco Earthquake* (1906), *First Wright Flight in France* (1908), *Meeting of the Motion Picture Patents Co.* (1912), *Miss Davidson's Funeral* (1913), and *Sinking of the Austrian Battleship St. Stephen* (1915).

Availability: The Museum of Modern Art

EARLY GERMAN FILMS (29 mins/16mm)

A package of German films by Max Skladanowsky, Oskar Messter and an unknown director, compiled by the Museum of Modern Art: a series of primitive shorts by Skladanowsky, Messter's *Don Juan's Wedding* (1909) and *Misunderstood* (circa 1912), directed by an unknown, with Henny Porten.

Availability: The Museum of Modern Art

EARLY SOUND FILMS (2 reels/23 mins/16mm)

A selection of examples of pre-*The Jazz Singer* sound films, compiled by the British Film Institute. Included in this compilation are examples of Edison's experiments with sound, Gaumont Chronophone sound films from the early 1900s, Coquelin in *Cyrano de Bergerac* (circa 1912), Harry Relph in *Little Tich and His Big Boots* (1902), and a De Forest Phonofilm of Bransby Williams in a scene from *Bleak House*. Some of the extracts are from an unidentified French reconstruction of early sound experiments.

Availability: British Film Institute, London (no American distributor)

EARLY TRICK FILMS (1 reel/15 mins/35mm)

A package of European trick films, produced between 1895 and 1912, compiled by the British Film Institute: *The House That Jack Built* (1900), *Upside Down* (1898), *The Brahmin and the Butterfly* (1900), *The Motorist* (1906), *The Magic Screen* (1912), and *Dante's Inferno* (1909)

Availability (35mm and 16mm): British Film Institute, London (no American distributor)

ECHO OF APPLAUSE (4, 350 ft. /35mm)

G.B. Warner Bros. 1946. Producer: Burt Hyams. Written, Devised and Directed by James M. Anderson. Photography: Charles Francis, Bunny Onions and Billie Williams. Music Arranged by H. Crisp. Piano Improvisation: Florence DeJong. Recording: Tom Druce and Ken Wiles. Narrator: Frederick Grisewood.

With Anne Wrigg, Kenneth Firth and Max Melford.

Highlights of the history of the motion picture, including the first Lumière films to be screened in London, the first newsreel film of the Derby, newsreel film of the departure of the Gordon Highlanders for the Boer War, and clips of a variety of early film personalities including Max Linder, John Bunny, Florence Turner, Maurice Costello, Broncho Billy Anderson, and Britain's first professional film actor, Johnny Butt. Material used in this compilation was provided by the National Film Archive, the Royal Photographic Society and the Science Museum.

Availability: None

EDDIE CANTOR STORY, THE (115 mins/35mm)

U.S. Warner Bros. 1953. Producer: Sidney Skolsky. Director: Alfred E. Green. Screenplay: Jerome Weidman, Ted Sherdeman and Sidney Skolsky. Based on an Original Story by Sidney Skolsky. Photography: Edwin DuPar. Technicolor Consultant: Mitchell G. Kovaleski. Art Director: Charles H. Clarke. Music Director: Ray Heindorf. Musical Numbers Staged and Directed by LeRoy Prinz. Film Editor: William Ziegler. Sound: C. A. Riggs and David Forrest. Assistant Director: Al Alleborn.

With Keefe Brasselle (Eddie Cantor), Marilyn Erskine (Ida Cantor), Aline MacMahon (Grandma Esther), Arthur Franz (Harry Harris), Gerald Mohr (Rocky Kramer), Alex Gerry (David Tobias), Greta Granstedt (Rachel Tobias), William Forrest (Ziegfeld), Jackie Barnett (Durante), Douglas Evans (Leo Raymond), Hal March (Gus Edwards), Ann Doran (Lillian Edwards), Richard Monda (Eddie, at age 13), Susan Odin (Ida as a girl), Will Rogers, Jr. (Will Rogers), Marie Windsor (Cleo Abbott), and James Flavin (Kelly, the Cop).

Exactly what its title suggests; another film biography from the Skolsky and Green team that brought you The Jolson Story. Eddie and Ida Cantor appear briefly before and after the story.

Availability (16mm): Roa's

EDISON ALBUM, AN (1 reel/16mm)

A compilation by Blackhawk Films of the following Edison subjects: The Kiss (1896), The Old Maid in the Drawing Room (1900), Street Car Chivalry (1901), Romance of the Rails (1902), and an excerpt from Rescued from an Eagle's Nest (1907).

Availability (16mm and 8mm): Blackhawk (sale only)

EDISON COLLECTION #1 (1 reel/16mm)

A compilation of nine early Edison productions from 1895-1904, including The Kiss, Street Car Chivalry and Old Maid in a Drawing Room.

Availability: Em Gee

EDISON COLLECTION #2 (1 reel/16mm)

A collection of thirteen Edison productions from 1895-1902, including Spooks in the Barber Shop.

Availability: Em Gee

EDISON PRIMITIVES (1 reel/16mm)

A compilation by Blackhawk Films of Edison production from 1893 through 1903 from the Library of Congress Paper Print Collection.

Availability (8mm): Blackhawk (sale only)

EDISON, THE MAN (111 mins/35mm)

U.S. M-G-M. 1940. Producer: John W. Considine Jr. Associate Producer: Orville O. Dull. Director: Clarence Brown. Screenplay: Talbot Jennings and Bradbury Foote. Based on an Original Story by Dore Schary and Hugo Butler. Photography: Harold Rosson. Music: Herbert Stothart. Art Directors: Cedric Gibbons and John S. Detlie. Film Editor: Frederick Y. Smith. Assistant Director: Robert A. Golden.

With Spencer Tracy (Thomas A. Edison), Rita Johnson (Mary Stillwell), Lynne Overman (Bunt Cavatt), Charles Coburn (General Powell), Gene Lockhart (Mr. Taggart), Henry Travers (Ben Els), Felix Bressart (Michael Simon), Peter Godfrey (Ashton), Guy D'Ennery (Lundstrom), Byron Foulger (Edwin Hall), Milton Parsons ("Acid" Graham), Arthur Aylesworth (Bigelow), Gene Reynolds (Jimmy Price), Addison Richards (Mr. Johnson), Grant Mitchell (Snade), Irving Bacon (Sheriff), George Lessey (Toastmaster), Jay Ward (John Schofield), Ann Gillis (Nancy Grey), Edward Earle (Broker), Eddie Gribbon (Cashier), Maurice Costello and Wilfred Lucas (Brokers), and Billy Bletcher (Reporter).

Thomas Alva Edison's life story from 1869 through 1882. Edison, the Man is chiefly concerned with the invention of the electric light, and does not cover the invention of motion pictures. See also Young Tom Edison.

Availability (16mm): Films Incorporated

EDWARDIAN NEWSREEL (6 reels/55 mins/35mm)

G.B. The National Film Archive/British Film Institute. 1948. Compiler: Charles Oakley. Assistant: Philip M. Hall. Music: Thomas Best. Narrator: Francis Howard

A film record of some of the main events and leading personalities of the reign of King Edward VII, compiled from contemporary newsreels in the National Film Archive, London. Events covered include Queen Victoria's Diamond Jubilee and her funeral, the Boer War, the coronation of King Edward VII, and the Delhi Durbar in celebration of King George V's coronation.

Availability (35mm and 16mm): British Film Institute, London (no American distributor)

EDWARDIAN SHOWMAN'S COLLECTION, AN (2 reels/16 mins/16mm)

G.B. Debonair Productions. 1964. Editor and Compiler: Philip Jenkinson. Piano Accompaniment: Arthur Dulay.

A typical program of films screened by traveling showmen at English fairgrounds in the early 1900s. The following films are included: Skating Carnival (Britain, 1910), Japanese Wrestlers (Britain, 1911), A Runaway Horse (France, circa 1910), A Bolt from the Blue (Britain, 1910) and Little Willie Goes Cycling (France, 1910).

Availability: British Film Institute, London (no American distributor)

EDWIN S. PORTER PROGRAM (55 mins/16mm)

A package of five Edison productions, directed by Edwin S. Porter, compiled by the Museum of Modern Art: The Life of an American Fireman (1903), Uncle Tom's Cabin (1903), The Great Train Robbery (1903), The Dream of a Rarebit Fiend (1906), and Rescued from an Eagle's Nest (1907). Note: Since this package of films was prepared, research has indicated that Rescued from an Eagle's Nest was probably directed by J. Searle Dawley, not Porter.

Availability: The Museum of Modern Art/Images (rental and sale)

1895--ELOKUVA ELOKUVASTA / 1895--HOW THE MOVIES ARE MADE (1,620 ft. /18 mins/35mm)

Finland. Filmiryhmä Oy. 1972. Director and Screenplay: Aito Mäkinen. Photography: Virke Lehtinen. Animation/Film Editor: Elina Katainen. Narrators: Bo Carpelan, Carl Henning and Joe Brady.

A short account of the birth of the cinema, with interviews with those who remember the first film programs in Finland. The various components which went into the invention of the cinema--optical toys, the discovery of the persistence of vision, the invention of sound recording, etc.--are discussed.

Availability: None

EISENSTEIN AND PROKOFIEV (7 reels/35mm)

U.S.S.R. Moscow Television Studio. 1964. Director: E. Kovylkina. Screenplay: Leonid Kozlov.

A documentary in part on the life and career of the Soviet film director, Sergei Eisenstein.
Availability: None

EISENSTEIN: HIS LIFE AND TIMES see SERGEI EISENSTEIN

ELOQUENTS, LES (25 mins/35mm)

France, Polyfilms, 1955. Director: Jacques Guillon.

A delightful documentary, which should be sub-titled in English and made more widely available. An errand boy from the Cinemathèque Française delivers reels of film to various French film-makers of the Twenties. We see them as they look today in their present work, and then a short extract from one of their films follows. Among those taking part are Françoise Rosay, Marcel L'Herbier, Claude Autant-Lara, Ladislas Starevich, Charles Ford, and Abel Gance.
Availability (16mm): F. A. C. S. E. A.

ELSTREE STORY (5, 257 ft. /62 mins/35mm)

G. B. Associated British Pictures. 1952. Producer and Director: Gilbert Gunn. Commentary Written by Jack Howells. Photography: Stanley Grant. Production Manager: Gerry Mitchell. Film Editor: Richard Best. Sound: Harold V. King. Music: Philip Green. Music Director: Louis Levy. Introduced by Richard Todd.
With the voices of George Henschel, Norman Shelley, Leonard Sachs, Warwich Ward, Peter Du Roch, Ken Connor, and Peter Jones.

A documentary on the first twenty-five years of Elstree Studios. Richard Todd introduces the various components of film-making at a large studio; a film editor discusses cutting and assembling films in the Twenties; a screenwriter talks about adapting novels and plays into films; a casting director discusses his work, etc. Among the film extracts used are: The White Sheik (1927, with Warwick Ward in the first Elstree production), A Little Bit of Fluff (1928, with Syd Chaplin and Betty Balfour), Blackmail (1929, with John Longden, Anny Ondra and Donald Calthrop), The

Informer (1929, with Warwick Ward, Lya de Putti and Lars Hanson), Piccadilly (1929, with Anna May Wong and Charles Laughton), Murder (1930, with Herbert Marshall), Atlantic (1930, with John Stuart and Madeleine Carroll), Josser Joins the Army (1930, with Ernie Lotinga), Lord Camber's Ladies (1933, with Sir Gerald Du Maurier and Benita Hume), Blossom Time (1934, with Richard Tauber and Jane Baxter), Red Wagon (1934, with Charles Bickford, Raquel Torres and Greta Nissen), Radio Parade of 1935, (with Ted Ray and the Western Brothers), I Give My Heart (1935, with Gitta Alpa singing the title song), Mimi (1935, with Douglas Fairbanks, Jr. and Gertrude Lawrence), The Housemaster (1938, with Otto Kruger and Kynaston Reeves), Just William (1939, with Dickie Lupino and Roddy McDowall), The Hasty Heart (1949, with Richard Todd), The Dancing Years (1949, with Patricia Dainton), Murder without Crime (1950, with Derek Farr and Joan Dowling), and Happy Go Lovely (1950, with Vera-Ellen). As Variety's Myro (February 25, 1953) noted, "In its treatment of its own history the Elstree producers have been able to laugh at their own masterpieces in a manner which reflects the changing style and tempo of film production." For more information, see The Monthly Film Bulletin (February, 1953), page 27.

Availability: None (This feature is preserved in Britain's National Film Archive)

ELVIS--THAT'S THE WAY IT IS

Although this 1970 feature has been described as a documentary on Elvis Presley, it is in fact a study of a Presley concert tour, and does not concern itself with the actor-singer's film career.

EMILE COHL COMPILATION (17 mins/16mm)

A compilation of four films by French pioneer Emile Cohl: Fantasmagorie, The Dentures, Professor Bonehead Is Shipwrecked, and The Automatic Moving Company. Also known as Emile Cohl Primitives # 1.

Availability: Images

EMILE COHL FILMS (Thunderbird release) see EMILE COHL PRIMITIVES # 1

EMILE COHL PRIMITIVES #1 (1 reel/16mm)

A compilation of four early films by French pioneer animator Emile Cohl, with an added music track: Fantasmagorie, Le Ratelier, The Automatic Moving Company, and Professor Bonehead Is Shipwrecked.
Availability: Em Gee/Thunderbird (sale only)

EMILE COHL PRIMITIVES #2 (1 reel/16mm)

A compilation of three early films by French pioneer animator Emile Cohl: Joyeux Microbes, Le Peintre Neo-Impressioniste and The Pumpkin Race.
Availability: Em Gee

EN COMPAGNIE DE MAX LINDER / LAUGH WITH MAX LINDER (7,920 ft./88 mins/35mm)

France. Films Max Linder. 1963. Compiler: Maude Max Linder. Production Assistants: Roger Morand, Henri Dutrannoy, Sophie Dominiecki, Nicole Chamson, and Annick Vercier. Technical Collaborators: Yannick Bellon, Albert Jurgenson, Renée Deschamps, Jean Nény, and Jean Fouchet. Music: Gérald Calvi. Music Associate: Maurice Blanchot. Sound Effects: Serge Depannemacker. Narrator: René Clair.

Extracts from three of the great French comedian Max Linder's American features: Be My Wife (1921), The Three Must-Get-Theres (1922) and Seven Years Bad Luck (1923). A well-made compilation which is deserving of wider distribution. It was shown with considerable success at both the London and Venice film festivals. After seeing the compilation at the latter festival, Variety's Mosk wrote (September 11, 1963): "Besides its historical values the film has enough laughs to please both popular and selective audiences. His was a true visual approach without vulgarity, and he was also one of the first complete comic personalities of the screen. Max Linder deserves both belated recognition and commercial interest." For more information, see The Monthly Film Bulletin (November, 1964), pages 160-161.
Availability: None

ENCHANTED STUDIO, THE (2 reels/16mm)

U.S. Blackhawk Films. 1976. Compiled and Annotated by Anthony Slide.

A compilation, with historical notations, of productions by the French Pathé Frères Company: The Policeman's Little Run (1907), The Dog and His Various Merits (1908), A Diabolical Itching (1908), and Red Spectre (1907). See also More from the Enchanted Studio.

Availability (16mm and 8mm): Blackhawk (sale only)/ Images

ENTER LAUGHING

1967 feature based on Carl Reiner's highly successful novel and play concerning his attempts to break into show business, which does not deal with his film career.

EPIC THAT NEVER WAS, THE (60 mins/35mm)

G.B. BBC Television. 1965. Producer and Screenplay: Bill Duncalf. Narrator: Dirk Bogarde.

A documentary on Josef von Sternberg's abortive film project, I Claudius, which the director had begun shooting in February of 1937. The Epic That Never Was includes extant footage from I Claudius, together with interviews with many of the principals, including von Sternberg, Merle Oberon, Robert Newton, Emlyn Williams, and Flora Robson. The anonymous writer of promotional material for the 1969 New York Film Festival, at which the documentary was screened with great success, describes The Epic That Never Was as "a posthumous confrontation between a dictatorial director and an anarchic actor." The Epic That Never Was was first televised on December 24, 1965. The most detailed analysis of the I Claudius footage can be found in The Cinema of Joseph von Sternberg by John Baxter (A. S. Barnes, 1971).

Availability (16mm): Images/Twyman

EROTIKUS (90 mins/16mm)

U.S. A Hand-in-Hand Films Release of a Times Films

Production. 1973. Producer: Tom DeSimone. Director: Nicholas Grippo. Narrator: Fred Halsted.

A compilation of gay pornographic films illustrating the progress (?) made in the field. Among those seen in the various clips are Ed Fury, Casey Donovan, Monty Hanson, Glenn Corbett, and Gary Conway. The film claims that the first artistic gay short was Yes (1969), the first artistic gay feature was The Collector (1970), and the first orgasm shot was in a documentary on teenage masturbation titled One. Films excerpted in this compilation include Boys in the Sand, Confessions of a Male Groupie, Dust unto Dust, and L.A. Plays Itself, together with early works from the Athletic Model Guild and Pat Rocco.

Availability: None

ETERNAL TRAMP, THE (55 mins/35mm)

U.S. A Film by Harry Hurwitz. 1967. Producer, Director and Screenplay: Harry Hurwitz. Additional Photography: Charles Hawkins Jr. and Victor Petrochevic. Music: Stuart Oderman. Titles: Emil Antonucci. Narrator: Gloria Swanson.

A study of Chaplin's early, pre-1920 work, utilizing newsreel footage, stills and film clips from the comedian's public domain--Keystone, Essanay and Mutual--comedies. Hurwitz analyzes Chaplin's art and technique, and discusses the evolution of the Tramp character.

Availability (16mm): Macmillan/Select/Indiana University Audio-Visual Center

EXTRAORDINARY ILLUSIONS OF 1904 (1 reel/16mm)

A compilation by Reel Images of two 1904 Georges Méliès productions: The Untameable Whiskers (featuring Méliès as the sole performer) and Tchin-Chao, the Chinese Conjuror.

Availability: Reel Images

EYE HEARS, THE EAR SEES, THE (58 mins/16mm)

Canada. National Film Board of Canada in association with the BBC. 1970. Director: Gavin Millar.

An introduction to the work of Canadian film-maker Norman McLaren, in which he talks about his entry into films and the various film-making techniques that he has introduced and used. A number of extracts are used including some from the following productions: Hen Hop, La Poulette Grise, Neighbours, Fiddle-de-Dee, Blinkity Blank, Spheres, Mosaic, and Pas de Deux.

Availability: International Film Bureau/Learning Corporation of America/Indiana University Audio-Visual Center

FABULOUS MUSICALS, THE see HOLLYWOOD AND THE STARS

FANTASIES OF MELIES, THE (1 reel/16mm)

A compilation by Blackhawk Films of three Georges Méliès productions from 1903: Extraordinary Illusions, The Enchanted Well and The Apparition.

Availability: Em Gee (formerly available for sale on 8mm and 16mm from Blackhawk Films)

FASHIONS IN LOVE (1 reel/10 mins/35mm)

U.S. Paramount. 1936. Film Editors: Fred Waller and Milton Hocky. Narrator: Alois Havrilla.

A compilation of famous screen lovers and famous screen love scenes, basically from Paramount features, and including Valentino in Monsieur Beaucaire, Clara Bow in It and Mae West in She Done Him Wrong.

Availability (16mm): Em Gee (This short was available for sale on 16mm for many years)

FERDINAND ZECCA PROGRAM (51 mins/16mm)

A package of seven films produced by Ferdinand Zecca, compiled by the Museum of Modern Art: Whence Does He Come? (circa 1906), Scenes of Convict Life (1905), Slippery Jim (1905), A Father's Honor (1905), Fun after the Wedding (circa 1907), The Runaway Horse (circa 1907), and Rebellion, Mutiny in Odessa (1906).

Availability: The Museum of Modern Art

FILM AND REALITY (10 reels/105 mins/35mm)

G.B. The British Film Institute. 1942. Compiler: Alberto Cavalcanti.

An historical survey of the documentary film in its various forms, newsreels, scientific films, factual films, travelogues, etc. Among the films covered are Nanook of the North (1922), Moana (1923), Grass (1925), Berlin (1927), Turksib (1929), The General Line (1929), Drifters (1929), Industrial Britain (1931), Man of Aran (1932), Song of Ceylon (1935), Night Mail (1936), The Plow That Broke the Plains (1936), and Spanish Earth (1937), together with historical reconstruction films such as The Covered Wagon (1923), Battleship Potemkin (1925) and The Life of Emile Zola (1937), and three fictional films notable for their realism, Kameradschaft (1931), La Grande Illusion (1937) and Farewell Again (1937). Cavalcanti perhaps over-concentrates on British films, and his survey is obviously dated. Film and Reality is divided into five parts: The Early Realist Film and Its Divorce from Film Drama, The Foundation of the Realist Film, The Romantic Documentary of Distant Lands, The Realistic Documentary of Life at Home, and Realism in the Story Film.

Availability (16mm): Contemporary-McGraw Hill (Distributed in England by the British Film Institute in both 16mm and 35mm)

FILM D'ART, THE (96 mins/16mm)

A package of two early French productions, compiled by the Museum of Modern Art: The Assasination of the Duc de Guise (1908) and Queen Elizabeth (1912).

Availability: The Museum of Modern Art

FILM FIRSTS: Chapter One (The History of the Motion Picture/Silents Please series)

A fascinating anthology of early film footage, including clips from Gertie the Dinosaur, Musketeers of Pig Alley, The Nihilists, The Great Train Robbery, and Mae Irwin and John Rice in The Kiss. The highspot is an all-too-brief interview with G.M. "Broncho Billy" Anderson. An excellent film for teaching the early history of the cinema in thirty minutes. Produced by Paul Killiam and Saul J. Turell, and written by Paul Killiam. For more information, see The History of the Motion Picture series.

Availability: Blackhawk (sale)/Killiam Shows (rental)/ University of California Extension Media Center/Budget

FILM FIRSTS: Chapter Two (The History of the Motion Picture/Silents Please series)

More fascinating film clips from the silent era, including Brute Force, The Lost World, 20,000 Leagues under the Sea, Resurrection, The Spoilers, and She, all proving that whatever film-makers did after the coming of sound, it all had been done before in the 'teens and Twenties. An excellent film for teaching the early history of the cinema in thirty minutes. Produced by Paul Killiam and Saul J. Turell, and written by Paul Killiam. For more information, see The History of the Motion Picture series.

Availability: Blackhawk (sale)/Killiam Shows (rental)/ University of California Extension Media Center/Budget

FILM FUN (851 ft./9 mins/35mm)

U.S. RKO "Screenliner" Series. 1955. Producer: Burton Benjamin. Music: Herman Fuchs. Narrator: Ward Wilson.

One of a series of short films designed to poke fun at early film dramas, in this case a Biograph production with Lillian Gish and Lionel Barrymore and a Vitagraph melodrama.

Availability: Jackson Dube

FILM HISTORY--BEGINNINGS OF CINEMA see BEGINNINGS OF CINEMA

FILM MAKERS: KING VIDOR, THE (28 mins/16mm)

U.S. NET. 1965. Producer and Director: Michael Vidor.

Pioneer director King Vidor talks about his career, and introduces sequences from his production, Our Daily Bread (1934).

Availability: Indiana University Audio-Visual Center

FILM PARADE, THE (circa 60 mins/35mm)

The following piece first appeared in Films in Review (February, 1978), and is reprinted with permission:

On February 13, 1933, the Los Angeles Times editorialized, "Turning introspective, the movies are beginning to discover that they have a history and a past. J. Stuart Blackton, pioneer producer and most ambitious of the celluloid archeologists, has made a feature out of his reminiscences and called it The Film Parade. Curious fans will welcome it, and many, remembering, will feel suddenly old."

The Film Parade, also known as March of the Movies --not to be confused with the March of Time documentary on the film activities of the Museum of Modern Art--and Cavalcade of the Movies, occasionally surfaces in the form of used 16mm prints. It's a fascinating document, the story of whose making should be recorded.

I became actively involved with the film when, as the American Film Institute's Associate Archivist, I worked on its restoration with Robert Gitt, who was then the AFI's Technical Officer and is now Associate Curator of the UCLA Film Archives. The problem was that Blackton kept reshaping the film after its initial release, rather in the manner in which Griffith reworked his early features. He would change the music track, his commentary, some of the clips, and, towards the end of his life, took to presenting the film, silent with a live narration. All 16mm prints available today have splices, sections missing, and none retains the first narration track from the 1933 release. Using several 16mm prints plus miscellaneous reels of 35mm nitrate prints and negative, Robert Gitt and I were able to produce the most complete, but by no means definitive, 16mm version, the negative of which now resides in the National Film Collection at the Library of Congress.

So why is The Film Parade so important? The answer is twofold: first, it is one of the earliest compilations on the history of the cinema, and second, it was compiled by one of the great pioneers of the cinema, J. Stuart Blackton, and reflects his personal, truly joyful, feeling towards the film industry which he had done so much to create.

The Film Parade did not receive much attention on its initial appearance. Variety (December 26, 1933) reviewed the film at Loew's Theatre, NY, and commented, "A novel idea which makes interesting entertainment but it could have been developed into far more outstanding value. Picture was here for one day along with a western on a twin bill. That's about its booking value but among the dualers it should have pretty wide circulation, if for no other reason than that it's a change from the usual diet."

It seems that Blackton first became interested in film compilations on the history of the cinema in the Twenties. On January 21, 1926, he presented a short compilation, Reminiscences of 1915, as a preface to his feature, Bride of the Storm, at the Writers Club in Los Angeles. Reminiscences of 1915, which, alas, no longer survives, included shots of the Vitagraph Studios and its founders, together with extracts from a hundred Vitagraph productions from 1910 through 1915.

The idea for The Film Parade originated with one of the Vitagraph Company's leading directors of the 'teens, William P. S. Earle, who had retired financially secure in the Twenties, lost everything in the Wall Street crash, and by the early Thirties was reduced to selling vacuum cleaners from door to door. Earle and Blackton combined resources, with Earle taking care of the camera and handling the special effects, and his former boss acting as producer, director, and occasional actor. The partners rented a small loft above the former headquarters of a soap company at 919 Lillian Way in the heart of Hollywood, and to assist them in this venture enlisted the aid of Blackton's daughter, Marian, his son Jim and Jim's wife, Melvia, Ben Hendricks, Jr., and former silent actress, Margerie Bonner, who was later to marry novelist Malcolm Lowry.

Blackton and Earle utilized some original footage already in their possession, persuaded the studios to give them some material, in particular, sequences from The Big Parade and Steamboat Willie. When money ran out, (not that there was too much money to begin with), Blackton was able to continue by selling newsreel footage of Czar Nicholas of Russia, which he owned, for $2,000 to Metro-Goldwyn-Mayer, which was in the process of producing Rasputin and the Empress.

William P. S. Earle owned a copy of a film set in ancient Egypt, shot by his brother Ferdinand Pinney Earle in the Twenties, so rather than waste it, Blackton revised film history, and utilized the footage to demonstrate that it was the ancient Egyptians who had discovered the theory of the persistence of vision. Blackton also decided that the Zoetrope was named after the Egyptian God, Zoe!

Where footage did not survive, Blackton and Earle recreated it. They did not have the Edison film of Fred Ott's sneeze, so Earle recreated that great moment in film history and impersonated Ott. The Vitagraph films of A Visit to the Spiritualist and His Sister's Beau were recreated, with Marian Blackton, heavily padded, appearing in the latter as the sister and Ben Hendricks as the Beau. The 1899 Blackton film of The Battle of Manila Bay did not survive, so just as J. Stuart Blackton and his partner Albert E. Smith had faked it back then with a water tank, cardboard cut-out model ships and Blackton's cigar smoke, the partners did it again.

Marian Blackton remembers, "My father and A. E. [Smith] seldom met after my father's financial nosedive. But I was amazed when A. E. turned up the day we made the filming of the Manila Bay scene. My father must have asked him to join us. But he never told me that he had. A. E. was fond of me and I of him. We had a lovely, cozy chat after the filming was finished. I remember him well, looking around the shabby loft and sighing and then pressing my hand ... and I could swear that there were tears in his eyes."

Perhaps the most extraordinary Blackton recreation was that of Al Jolson in The Jazz Singer. Warner Bros. refused to give Blackton any footage, so he donned blackface himself and sang "Mammy" just for The Film Parade.

The whole production may seem quaint to many, but to all those who know of the activities of J. Stuart Blackton and the Vitagraph Company, it is exceedingly moving. Whatever one may think of it, The Film Parade must take its place as the last major Blackton production, a fitting close to a great man's career. It is touching that Blackton chose to dedicate the film to Thomas Edison, whose contribution to the cinema has been downgraded in recent years, but who obviously meant a lot to pioneer Blackton.

The Film Parade contains glimpses of many who played an important part in Blackton's life and career. There is his one-time Oyster Bay neighbor, Theodore Roosevelt. The producer's second wife, Paula, is seen in the Vitagraph production of Monsieur Beaucaire, which Blackton claims was his last film as an actor. Among the glimpses of major stars such as Mary Pickford, Blanche Sweet, Richard Barthelmess, and Harold Lloyd, there is a sequence of John Lowell and his daughter Evangeline Russell in The Big Show (1926). Evangeline Russell was to be Blackton's last wife, and after his death she married William P. S. Earle.

Footage from The Film Parade has turned up in countless compilations since. In the Forties, Bell and Howell released a twenty-minute version--it originally ran for a little under an hour--with the title of Silver Shadows;

it is presently available from Thunderbird Films in 16mm and 8mm. When Albert E. Smith wrote Two Reels and a Crank, he appeared on the Art Baker television show, You Asked for It, and introduced some of Blackton's recreations with the proud boast that he had directed these in the early 1900s.

Marian Blackton recalls that one day her father's then-current wife, Helen Stahle, visited the loft studio and sadly commented, "You are all working so hard ... and none of it will get you anywhere." Well, The Film Parade did not get Blackton much during the last years of his life perhaps, although he certainly enjoyed its production and, as daughter Marian says, it made him a "happy has-been," but the film is now in the Library of Congress, and that does assure Blackton a place in posterity. I am sure he would be proud of that, just as I am very proud to have been in some small way associated with The Film Parade.

FILM PORTRAIT (7, 290 ft. /81 mins/35mm)

U.S. Jerome Hill-Heptagon/Noël Productions. 1972. Producers: Barbara and David C. Stone. Director, Screenplay, Photography, Music, and Narrator: Jerome Hill. Assistant Director: Antoine Vernier. Opticals: Cineffects. Film Editor: Henry Sundquist. Orchestrations: Alex Wilder. Music Directors: Samuel Baron and Milton Kaye. Musicians: Paul Wolfe (Harpsichord), Judd Woldin (Piano), and the New York Woodwind Quintet. Sound: Robert C. Fine. Mechanical Snuff Boxes: Dr. Maurice Sandoz. Louis C. Tiffany Objects: Lillian Nassau. Period Music: "The Flight of the Swallows," "The Whistler and His Dog," "Rings on My Fingers," and "Yip-I-Adee." Blackfoot Indian Music by Alan Downs. Collaborators: John D. Barrett, William Hinkle, Lani Ryland, Marie Hersey, Tina Louise, Melvina Boykin, Harry Rigby, Lester Judson, Brigitte Bardot, Lony Giltray, the Hill Family, Charles Rydell, Mabelle Nash, Nellie Barrett, Edwina St. Clair, Louis Rush, Cyd Charisse, Gwen Davies, Ellen Martin, Louise Husted, Joanna Hill, C. C. Jung, Susanne Schroll, Virginia Hood, Grandma Moses, Ernest Borgnine, Jack Hersey, Maud Oakes, Beaver Woman, John Holland, Luggi Foger, Jerry Reilly, Ed Hersey, Roger Stearns, John Perkins, Jeanne Daour, Albert Schweitzer, Valerie Beattie, Fish Wolf Robe, Susana de Mello, Ghislain Dussart, Two Guns White Calf, Christopher Schroll, and Julia Knowlton.

"Jerome Hill (1905-72), the independent American

film-maker, reflects on the importance and influence of cinema in his life, and on the nature of passing time, with reference to filmed material shot during his childhood in St. Paul, Minnesota; during a visit to Rome in 1927; in the South of France in 1932, and more recently of himself at work."--Tim Pulleine in The Monthly Film Bulletin (July, 1977). Film Portrait includes extracts from the following Jerome Hill films: The Magic Umbrella (1927), The Fortune Teller (1932), Grandma Moses (1950), The Sand Castle (1961), Open the Door and See All the People (1964), Schweitzer and Bach (1965), and Merry Christmas (1969).

Availability: None

FILM THAT WAS LOST, THE (1 reel/10 mins/35mm)

U.S. Metro-Goldwyn-Mayer. John Nesbitt's "Passing Parade" Series. Released: October 31, 1942. Director: Sammy Lee.

A short illustrating the work of the Museum of Modern Art Film Library in preserving and restoring early films. Among the footage used were clips of Queen Victoria, Lenin, King George V, Kaiser Wilhelm, Theodore Roosevelt, and Woodrow Wilson. "An appealing and informative subject for today's motion picture audiences," commented Motion Picture Herald (October 24, 1942).

Availability: Films Incorporated

FILMS OF GEORGES MELIES, THE (Each Part: 1 reel/11 mins/16mm)

A three-part package of George Méliès productions, compiled by the British Film Institute. Part One: The Vanishing Lady (1896), The Brahmin and the Butterfly (1900), The Indiarubber Head (1901), and The Coronation of King Edward VII (1902). Part Two: A Trip to the Moon (1902), The Mysterious Box (1903), and The Marvellous Wreath (1903). Part Three: The Melomaniac (1903), The Bewitched Trunk (1904), The Four Hundred Faces of the Devil (1906), and The Knight of the Black Art (1908).

Availability: British Film Institute, London (no American distributor)

FILMS OF GEORGES MELIES, THE (60 mins/16mm)

U.S. KQED-TV. 1964.

A documentary on the French film pioneer, utilizing film clips, photographs and the personal recollections of his granddaughter.

Availability: Indiana University Audio-Visual Center

FILMS OF OSCAR FISCHINGER, THE (Part One: 13 mins, Part Two: 11 mins, Part Three: 10 mins/16mm)

A three-part package of films by the experimental animator Oscar Fischinger, compiled by the Museum of Modern Art. Part One consists of Study No. 6 (1929), Study No. 7 (1930) and Study No. 8 (1931). Part Two consists of Composition in Blue (1933), Circle (1933) and An American March (1939). Part Three consists of Motion Painting No. 1 (1949).

Availability: The Museum of Modern Art

FILMS OF THE 1890s (18 mins/16mm)

A package of the following films compiled by the Museum of Modern Art: Chinese Laundry (1894), The Execution of Mary Queen of Scots (1895), Dickson Experimental Sound Film (circa 1895), The Irwin-Rice Kiss (1896), Feeding the Doves (1896), Morning Bath (1896), Burning Stable (1896), The Black Diamond Express (1896), New York Street Scenes (circa 1896-1898), Fatima (1897), A (W)ringing Good Joke (1899), and Dewar's Scotch Whisky (1897). These films represent the releases of two companies, Edison and the International Film Company.

Availability: The Museum of Modern Art/Images (rental and sale)

FILMS OF THE TURN OF THE CENTURY (1 reel/16mm)

A collection of short films--comedies, newsreels, etc.--by pioneers such as Cecil Hepworth and R. W. Paul, compiled by Breakspear Films.

Availability (16mm and 8mm): Breakspear Films (sale only)

FIRST FLICKERS, THE (27 mins/16mm)

U.S. WRC-TV. 1969. Director: Charles Stopak.

A documentary on the Library of Congress Paper Print Collection, illustrating its restoration and preservation. Extracts from a number of films in the Collection are shown.

Availability: Films Incorporated/Twyman/Indiana University Audio-Visual Center

FIRST (MOTION) PICTURE SHOW, THE (26 mins/16mm)

U.S. Geoffrey Bell Productions. 1976. Producer and Director: Geoffrey Bell. Screenplay: Jameson Goldner and E. G. Valens. Photography: Joe Winters. Film Editor: Lela Smith. Music: Sam Hall.

"Historic photographs, animation, authentic newspaper clips, illustrate the successive stages leading to the first successful public motion picture demonstration at the San Francisco Art Association, May, 1880. A dramatic framework is provided through the 'reportage' of a newspaper writer who presents the background information about Leland Stanford, who funded the project, and Eadweard Muybridge who synthesized the work of earlier pioneers in photography --as well as in projection and in animation."--Geoffrey Bell.

Availability: University of California Extension Media Center

FIRST PROGRAMS, THE (21 mins/16mm)

A collection of the first films of the Lumière Brothers, first exhibited on opening nights in Paris, London and New York, compiled by the Museum of Modern Art.

Availability: The Museum of Modern Art

FIRST TWENTY YEARS, THE (16mm)

A compilation in twenty-six parts of films from the Paper Print Collection of the Library of Congress, prepared by Kemp R. Niver. The films date from 1898 through 1912, and include works by D. W. Griffith, Georges Méliès, British producers, the Nordisk Film Company, and the Lubin, Selig and Edison Companies. A 176-page book is available for us in connection with the films, which have musical tracks. Parts One through Four cover Edison productions; Parts Five through Sixteen, American Mutoscope and Biograph productions; Parts Seventeen through Nineteen, D. W. Griffith productions at Biograph; Part Twenty, Lubin productions 1904-1909; Part Twenty-One, American Independents 1899-1908; Part Twenty-Two, France and Georges Méliès; Part Twenty-Three, Great Britain, Comedy 1903-1904; Part Twenty-Four, Great Britain, Drama 1903-1904; and Parts Twenty-Five through Twenty-Six, Denmark and the Nordisk Company.

Availability: Pyramid (sale and rental)/USC Film Library

FLAHERTY AND FILM (Each Part: 60 mins/16mm)

U.S. WGBH-TV. 1961.

Four sixty-minute programs in which Frances Flaherty, widow of the documentary film-maker, discusses his work on Nanook of the North, Moana, Man of Aran, and Louisiana Story. The first thirty minutes of the program consists of Mrs. Flaherty's reminiscences and the second part is comprised of clips from the features.

Availability: Indiana University Audio-Visual Center

FLASHBACKS (6, 300 ft. /70 mins/35mm)

G.B. Charles B. Cochran Productions. 1938. Director and Narrator: R. E. Jeffrey. Screenplay: A. Barr-Smith and Lester Powell.

Described by The Cinema (December 7, 1938) as an "informative survey of genesis and development of screen entertainment. Treatment falls into two clear-cut sections, one presenting old films of outstanding national and royal events, other depicting scenes from old-time epics featuring then world-famous names, latter departure scoring richly on unconscious hilarities of exaggerated acting or emotional banalities emphasized by amusingly facetious commentary by R. E. Jeffrey."

Availability: None

FLICKER FLASHBACKS

A series of one-reel shorts, produced by RKO Pathé between 1943 and 1948. Each short consisted of one or two highly truncated versions of films from the early 'teens, complete with music, sound effects and a comedy narration. A series of seven shorts were produced each season from the first, 1943-1944, through the last season, 1947-1948. The final "Flicker Flashback" was released by RKO on July 2, 1948. In its early years, the series was produced and directed by Richard Fleischer, who recalled for Leonard Maltin, in The Great Comedy Shorts (Crown, 1972), "Pathé didn't own anything. I had to dig it all up myself, from various sources all over the country and, in fact, all over the world. I made a trip to Buenos Aires to pick up a few reels. When I read the Library of Congress had found these old films that were printed on paper, I went down there and made a deal with them. I got some through private sources. I went everywhere to get the films. While I was working on these short subjects, Ike Kleinerman was my assistant, and he is now one of the biggest producers in television; he did The 21st Century. Also when I worked out here on the films, Carl Hunt was cutting them, and he is now the president of DeLuxe Labs."

Availability (16mm): Jackson Dube

FLICKER MEMORIES (1 reel/10 mins/35mm)

U.S. M-G-M. 1941. A Pete Smith Speciality. Director: George Sidney.

A salute to the cinema's nickelodeon days.

Availability: M-G-M

FLICKS I AND II (Each Part: 27 mins/16mm)

U.S. National Educational Television. 1971.

Flicks I traces the evolution of the motion picture from shadow plays to the present, and includes film clips of Al Jolson, Lon Chaney, and Laurel and Hardy, among others. Flicks II studies the history of the animated film from 1892 through Walt Disney's Skeleton Dance.

Availability: Indiana University Audio-Visual Center

FOLLIES, FOIBLES AND FASHIONS, 1903-1905 (1 reel/ 16mm)

A sampling of typical non-fiction subjects produced by the American Mutoscope and Biograph Company between 1903 and 1905, copied by Blackhawk Films from the Paper Print Collection at the Library of Congress.

Availability: None (formerly available for sale on 8mm and 16mm from Blackhawk Films)

FOTO: SVEN NYKVIST (900 ft. /25 mins/16mm)

G.B. Bayley Silleck Productions. 1973. Producer: Philip Strick. Photography: Stephen Goldblatt. Film Editor: Colin Sherman. Sound: Ian Bruce. Narrator: Sven Nykvist.

A study of the Swedish cinematographer, Sven Nykvist, who has been so closely associated with the films of Ingmar Bergman. Nykvist is seen working on Bergman's Scenes from a Marriage, and there are also film clips from Through a Glass Darkly, Persona, Shame, Winter Light, and A Passion, together with comments by Ingmar Bergman, Liv Ullmann and Erland Josephsson.

Availability: Films Incorporated

4 CLOWNS (8, 621 ft. /97 mins/35mm)

U.S. Twentieth Century-Fox. 1970. Producer and Screenplay: Robert Youngson. Assistant Producers: Herbert Gelbspan and Alfred Dahlem. Music: Manny Albam. Musical Supervision: Angelo Ross. Sound Effects: Alfred Dahlem. Sound Recording: Henry Markosfeld of Ross-Gaffney Inc. Research Supervisor: Jeanne Youngson. Opticals: Movielab. Narrator: Jay Jackson.

The clowns in question are Stan Laurel, Oliver Hardy, Charlie Chase, and Buster Keaton. Keaton is seen in a condensed version of his 1925 feature, Seven Chances. Oliver Hardy is seen in His Day Out (1918), The Hobo (1917) and No Man's Law (1927). Laurel and Hardy appear together in The Second Hundred Years (1927), Putting Pants on Philip (1927), Two Tars (1928), and Their Purple Moment (1928). Charlie Chase is featured in Us (1927), Fluttering Hearts (1927), The Family Group (1928), and Limousine Love (1928).

4 Clowns opens with shots of Broadway in the Twenties. This Robert Youngson compilation was described by Boxoffice (June 15, 1970) as containing "some of the funniest material yet."

Availability (16mm): Films Incorporated

FRANCES FLAHERTY: HIDDEN AND SEEKING (56 mins/ 16mm)

U.S. Werner Productions. 1972. Director: Peter Werner.

At the age of eighty-seven, Frances Flaherty, the widow of documentary film-maker, Robert Flaherty, recalls their years together.

Availability: Peter Werner

FRANK CAPRA: THE MAN ABOVE THE TITLE (42 mins/ 16mm)

U.S. United States Information Agency. 1975. Producer and Director: Lawrence L. Ott, Jr. Screenplay: Martin Spinelli. Sound: Earle Johnson.

Frank Capra discusses his career with critic Richard Schickel and archivist and historian John Kuiper. Clips from the following films are included: Fultah Fisher's Boarding House, It Happened One Night, Lost Horizon, Mr. Deeds Goes to Town, and Mr. Smith Goes to Washington.

Availability: None

FROM LUMIERE TO LANGLOIS (135 mins/35mm)

A special compilation by Henri Langlois of the Cinemathèque Française for the 1970 New York Film Festival, presented with a live piano accompaniment by Arthur Kleiner.

Availability: None

FROM MAGIC LANTERN TO TODAY/FROM THE MAGIC LANTERN TO TODAY (30 mins/16mm)

This production is distributed without credits and without a main title. It was apparently a 1963 KCET television production.

A documentary on the development of the animated film from the magic lantern through the present, and including the work of Emile Reynaud, Emile Cohl, Winsor McCay, Paul Terry, Walt Disney, John Hubley, and Norman McLaren. The narration is overly simplistic, and the clips from color cartoons are shown in black-and-white.

Availability: Em Gee (rental)/Cinema Eight (purchase)/Reel Images (purchase)

FUN FACTORY, THE (The History of the Motion Picture/ Silents Please series)

The rise to fame of Mack Sennett, with a look at a number of the comedy producer's stars, including Chaplin, Ben Turpin, Marie Dressler, the Keystone Kops, and Carole Lombard, co-produced and written by Paul Killiam and Saul J. Turell. For more information see The History of the Motion Picture series.

Availability (16mm): Blackhawk (sale)/Killiam Shows (rental)/USC Film Library/Select/Budget

FUNNIEST MAN IN THE WORLD, THE (102 mins/35mm)

U.S. Funnyman Inc. 1967. Producers: Vernon P. Becker and Mel May. Associate Producer: Mitchell R. Leiser. Production Consultants: John E. Allen, William K. Everson, Gerald McDonald, and Edward Sutherland. Screenplay: Vernon P. Becker. Visual Effects: Film Formation Inc. and Cinema Research Inc. Film Editor: William C. Dalzell. Art Director: Tony Garcia. Music: Albert Hague. Musical Director: Johnny Douglas. Sound: Albert Gramaglia. Sound Recording: Keith Grant. Film Restoration: Rapid Film Techniques, Inc. Narrator: Douglas Fairbanks, Jr.

A compilation on the early career of Charles Chaplin, including his birth, early life and stage career, and ending with the formation of United Artists by Chaplin, Pickford, Griffith, and Fairbanks. The Funniest Man in the World concentrates only on the Chaplin shorts which are now in the public domain in the United States, and includes clips from Making a Living, Kid Auto Races at Venice, Between Showers, Mabel at the Wheel, Caught in a Cabaret, The Rounders, Tillie's Punctured Romance, His Prehistoric Past, His New Job, A Night Out, The Tramp, The Rink, The Immigrant,

Police, and Easy Street. Of particular interest is footage of Chaplin imitators including Billy Ritchie and Billie West. For more information, see the review of the shortened--69 minutes--British version in The Monthly Film Bulletin (December, 1968), pages 205-206.

Availability (16mm): Grove Press

FUNNY MEN, THE see HOLLYWOOD AND THE STARS

FURTHER PERILS OF LAUREL AND HARDY, THE (8,910 ft. /99 mins/35mm)

U.S. Twentieth Century-Fox. 1967. Producer and Screenplay: Robert Youngson. Associate Producers: Herbert Gelbspan, Alfred Dahlem and the Hal Roach Studios. Music: John Parker. Music Supervisor: Angelo Ross. Sound: Val Peters, Harry Hirsch and Ross-Gaffney, Inc. Opticals: Berkey Industries. Production Manager: I. Hill Youngson. Narrator: Jay Jackson.

A sequel to Youngson's Laurel and Hardy's Laughing 20s. Aside from its star performers, this feature also offers glimpses of Jimmy Finlayson, Edgar Kennedy, Billy West, Charlie Chase, Snub Pollard, and Jean Harlow. The opening sequence from the lesser-known You're Darn Tootin' (1928), with Edgar Kennedy, is a delight, as is a fascinating glimpse of The Unkissed Man (1929) with Bryant Washburn and a young Jean Harlow. For more information, see The Monthly Film Bulletin (September, 1967), page 144.

Availability (16mm): Films Incorporated

GABLE AND LOMBARD (131 mins/35mm)

U.S. Universal, an MCA Company presentation of a Sidney J. Furie Film, A Harry Korshak Production. 1976. Producer: Harry Korshak. Director: Sidney J. Furie. Screenplay: Barry Sander. Photography: Jordan S. Cronenweth. Production Designer: Edward C. Carfagno. Film Editor: Argyle Nelson. Costumes: Edith Head. Music: Michel Legrand. Set Decorator: Hal Gausman. Sound: Don Sharpless and Robert L. Hoyt. Unit Production Managers: Jim Fargo and Fred Slark. First Assistant Director: James A. Westman. Second Assistant Directors: Mike Messinger and Jon Triesault. Party Consultant: Bernie Richards.

With James Brolin (Clark Gable), Jill Clayburgh

(Carole Lombard), Allen Garfield (Louis B. Mayer), Red Buttons (Ivna Cooper), Joanne Linville (Ria Gable), Melanie Mayron (Dixie), Carol McGinnis (Noreen), S. John Launer (Judge), William Bryant (Colonel), Noah Keen (A. Broderick), Alan D. Dexter (Sheriff Ellis), Alice Backes (Hedda Hopper), John Lehne (Attorney Kramer), Robert Karnes (Gable's Director), Betsy Jones-Moreland (Party Guest), Ross Elliott (Lombard's Director), and Morgan Brittany (Vivien Leigh).

A comedy concerning the years Clark Gable and Carol Lombard spent together. Brolin looks like Gable; Clayburgh doesn't look like Lombard.

Availability (16mm): Twyman/Swank

GASLIGHT FOLLIES (110 mins/35mm)

U.S. Producers: Joseph E. Levine and Maxwell A. Finn. Narrator: John B. Kennedy. No other credit information or date of production available.

This production, whose sole intention is to poke fun at the past, is divided into four parts. Part One features "more than 100 stars of yesteryear." The second part, subtitled "Time Marches Back," takes a look at early newsreels. Part Three features a melodrama titled The Drunkard, "filmed as it has been seen on the stage in Los Angeles for the past 13 years." The American Biograph production of East Lynne comprises Part Four of Gaslight Follies, and while it is being screened Milton Cross and Ethel Owen heckle from the soundtrack.

Availability (16mm): Macmillan

GENTLEMAN TRAMP, THE (78 mins/35mm)

U.S. Filmverhuurkantoor "De Dam" B.V. Production and Release, in Association with Audjeff, Inc. 1975. Producer: Bert Schneider. Director, Screenplay and Film Editor: Richard Patterson. Original Music: Charles Chaplin. Photography: Nestor Almendros. Associate Producer: Artie Ross. Production Advisor: Pierre Cottrell. Narrator: Walter Matthau. Passages from My Autobiography Read by Laurence Olivier. Academy Award Citation Read by Jack Lemmon.

An affectionate and pleasing tribute to the life and

work of Charles Chaplin, with clips from seventeen of his films, newsreel footage, still photographs, dramatized voices, behind-the-scenes footage from Chaplin's own collection, and Oona O'Neill Chaplin's home movies. As John H. Dorr commented in The Hollywood Reporter (March 21, 1975), "a tremendously moving and well-constructed document." For more information, see Emily S. Jones' review in Film News (September-October, 1976), page 12.

Availability (35mm and 16mm): rbc films

GEORGE RAFT STORY, THE (9,497 ft./105 mins/35mm)

U.S. Allied Artists. 1961. Producer: Ben Schwalb. Director: Joseph M. Newman. Production Supervisor: Edward Morey, Jr. Screenplay: Crane Wilbur. Photography: Carl Guthrie. Original Music and Adaptations: Jeff Alexander. Art Director: David Milton. Set Decorator: Joseph Kish. Choreography: Alex Romero. Film Editor: George White. Music Editor: Eve Newman. Sound Editor: Monty Pearce. Set Continuity: Virginia Barth. Sound: Ralph Butler. Wardrobe Supervisor: Roger J. Weinberg. Wardrobe: Norah Sharpe. Makeup: Norman Pringle. Hairdresser: Alice Monte. Construction Supervisor: James West. Property Master: Ted Mossman. Assistant Director: Lindsley Parsons, Jr.

With Ray Danton (George Raft), Jayne Mansfield (Lisa), Julie London (Sheila), Barrie Chase (June), Barbara Nichols (Texas), Frank Gorshin (Moxie), Margo Moore (Ruth), Brad Dexter (Benny), Neville Brand (Capone), Robert Strauss (Frenchie), Joe De Santis (Frankie), Argentina Brunetti (Mrs. Raft), John Bleifer (Mr. Raft), Pepper Davis and Tony Reese (M.C.s), Jack Lambert (Fitzpatrick), Cecile Rogers (Charleston Dancer), Tol Avery (Mizner, the Wit), Robert H. Harris (Harvey), and Herschel Bernardi (Sam).

The George Raft Story was described at the time of its original release as more of a gangster story than the film biography of George Raft.

Availability (16mm): Hurlock Cine-World

GEORGES MELIES (22 mins/16mm)

France. Les Amis de Georges Méliès. 1969. Director: Claude Leroy.

Mêliès' life is retraced through the use of sets, designs, costumes, and photographs.
Availability: F. A. C. S. E. A.

GEORGES MELIES: CINEMA MAGICIAN (26 mins/16mm)

U. S. A Film by Patrick Montgomery and Luciano Martinengo, distributed by Blackhawk Films. 1979.

A general overview of the life and career of Georges Mêliès, including clips from several of his productions not generally available in recent years.
Availability: Blackhawk

GEORGES MELIES PROGRAM (75 mins/16mm)

A package of five films produced by Georges Mêliès, compiled by the Museum of Modern Art: The Conjuror (1899), A Trip to the Moon (1902), The Palace of the Arabian Nights (1905), The Doctor's Secret (1908), and The Conquest of the Pole (1912).
Availability: The Museum of Modern Art

GERMAN CLASSIC COMPILATION: Part One (73 mins/16mm)

Clips from the following German films of the late 'teens and Twenties, with brief narration and evaluation of each production: Madame Dubarry, The Cabinet of Dr. Caligari, The Golem, The Rail, Destiny, Backstairs, Waxworks, and The Last Laugh.
Availability: Em Gee

GERMAN CLASSIC COMPILATION: Part Two (61 mins/16mm)

Similar in format to Part One, but including lengthy clips from Joyless Street, Metropolis, Faust, Berlin, Mother Krausen's Journey to Happiness, and Such Is Life.
Availability: Em Gee

GIRLS IN DANGER (The History of the Motion Picture/Silents Please series)

Leading ladies of the silent era, including Mae Marsh, Leatrice Joy and Gloria Swanson, face a variety of dangers, which could only happen to screen heroines, co-produced and written by Paul Killiam and Saul J. Turell. For more information, see The History of the Motion Picture series.

Availability (16mm): Blackhawk (sale)/Killiam Shows (rental)/Indiana University Audio-Visual Center (rental)/Budget (rental)

GLIMPSES OF INDIAN CINEMA (20 mins/16mm)

A documentary on the growth and development of the Indian cinema during the past fifty years.

Availability: Information Service of India

GOLDEN AGE OF COMEDY, THE (78 mins/35mm)

U.S. Ro-Co Productions/Distributors Corporation of America. 1958. Producer and Screenplay: Robert Youngson. Music: George Steiner. Narrators: Dwight Weist and Ward Wilson.

The first Robert Youngson feature-length comedy compilation, which concentrated on the best of the Mack Sennett and Hal Roach comedies of the Twenties. Featured comedians include Laurel and Hardy (with the greatest amount of footage), Will Rogers, Carole Lombard, Jean Harlow, Ben Turpin, Harry Langdon, Charlie Chase, Billy Bevan, Andy Clyde, Charlie Murray, Harry Gribbon, Daphne Pollard, Vernon Dent, Marie Mosquini, Louise Carver, and the Keystone Kops.

Availability (16mm): Budget Films/Kit Parker Films/Macmillan/Swank/Twyman

GOLDEN SILENCE see SILENCE EST D'OR, LE

GOLDEN TWENTIES, THE (66 mins/35mm)

U.S. RKO/March of Time. 1950. Producer: Richard de Rochemont. Assistant Producer: Samuel Wood Bryant.

Original Story by Frederick Lewis Allen and Samuel Wood Bryant. Music Director: Jack Shaindlin. Film Editor: Leo Zochling. Research: Whitfield Davis, Lois Jacoby, Leona Carney, and Nancy Pessac. Narrators: Frederick Lewis Allen, Robert Q. Lewis, Allen Prescott, "Red" Barber, and Elmer Davis.

A compilation of newsreel footage from the Twenties in the "March of Time" manner. Robert Q. Lewis handles the narration of the entertainment section of the production, which includes footage of many entertainment personalities from the Twenties, including Douglas Fairbanks, Greta Garbo, Peggy Hopkins Joyce, Thomas Edison, Al Jolson, Helen Morgan, Rudy Vallee, Texas Guinan, Harry Houdini, John Gilbert, Charles Chaplin, Anna Pavlova, and Gallagher and Shean. Very well received by critics at the time of its initial release.

Availability (16mm): Twyman/Macmillan

GOOD OLD CORN (20 mins/35mm)

U.S. Warner Bros. 1945. Narrator: Knox Manning.

One of a series of Warner Bros. compilations utilizing Mack Sennett film clips.

Availability: United Artists 16

GOOFY'S GOLDEN GAGS (400 ft. /8mm)

Excerpts from five Walt Disney/Goofy cartoons: Goofy's Glider (1940), Baggage Buster (1941), The Art of Self-Defense (1941), Tiger Trouble (1945), and Knight for a Day (1946).

Availability: Walt Disney 8mm

GRACE KELLY (26 mins/16mm)

U.S. Wolper Productions, released by Official Films. 1963. Producer: David L. Wolper. Music: Jack Tillar. Host/Narrator: Mike Wallace.

A documentary on the life and career of Grace Kelly, utilizing a considerable amount of newsreel footage. A film in the "Biography" television series.

Availability: Sterling

GRAND MELIES, LE (2,700 ft./30 mins/35mm)

France. Armor Films. 1952. Producer: Fred Orain. Director and Screenplay: Georges Franju. Photography: Jacques Mercanton. Art Director: Henri Schmitt. Music: Georges Van Parys.

A charming tribute to the French film pioneer, with dramatic reconstructions of incidents in his life, clips from his films, and shots of his widow taking flowers to his grave. The music in Le Grand Méliès is based on a waltz which Méliès composed for his wife. For more information, see The Monthly Film Bulletin (August, 1954), page 123.

Availability: F.A.C.S.E.A.

GREAT ACTRESSES OF THE PAST (71 mins/16mm)

A package of films, capturing the art of the most famous stage actresses of their day, compiled by the Museum of Modern Art: Gabrielle Réjane in Madame Sans-Gêne (1911), Sarah Bernhardt in La Dame aux camélias (1912), Minnie Maddern Fiske in Vanity Fair (1915), and Eleanora Duse in Cenere (1916).

Availability: The Museum of Modern Art

GREAT ADVENTURES (13 mins/35mm)

"Produced for exclusive use by those colleges and universities actively enrolled as participants in the Warner Bros.-NEC Film Project.... Thrilling the world with scenes of great daring and drama, spectacular adventure stories have charged the screen with excitement. Westerns and sea dramas, sweeping outdoor spectacles, here are historic film highlights from the screen's great adventures. Narrated by James Stewart."--description in Warner Bros. catalogue.

Availability (16mm): Warner Bros.

GREAT CHASE, THE (79 mins/35mm)

U.S. A Saul J. Turell and Paul Killiam Presentation. 1962. Producers: Saul J. Turell and Paul Killiam. Director: Harvey Cort. Screenplay: Harvey Cort, Saul J. Turell and Paul Killiam. Music Composed and Played by Larry Adler. Music Arranger and Conductor: George Bassman.

Film Editors: Harvey Cort and Saul J. Turell. Main Titles: Ted Trinkaus. Narrator: Frank Gallop.

A series of film clips illustrating how the cinema has used the chase, from The Great Train Robbery, through A Girl and Her Trust and Way Down East, to The General. Also included are sequences with Douglas Fairbanks, Noah Beery and Rod La Roque, Pearl White, Ruth Roland, and William S. Hart. In 1975 additional sequences, showing Mack Sennett and Mabel Normand, were added to the compilation.

Availability (16mm): Janus

GREAT COMEDIES (13 mins/35mm)

"Produced for exclusive use by those colleges and universities actively enrolled as participants in the Warner Bros.-NEC Film Project.... Many great comedians have made the world laugh in light-hearted films designed to amuse and entertain. From slapstick to drawing-room satire, here are historic highlights of humor, scenes to enjoy again and again from great comedies. Narrated by Jack Benny."--description in Warner Bros. catalogue.

Availability (16mm): Warner Bros.

GREAT DIRECTOR, THE (62 mins/16mm)

G.B. BBC. 1966. Producer and Director: John Boorman. Commentary Written by John Lloyd. Researched and Compiled by William K. Everson, John Merritt and John Boorman. Narrator: Clive Swift.

A well-made documentary on the career of D. W. Griffith, concentrating on The Birth of a Nation and Intolerance, and also including an all-too-brief interview with Lillian Gish. What The Great Director features and says is good, but it could have presented a great deal more in the way of interviews and film clips--and the clips could have been of better pictorial quality.

Availability: Killiam Shows

GREAT DIRECTORS, THE see HOLLYWOOD AND THE STARS

GREAT LOVE SCENES (13 mins/35mm)

"Produced for exclusive use by those colleges and universities actively enrolled as participants in the Warner Bros.-NEC Film Project.... Great love scenes ... inspiring, thrilling scenes to touch the heart, many lustrous love stories have found their place in the lasting legends of the screen. Here are historic highlights from great romantic films. Narrated by Joan Crawford."--description in Warner Bros. catalogue.

Availability (16mm): Warner Bros.

GREAT LOVERS, THE see HOLLYWOOD AND THE STARS

THE GREAT PRIMITIVES: LANDMARK FILMS FROM THE FIRST DECADE OF MOTION PICTURE HISTORY (43 mins/16mm)

A compilation of the following early films. From the Edison Company: Fred Ott's Sneeze (1894), Sandow Flexing His Muscles (1894), The Kiss (1896), Boxing Cats (circa 1897), Pie Eating Contest (1897), and Ella Lola's Turkish Dance (1898). From the Lumiere Brothers: Workers Leaving the Lumière Factory, Arrival of the Train at La Ciotat, Firemen Answering the Call, Snowball Fight, Demolition of a Wall, Watering the Gardener, Feeding the Baby, Quarreling Infants, A Game of Cards, Children Digging Shrimp, Swimming in the Sea (all produced between 1895 and 1898). From Georges Méliès: A Trip to the Moon (1902). From Edwin S. Porter: Uncle Josh at the Moving Picture Show (1902), The Life of an American Fireman (1903) and The Great Train Robbery (1903). From Cecil Hepworth: Rescued by Rover (1905).

Availability: Berkeley Films

GREAT RADIO COMEDIANS (Part One: 35 mins, Part Two: 26 mins, Part Three: 27 mins/16mm)

U.S. WNET-TV. 1974. Producer and Director: Perry Miller Adato. Associate Producer: Aviva Slesin. Playhouse New York Executive Director: Jac Venza.

A three-part study of the great radio comedians--Bob Hope, Eddie Cantor, George Burns and Gracie Allen, Fanny

Brice, W. C. Fields, Edgar Bergen and Charlie McCarthy, and Fred Allen--utilizing still photographs, radio transcriptions, newsreel footage, and clips from motion pictures. In Part One, George Burns talks about the transition from vaudeville to radio. In Part Three, Minerva Pious, Kenny Delmar, Parker Fennelly, and Peter Donald present a new version of Allen's Alley, scripted by Harry Bailey, who wrote the original shows.

Availability (16mm and videotape): McGraw-Hill (rental and sale)

GREAT STONE FACE, THE (93 mins/35mm)

U.S. Funnyman Productions. 1968. Producer and Director: Vernon P. Becker. Film Editor: William C. Dalzell. Narrator: Henry Morgan.

An amusing documentary on the life and career of Buster Keaton, with clips from a number of his films including Coney Island (1917), Cops (1922), Daydreams (1922), Balloonatics (1923), and The Railrodder (1965). Almost half of the film is taken up with a condensed version of Keaton's 1926 feature, The General.

Availability (16mm): Twyman/Kit Parker Films/Select.

GREAT WESTERNS (13 mins/35mm)

"Produced for exclusive use by those colleges and universities actively enrolled as participants in the Warner Bros.-NEC Film Project.... A part of the heritage of our American West, sweeping adventure, brawling action and pioneering drama have been portrayed on the screen by stars of great stature in many notable motion pictures. Here are historic film highlights--memorable scenes from great westerns. Narrated by John Wayne."--description in the Warner Bros. catalogue.

Availability (16mm): Warner Bros.

GRIERSON (58 mins/16mm)

Canada. National Film Board of Canada. 1973. Producer: David Bairstow. Director: Roger Blais. Photography: Eugene Boyke, Lewis McLeod, Michel Thomas-d-Hoste, Magi Torruella, and Jacques Fogel. Film Editors: Les Halman and John Kramer. Narrator: Michael Kane.

A documentary on John Grierson, the father of the documentary film, including comments by many who knew and worked with him: Roberto Rossellini, Joris Ivens, Sir Arthur Elton, Edgar Anstey, Basil Wright, Stuart Legg, Stanley Hawes, Lorne Greene, Ross McLean, and Sydney Newman. "From the men and women who knew him, who listened to him and were influenced by what he said, a remembrance of John Grierson, the man who saw in films a means to realize the democratic idea."--from the catalogue of the National Film Board of Canada.

Availability: National Film Board of Canada (rental and sale)/Indiana University Audio-Visual Center

GRIFFITH BIOGRAPH PROGRAM (77 mins/16mm)

A package of five films directed by D. W. Griffith for the American Biograph Company, compiled by the Museum of Modern Art: A Lonely Villa (1909), A Corner in Wheat (1909), The Lonedale Operator (1911), The Musketeers of Pig Alley (1912), and The New York Hat (1912).

Availability: The Museum of Modern Art

HAPPY TIMES AND JOLLY MOMENTS (20 mins/35mm)

U.S. Warner Bros. "Broadway Brevities" series. 1943. Screenplay: James Bloodworth. Narrator: Lou Marcelle.

One of a series of Warner Bros. shorts utilizing footage from Mack Sennett comedies. "This Mack Sennett compilation includes the best moments of Ben Turpin and Fatty Arbuckle in some riotous comic escapades along with featuring the best moments of other silent comedy stars."--description in Swank catalogue.

Availability (16mm): Swank/United Artists 16

HARLOW (125 mins/35mm)

U.S. A Joseph E. Levine Production in Association with Paramount. 1965. Producer: Joseph E. Levine. Director: Gordon Douglas. Screenplay: John Michael Hayes. Based on the Book by Irving Shulman in Collaboration with Arthur Landau. Photography: Joseph Ruttenberg. Art Directors: Hal Pereira and Roland Anderson. Set Decorators: Sam Comer and James Payne. Gowns: Edith Head. Makeup Supervision: Wally Westmore. Hair Style Supervision: Nellie Manley. Carroll Baker's Hair Styled by Sydney Guilaroff. Unit Production Manager: Kenneth DeLand. Film Editors: Frank Bracht and Archie Marshek. Sound Recording: Stanley Jones and Charles Grenzbach. Music: Neal Hefti. Men's Costumes: Moss Mabry. Dialogue Coach: Leon Charles. Special Photographic Effects: Paul K. Lerpae. Process Photography: Farciot Edouart. Technicolor Consultant: Richard Mueller. Assistant Director: Dave Salven.

With Carroll Baker (Jean Harlow), Martin Balsam (Everett Redman), Red Buttons (Arthur Landau), Michael Connors (Jack Harrison), Angela Lansbury (Mama Jean Bello), Peter Lawford (Paul Bern), Raf Vallone (Marino Bello), Leslie Nielsen (Richard Manley), Mary Murphy (Studio Secretary), Hanna Landy (Mrs. Arthur Landau), Peter Hansen (Assistant Director of the Thirties), Kipp Hamilton (Girl at Pool), Peter Leeds (Director of the Thirties), Fritz Feld (Window Washer), Billy Bletcher (Burly Policeman), and Benny Rubin (Director).

Film biography of Jean Harlow, covering her life from 1928 through her death in 1937.

Availability (16mm): Films Incorporated

HARLOW (9,800 ft./108 mins/35mm)

U.S. Marshall Naify Presents a Bill Sargent Production, Released by Magna Pictures. 1965. Executive Producer: Brandon Chase. Producer: Lee Savin. Director: Alex Segal. Screenplay: Karl Tunberg. Photography: Jim Kilgore. Art Director: Duncan Cramer. Set Decorator: Harry Gordon. Music Arranged and Conducted by Nelson Riddle. Music Composed by Al Ham and Nelson Riddle. Costumes: Nolan Miller. Sound: Dave Forrest. Associate Producer: Frank Ray. Production Manager: Eddie Dodds. Production Assistant: Nanette Eiland. Casting: Marvin Paige. Wardrobe: Paul McCardle. Makeup: Mike Westmore. Hairdresser: Mary Westmoreland. Props: Ken Westcott. Assistant Directors: Greg Peters, Johnny Wilson and Dick Bennett.

With Carol Lynley (Jean Harlow), Efrem Zimbalist,

Jr. (William Mansfield), Barry Sullivan (Marino Bello), Hurd Hatfield (Paul Bern), Lloyd Bochner (Marc Peters), Hermione Baddeley (Marie Dressler), Audrey Totter (Marilyn), John Williams (Jonathan Martin), Michael Dante (Ed), Jack Kruschen (Louis B. Mayer), Celia Lovksy (Maria Ouspenskaya), Robert Strauss (Hank), Sonny Liston (First Fighter), James Dobson (Counterman), Cliff Norton (Billy), Paulle Clark (Waitress), Jim Plunkett (Stan Laurel), John "Red" Fox (Oliver Hardy), Joel Marston (Press Agent), Miss Christopher West (Bern's Secretary), Fred Conte (Photographer), Catherine Ross (Wardrobe Woman), Buddy Lewis (Al Jolson), Danny Francis (Casino Manager), Frank Scannell (Doctor), Maureene Gaffney (Miss Larsen), Nick Demitri (Second Fighter), Ron Kennedy (Assistant Director), Harry Holcombe (Minister), Lola Fisher (Nurse), Fred Klein (Himself), and Ginger Rogers (Mama Jean).

Film biography of Jean Harlow, who, according to publicity at the time of the film's release, had the same physical measurements as Carol Lynley.

Availability: None

HAROLD LLOYD'S FUNNY SIDE OF LIFE (99 mins/35mm)

U.S. Harold Lloyd Productions. 1963. Producer: Harold Lloyd. Associate Producer: Jack Murphy. Story Consultant: Harold Lloyd, Jr. Commentary Written by Arthur Ross. Music: Walter Scharf. Song, "There Was a Boy, There Was a Girl," by Ned Washington and Walter Scharf. Music Editor: Sid Sidney. Film Editor: Duncan Mansfield.

A sequel to Harold Lloyd's World of Comedy, and equally funny. Harold Lloyd's Funny Side of Life features clips from For Heaven's Sake (1926), Girl Shy (1924) and The Kid Brother (1927), together with a slightly edited version of The Freshman (1925). Lloyd's comic genius is very much in evidence in the clips, which are introduced by the comedian himself. The music score is particularly pleasing, as is a song which should have been intrusive but is not.

Availability: None

HAROLD LLOYD'S WORLD OF COMEDY (8,727 ft./97 mins/35mm)

U.S. Harold Lloyd Productions. 1962. Producer:

Harold Lloyd. Associate Producer: Jack Murphy. Story Consultant: Harold Lloyd, Jr. Narration Written and Spoken by Art Ross. Music: Walter Scharf. Orchestrations: Lew Shuken and Jack Hayes. Music Editor: Sid Sidney. Music Recordings: Vinton Vernon. Film Editor: Duncan Mansfield. Sound Effects: Del Harris.

Harold Lloyd emerged from retirement with this compilation of clips from some of his greatest comedy features, painstakingly put together and tested before preview audiences in much the same manner in which Lloyd produced his silent features. Harold Lloyd's World of Comedy features extracts from the following films: Safety Last (1923), Why Worry (1923), Hot Water (1924), Girl Shy (1924), The Freshman (1925), Feet First (1930), Movie Crazy (1932), and Professor Beware (1938). The film received excellent critical response at the time of its initial release but little public attention. I can only echo Brendan Gill in The New Yorker (June 9, 1962), "Those were the days, and here they are, bathed in more sunlight than any actual day can hold."

Availability: None

HEARTS OF THE WEST (102 mins/35mm)

U.S. M-G-M Presents a Bill/Zieff Production. 1975. Producer: Tony Bill. Director: Howard Zieff. Screenplay: Rob Thompson. Photography: Mario Tosi. Music: Ken Lauber. Special Musical Artists: Nick Lucas, Roger Patterson and Merle Travis. Art Director: Robert Luthardt. Set Decorator: Charles R. Pierce. Film Editor: Edward Warschilka. Sound: Jerry Jost and Harry W. Tetrick. Assistant Film Editor: Freeman Davies, Jr. Costume Designer: Patrick Cummings. Costumers: Don Vargas and Lynn Bernay. Makeup: Bob Stein. Hair Styles: Dorothy Byrne. Casting: Dianne Derfner Crittenden. Unit Production Manager: Clark L. Paylow. Assistant Director: Jack B. Bernstein. Second Assistant Director: Alan Brimfield. Script Supervisor: Joan Eremin. Property Master: Ted Mossman. Music Supervisor: Harry V. Lojewski. Music Editor: Bill Saracino. Sound Effects Editor: John P. Riordan. Publicity: Regina Gruss. Choreography: Sylvia Lewis. Assistant to the Producer: Tina Calvo. Assistant to Mr. Zieff: Gina Ehrlich.

With Jeff Bridges (Lewis Tater), Andy Griffith (Howard Pike), Donald Pleasance (A. J. Nietz), Blythe Danner (Miss Trout), Alan Arkin (Kessler), Richard B. Shull (Stout

Crook), Herbert Edelman (Polo), Alex Rocco (Earl), Frank Cady (Pa Tater), Anthony James (Lean Cook), Burton Gilliam (Lester), Matt Clark (Jackson), Candy Azzara (Waitress), Thayer David (Bank Manager), Wayne Storm (Lyle), Marie Windsor (Woman in Nevada), Anthony Holland (Guest at Beach Party), Dub Taylor (Nevada Ticket Agent), Raymond Guth (Wally), Herman Poppe (Lowell), William Christopher (Bank Teller), Jane Dulo (Mrs. Stern), Dave Morick (Cameraman), Jacques Foti (Musical Director), Stuart Nisbet (Lucky), Tucker Smith (Noodle in Pith Helmet), Richard Stahl (Barber), Linda Borgeson (Western Ingenue), Titus Napoleon (Native Drummer), Barbara Brownell (Nietz' Girlfriend), and Granville Van Dusen (World War One Pilot).

A comedy set against a background of the making of "B" Westerns in the Hollywood of the Thirties. Murf in Variety (October 1, 1975) commented, "The structure of the film is notable in that it tells its story in the manner of films of 40 years ago, while in turn keeping separate the ways in which period films of 40 years were then artistically conceived and executed."

Availability (16mm): Films Incorporated

HEDDA HOPPER'S HOLLYWOOD (1 reel/35mm)

U.S. Paramount. 1941 and 1942. Producer: Herbert Moulton. Associate Producer: Whitney Williams. Photography: Robert C. Bruce and Frank W. Young. Film Editor: Duke Goldstone. Narrator: Hedda Hopper.

A series of six shorts--the first two released in 1941 and the remaining four released in 1942--in which Hedda Hopper looks at some interesting and some extremely dull aspects of the Hollywood scene. Among the items included in the series are Carl Spitz' Dog Training School (# 3), A Garden Party at Pickfair (# 1), Jane Withers' Sixteenth Birthday Party (# 4), the Dedication of the Motion Picture Country House (# 2), A Visit to the Mocombo Nightclub (# 2), Constance Bennett, John Howard and Lum an' Abner at Home (# 5), Kay Kyser (# 6), and Gary Cooper, Ernest Hemingway and Howard Hawks on a Shooting Party at Sun Valley (# 3). Of historical interest are a visit to William S. Hart at his Newhall Ranch (# 6) and William Farnum reminiscing about his career in silent films and showing a clip from Hedda Hopper's first film, in which he co-starred (# 2).

Availability: National Telefilm Associates (16mm

prints are available for study at the Academy of Motion Picture Arts and Sciences)

HELEN HAYES: PORTRAIT OF AN AMERICAN ACTRESS (90 mins/16mm)

U.S. NET. 1973. Producer and Director: Nathan Kroll. Screenplay: Claire Birsch Merrill. Photography: Arthur Ornitz. Film Editor: Marion Arsham.

A study of Helen Hayes' career on stage and in films from the early 1920s through the present. George Abbott, Robert Whitehead, Marc Connelly, and Maureen Stapleton discuss working with Miss Hayes, who is seen in a number of roles, including Queen Victoria in Victoria Regina, Mary Stuart in Mary of Scotland and Catherine in A Farewell to Arms. The New York Times described this documentary as an "articulate living history of the theatre."

Availability: Phoenix Films (rental and sale)/Budget

HELEN MORGAN STORY, THE (127 mins/35mm)

U.S. Warner Bros. 1957. Producer: Martin Rackin. Director: Michael Curtiz. Screenplay: Oscar Saul, Dean Riesner, Stephen Longstreet, and Nelson Gidding. Photography: Ted McCord. Art Director: John Beckman. Set Decorator: Howard Bristol. Film Editor: Frank Bracht. Sound: Francis J. Scheid and Dolph Thomas. Musical Numbers Staged by LeRoy Prinz. Songs Sung by Gogi Grant. Costumes: Howard Shoup. Dialogue Supervisor: Norman Stuart. Vocal Arrangements: Charles Henderson. Makeup: Gordon Bau. Assistant Director: Paul Helmick.

With Ann Blyth (Helen Morgan), Paul Newman (Larry Maddux), Richard Carlson (Russell Wade), Gene Evans (Whitey Krause), Alan King (Ben Weaver), Cara Williams (Dolly Evans), Virginia Vincent (Sue), Walter Woolf King (Ziegfeld), Dorothy Green (Mrs. Wade), Ed Platt (Haggerty), Warren Douglas (Hellinger), Sammy White (Sammy), Peggy De Castro, Cheri De Castro and Babette De Castro (Singers), Jimmy McHugh (Himself), Rudy Vallee (Himself), and Walter Winchell (Himself).

The life story of the nightclub and vaudeville singer and occasional film star.

Availability: None

HELL OF A GOOD LIFE: HOWARD HAWKS--19 CHAPTERS FROM THE MEMORY OF A STORY TELLER, A (58 mins/16mm)

Germany. Sunset Mark Productions (Munich) in association with Bayerischen Rundfunks. 1978. Director and Screenplay: Hans C. Blumenberg. Photography: Bodo Kesller. Film Editor: Inge Gielow. Sound: Pat Shea. Production Coordinator: Jürgen Hellwig.

Interviews with director Howard Hawks, filmed over a five-day period in November of 1977 in Palm Springs and Willow Springs, California. The director talks about his passion for planes and motor racing, his friendships with John Ford, Howard Hughes and Ernest Hemingway, his work with actors such as Gary Cooper, John Wayne and Cary Grant, and the women in his films, in particular Lauren Bacall and Carole Lombard. The producers of this film purposely avoided using clips from Hawks' productions.

Availability: None

HIGHLIGHT: THE SINGING CINEMA (58 mins/35mm)

G.B. Associated British-Pathe. 1963. Executive Producer: Terry Ashwood. Associate Producer: Lionel Hoare. Producer and Screenplay: Denis Gifford. Film Editor: Ron Glenister. Host: Pete Murray.

A pilot for an unrealized television series titled *Highlight*, *Highlight: The Singing Cinema* is a delightful compilation of musical numbers from the films of Associated British-Pathe, its predecessors and its subsidiaries, introduced by one-time British disc jockey Pete Murray. Extracts from the following films are used: *Piccadilly*, *Moulin Rouge*, *Elstree Calling*, *Indiscretions of Eve*, *Dance Band*, *Radio Parade of 1935*, *Invitation to the Waltz*, *Happy Go Lovely*, *Champagne Charlie*, *Trouble Brewing*, *Sally in our Alley*, *Please Teacher*, *Out of the Blue*, *Yes Madam*, *You Made Me Love You*, *Over She Goes*, *Gypsy Blood*, *Maid of the Mountains*, *Glamorous Nights*, *The Dancing Years*, *Chelsea Nights*, *Beloved Vagabond*, *I Give My Heart*, *My Song Goes Round the World*, *Blossom Time*, *Music Hath Charms*, *Jazz Time*, *Everything Is Rhythm*, *The Lady Is a Square*, *Tommy the Toreador*, and *Summer Holiday*.

Availability (16mm): British Film Institute, London (no American distributor)

HIGHLIGHTS OF HORROR (1 reel/10 mins/16mm)

A package of extracts, with no music or sound effects, from three silent Universal features: The Hunchback of Notre Dame, The Cat and the Canary and The Phantom of the Opera.
Availability: Swank

HIGHLIGHTS OF THE SINGING CINEMA see HIGHLIGHT: THE SINGING CINEMA

HISTORICAL STILL AND MOTION PICTURE PROJECTORS (11 mins/16mm)

A brief historical survey of film projectors, shown usually in the form of still photographs, with a commentary, produced by the University of Iowa in cooperation with the Archives and History Committee of the Division of Audio-visual Instruction of the National Education Association.
Availability: University of Iowa Audio-Visual Center

HISTORY BROUGHT TO LIFE see LET'S GO TO THE MOVIES

HISTORY OF ANIMATION (21 mins/35mm)

A shortened version of The Story of the Animated Drawing (q.v. for production credits), detailing the history of animation from the drawings of the primitive caveman through the sophisticated output of the Disney studios.
Availability (16mm): Walt Disney

HISTORY OF PORNOGRAPHY, THE

Aside from the content, as indicated by its title, no information has been uncovered concerning this production, first screened in Los Angeles at the Tiffany Theatre on December 23, 1970 by History Films.

HISTORY OF THE BLUE MOVIE, THE (140 mins/35mm)

U.S. A Screening Room Production, released by

Sherpix. 1970. Producer and Director: Alex de Renzy. Assistant Director: Paul Gerber. Film Editor: Jack Kerpan.

As its title indicates, this is a documentary compilation on the history of the pornographic movie, including a 1915 classic titled A Free Ride (photographed by Will B. Hard), On the Beach (featuring three nude women, a nude man and a goat) and Candy Barr's classic from the Forties, Smart Alec. Variety (November 11, 1970) described it as "overlong, but ... oddly quaint and commercial."

Availability: None

HISTORY OF THE CINEMA, THE (700 ft. /8 mins/35mm)

G.B. Halas and Batchelor. 1956. Director: John Halas. Story: John Halas and Nicholas Spargo. Photography: Bill Taylor and Roy Turk. Design: Ted Pettingell. Animation: Harold Whittaker. Music: Jack King. Narrator: Maurice Denham.

A highly entertaining animated history of the cinema, covering such topics as censorship, the coming of sound, the advent of television, and the introduction of the wide screen. This short debunks film history rather than records it.

Availability (16mm): Em Gee

HISTORY OF THE FRENCH CINEMA BY THOSE WHO MADE IT, A

A series of thirteen programs, directed by Armand Panigel for French television. The following are the various titles, with running times, of the programs in the series, all of which are in French with English sub-titles: The Birth of the Talkies (60 mins), 100% Sound and Songs (70 mins), The First Classics of the French Talkies (80 mins), Imagination and the Rise of the Popular Front, 1935-1936 (70 mins), Toward Poetic Realism, 1936-1938 (70 mins), From Munich to the "Funny War" (70 mins), The Grand Illusions, 1939-1941 (70 mins), A Classical Art under the Occupation and the Liberation (75 mins), A Certain Tradition of Quality, 1945-1955 (70 mins), You Have Seen Nothing at Hiroshima, 1956-1961 (75 mins), Disorder and Afterwards (85 mins), The First Age of French Cinema, 1895-1914 (75 mins), and The Golden Age of the Silent Film, 1915-1928 (90 mins).

Availability (16mm): F.A.C.S.E.A.

HISTORY OF THE MARCH OF TIME, THE (29 mins/16mm)

U.S. and Germany. Time-Life. 1975. Director: Lothar Wolff.

Originally produced for German television. A study of "The March of Time" from 1935 through 1951, including interviews with those associated with the newsreel.
Availability: Time-Life

HISTORY OF THE MOTION PICTURE, THE / SILENTS PLEASE series (26 mins/16mm)

U.S. Killiam-Sterling Films. 1960/1961. Producers and Screenplay: Saul J. Turell and Paul Killiam. Research and Additional Scripting: William K. Everson. Supervising Film Editor: Ray Angus. Film Editors: Howard Kuperman, Jerry Foreman, Graeme Ferguson, and Peter Galente. Consultants: Richard Griffith, William F. Brown and Theodore R. Kupferman. Narrator: Paul Killiam.

Perhaps the best series on the history of the silent film yet produced for television. The series theme song, "The Power of Love," indicated that television audiences, and later non-theatrical audiences, were about to witness an intelligent and loving tribute to the silent cinema. As an early publicity release on the series wrote, "Silents Please is a show of nostalgia, instruction, and most of all, solid entertainment that transcends any barriers of time. Above all, it treats the silent film with the dignity, respect and affection it so richly deserves." The initial thirty-nine episodes in the Silents Please series, whose title was changed because Paul Killiam felt the pun was a little too frivolous for the educational market, were as follows: Son of the Sheik, The General, Dr. Jekyll and Mr. Hyde (1920), Yankee Clipper, William S. Hart (q.v.), The Fun Factory (q.v.), Tempest, Orphans of the Storm (in two parts), The Hunchback of Notre Dame, The Black Pirate, The Serials (q.v.), Dracula (1922), The Eagle, Will Rogers (q.v.), The Thief of Bagdad, Variety, The Sad Clowns (q.v.), The Fall of Babylon, Girls in Danger (q.v.), America, The Road to Yesterday, Buster Keaton (q.v.), Don Juan (in two parts), Lilac Time, Slapstick (q.v.), Rin Tin Tin (actually a condensed version of Tracked by the Police), The Americano, The Garden of Eden, Blood and Sand, The Patent Leather Kit, The Sea Beast, The Clown Princes (q.v.), The Headless

Horseman, Hoodoo Ann, Films Firsts (q.v., in two parts), Old San Francisco, and The Three Musketeers (in two parts).
Availability (not all episodes): Blackhawk (sale)/Killiam Shows (rental)

HIT 'IM AGAIN (10 mins/35mm)

U.S. Warner Bros. 1953.

One of a series of Warner Bros. compilations utilizing Mack Sennett film clips.
Availability: None

HITS OF THE PAST (2 reels/16mm)

A compilation of clips from various Chaplin Keystone and other public domain comedies, including Caught in a Cabaret, Dough and Dynamite and The Rounders.
Availability: Em Gee

HOLLYWOOD AND THE STARS series (26 mins/16mm)

U.S. A David L. Wolper Production, released by United Artists Television. 1963/1964. Executive Producer: Jack Haley, Jr. Producer and Director: Irwin Rosten. Associate Producer: Julian Ludwig. Screenplay: Irwin Rosten, Al Ramrus and Jack Haley, Jr. Production Coordinator: Jim Schmerer. Film Editors: Larry Neiman and Hyman Kaufman. Title Music: Elmer Bernstein. Music Supervisor: Jack Tillar. Sound Effects Editor: Morton Tubor. Director of Research: William Edgar. Production Manager: Jack Mulcahy. Assistant Film Editor: Noel Nosseck. Film Librarian: John Orland. Staff Sound Engineer: Don Lusby Jr. Film Research: Madge Reynolds. Narrator: Joseph Cotten. (These technical credits were taken from The Oscars: Moments of Greatness, and may vary from episode to episode.)

Elmer Bernstein's memorable title music introduced Hollywood and the Stars, which was possibly the best television series ever produced on the history of the film industry. Research and film editing was always impeccable. Each episode would include not only appropriate film clips, but newsreel footage and interviews; for example, The Oscars:

Moments of Greatness included not only clips from Academy Award ceremonies and Academy Award-winning films, but also Conrad Nagel discussing the foundation of the Academy and Frank Capra reminiscing about a memorable moment in its history. First seen over the NBC television network between September, 1963 and September, 1964, the series comprised the following half-hour episodes: Anatomy of a Movie (1964), The Angry Screen (1964), Birth of a Star (1963), The Fabulous Musicals (1963), The Funny Men (1963, in two parts), The Great Directors (1964), The Great Lovers (1963), Hollywood Goes to War (1964), Hollywood U.S.A. (1963), How To Succeed as a Gangster (1963), The Immortal Jolson (1963), In Search of Kim Novak (1964), The Man Called Bogart (1964), Monsters We've Known and Loved (1964), Natalie Wood: Hollywood's Child (1964), The Odyssey of Rita Hayworth (1964), On Location: The Night of the Iguana (1964), The One and Only Bing (1963), The Oscars: Moments of Greatness (1964, in two parts), Paul Newman: Actor in a Hurry (1964), Sirens, Symbols and Glamour Girls (1963, in two parts), The Swashbucklers (1964), Teenage Idols (1963, in two parts), They Went That-a-Way (1963), The Unsinkable Bette Davis (1963), What a Way to Go (1964), and The Wild and Wonderful Thirties (1964).

Availability: United Artists Television

HOLLYWOOD BABYLON (87 mins/35mm)

U.S. Institute of Adult Education. 1972. Producers: L. K. Farbella and Van Guilder. Director: Van Guilder. Photography: Henning Schellerup.

With Jim Gentry, Myron Griffin, Ashley Phillips, and Uschi Digart.

A soft-core pornographic recreation of famous Hollywood scandals of the Twenties, interspersed with poor quality film clips of screen personalities from John Bunny to Sophia Loren. The film is based on the pirated, first American edition of Kenneth Anger's book, Hollywood Babylon.

Availability: None

HOLLYWOOD BOUND (5,466 ft./55 mins/35mm)

U.S. Hollywood Bound Corporation. 1949. Directors: Jean and Ronald Haines.

Billed as the "truly great story of a truly great actress's phenomenal rise to success," Hollywood Bound consists of three shorts--from 1927, 1930 and 1936--in which Betty Grable appears. As the anonymous reviewer in The Monthly Film Bulletin (May 31, 1949) commented, "Lacking a sequence from one of the star's recent films to demonstrate the degree of proficiency now achieved, there seems little point in the production."

Availability: None

HOLLYWOOD CAVALCADE (100 mins/35mm)

U.S. Twentieth Century-Fox. 1939. Executive Producer: Darryl F. Zanuck. Associate Producer: Harry Joe Brown. Director: Irving Cummings. Screenplay: Ernest Pascal. Based on a Story by Hilary Lynn and Brown Holmes and an Original Idea by Lou Breslow. Photography: Ernest Palmer and Allen M. Davey. Technicolor Director: Natalie Kalmus. Associate Technicolor Director: Henri Jaffa. Art Directors: Richard Day and Wiard Ihnen. Set Decorator: Thomas Little. Film Editor: Walter Thompson. Costumes: Herschel. Sound: Eugene Grossman and Roger Heman. Music Director: Louis Silvers.

With Alice Faye (Molly Adair), Don Ameche (Michael Linnett Connors), J. Edward Bromberg (Dave Spingold), Alan Curtis (Nicky Hayden), Stuart Erwin (Pete Tinney), Jed Prouty (Chief of Police), Buster Keaton (Himself), Donald Meek (Lyle P. Stout), George Givot (Englishman), Eddie Collins, Hank Mann, Heinie Conklin, and James Finlayson (Keystone Kops), Chick Chandler (Assistant Director), Robert Lowery (Henry Potter), Russell Hicks (Roberts), Ben Welden (Agent), Willie Fung (Valet), Paul Stanton (Filson), Mary Forbes (Mrs. Gaynes), Joseph Crehan (Attorney), Irving Bacon (Clerk), Ben Turpin (Bartender), Chester Conklin (Sheriff), Marjorie Beebe (Telephone Operator), Frederick Burton (Thomas), Lee Duncan (Himself), Rin-Tin-Tin Jr. (Himself), Edward Earle (Actor), Snub Pollard (Comic), and Victor Potel (Hamburger Man).

The program for the world premiere of Hollywood Cavalcade--at the Four Star Theatre in Los Angeles on October 4, 1939--contained the following note: "The Producers wish to express their appreciation to Al Jolson for his appearance in the early talking picture sequences of this picture, and also wish to thank Buster Keaton, Chester Conklin, Jed Prouty, Ben Turpin, Hank Mann, and Snub Pollard for their contribution to the silent screen sequences, which were directed by Malcolm St. Clair and supervised by Mack Sennett." Hollywood Cavalcade was described as "the first historical film about Hollywood," and dealt with the history of Hollywood film-making from 1913 through 1927.

Availability: None

HOLLYWOOD DREAM FACTORY, THE (1 reel/16mm)

A curiously dull Blackhawk Films compilation intended to illustrate the development of the film industry in Los Angeles. Most of the film clips are unidentified.

Availability (16mm and 8mm): Blackhawk (sale only)

HOLLYWOOD GOES TO WAR see HOLLYWOOD AND THE STARS

HOLLYWOOD MAGIC CAMP (45 mins/16mm)

Extracts from Hollywood productions of the Thirties which used special effects.

Availability: Creative Film Society

HOLLYWOOD--MY HOME TOWN (56 mins/16mm)

U.S. NBC Television. 1962. Producer and Director: William Martin. Screenplay: Royal Foster. Film Sequences by Ken Murray. Music: Georgie Stoll. Music Editor: Reg Browne. Orchestrations: Calvin Jackson, Leo Arnaud, Fred Katz, and Gerald Wilson. Theme Music: Georgie Stoll and Royal Foster. Vocals: Randy Van Horne Singers. Music Research by Bernard Brody. Opticals: Westheimer Company. Sound: Glen Glenn. Narrator: Ken Murray.

A collection of Ken Murray's home movies from 1927 through 1962, presented as the Du Pont Show of the Week on the NBC network on January 7, 1962. The following stars are represented in the film clips: Ben Alexander, Richard Arlen, Mary Astor, Lew Ayres, John Barrymore, Ralph Bellamy, Edgar Bergen, Charles Bickford, Ward Bond, Pat Boone, El Brendel, David Butler, Eddie Cantor, Frank Capra, Jack Carson, Charles Chaplin, Maurice Chevalier,

Lew Cody, Russ Colombo, Gary Cooper, Lou Costello, Bing Crosby, Bob Cummings, Blondie's dog Daisy, Bette Davis, Marie Dressler, Jimmy Durante, Douglas Fairbanks, Charles Farrell, W. C. Fields, Eddie Fisher, Errol Flynn, Glenn Ford, Clark Gable, Janet Gaynor, James Gleason, Cary Grant, Sid Grauman, Jon Hall, Mickey Hargitay, Jean Harlow, Susan Hayward, Van Heflin, Bob Hope, Leslie Howard, Allen Joslyn, Boris Karloff, Burt Lancaster, Jack Lemmon, Charles Lindbergh, Carole Lombard, Myrna Loy, Jayne Mansfield, Thomas Mitchell, Tom Mix, Harriet Nelson, Jack Oakie, Mary Pickford, Dick Powell, Tyrone Power, Buddy Rogers, Will Rogers, Mickey Rooney, Charles Ruggles, Jane Russell, Randolph Scott, Frank Sinatra, Robert Stack, Jimmy Stewart, Elizabeth Taylor, The Three Stooges, Spencer Tracy, Sonny Tufts, Rudolph Valentino, and Rudy Vallee.

Availability: None

HOLLYWOOD ON TRIAL (100 mins/35mm)

U.S. A Lumière Films release. A Stephen R. Friedman, Irwin Meyer and Peter Crane Presentation of a James C. Gutman/David Helpern, Jr. Production. 1976. Producer: James C. Gutman. Director: David Helpern, Jr. Writer and Interviewer: Arnie Reisman. Photography: Barry Abrams. Associate Producers: Frank Galvin and Juergen Hellwig. Production Manager and Location Sound: Max Kalmanwicz. Studio Re-Recording: Townsend Production Services. Sound Mixer: Jim Townsend. Assistant Film Editors: Bonnie Gangelhoff, Stephanie Tepper, Carol Stein, and Suzanne Pettit. Research: Bonnie Gangelhoff, Carol Stein, Leilani Hayes, Sue Wittenberg, John Rossi, and Mimi King. Gaffers: Stefan Czapsky, Don Clark and Bill Williams. Production Assistants: Dan Polan and Bob Kidwell. Second Unit Photography: Austin DeBesche and Don Clark. Second Unit Sound: Richard Bock. Post Production Services: Envision Corporation. Graphics and Photo Animation: Cine-Man/Red Lynde.

Described by its producers as a dramatic, historical reconstruction of the Blacklist era--the years of the House Committee on Un-American Activities from 1947 through 1955--Hollywood on Trial was nominated for an Academy Award for Best Feature-Length Documentary. It utilizes a considerable amount of historical footage of testimony by such Hollywood personalities as Gary Cooper, Adolphe Menjou, Louis B. Mayer, and Jack L. Warner, together with contemporary interviews with Walter Bernstein, Alvah Bessie, Lester Cole, Howard Da Silva, Edward Dmytryk, Millard Lampell, Ring Lardner, Jr., Albert Maltz, Ben Margolis, Zero Mostel, Otto Preminger, Ronald Reagan, Martin Ritt, Gale Sondergaard, Leo Townsend, Dalton Trumbo, and William Wheeler. Perhaps the most astonishing portion of the entire film is an interview with a complacent Ronald Reagan, who, as the-then President of the Screen Actors Guild, supported the Blacklist.

Availability (16mm): Corinth

HOLLYWOOD STORY (6,892 ft./76 mins/35mm)

U.S. Universal-International. 1951. Producer: Leonard Goldstein. Director: William Castle. Story and Screenplay: Frederick Kohner and Fred Brady. Photography: Carl Guthrie. Art Directors: Bernard Herzbrun and Richard H. Riedel. Set Decorators: Russell A. Gausman and Julia Heron. Sound: Leslie I. Carey and Glenn Anderson. Associate Producer: Billy Grady, Jr. Music Director: Joseph Gershenson. Film Editor: Virgil Vogel. Gowns: Rosemary Odell. Hair Stylist: Joan St. Oegger. Makeup: Bud Westmore.

With Richard Conte (Larry O'Brien), Julia Adams (Sally Rousseau), Richard Egan (Lt. Lennox), Henry Hull (Vincent St. Clair), Fred Clark (Sam Collyer), Jim Backus (Mitch Davis), Houseley Stevenson (Mr. Miller), Paul Cavanagh (Roland Paul), Katherine Meskill (Mary), Louis Lettieri (Jimmy), Joel McCrea (Himself), Betty Blythe (Herself), Helen Gibson (Herself), William Farnum (Himself), and Francis X. Bushman (Himself).

Murder mystery of a young film producer who makes a feature about a silent film director murdered at the studio where the producer now works. Obviously, very, very loosely based on the William Desmond Taylor murder. Of interest because of the silent stars who make brief appearances in the production, and of the shots of once-famous Hollywood landmarks such as the Chaplin Studios, Grauman's Chinese Theatre and the Trocadero. Variety (May 11, 1951) described Hollywood Story as "one of the few really legitimate Hollywood yarns every placed on celluloid."

Availability (16mm): Universal 16

HOLLYWOOD: THE DREAM FACTORY (52 mins/35mm)

U.S. M-G-M. 1972. Producers: Bud Friedgen and Irwin Rosten. Directors: Nick Noxon and Irwin Rosten. Music: George Romanis. Narrator: Dick Cavett.

A chronological history of M-G-M, with clips from more than sixty of the studio's films. Obviously a forerunner to That's Entertainment!

Availability (16mm): Films Incorporated/Indiana University Audio-Visual Center

HOLLYWOOD: THE FABULOUS ERA (54 mins/16mm)

U.S. Fountainhead International/David Wolper Productions. 1963. Producer and Director: David Wolper. Screenplay: Marshall Flaum. Music: Elmer Bernstein. Film Editor: Melvin Shapiro. Narrator: Henry Fonda.

A well-produced, intelligent history of Hollywood film production from the coming of sound to the present (i.e., 1963), utilizing film clips and newsreel footage.

Availability: None

HOLLYWOOD: THE GOLDEN YEARS (53 mins/35mm)

U.S. Wolper-Sterling Productions. 1961. Producer and Director: David L. Wolper. Associate Producer: Jack Haley, Jr. Production Supervisor: Mel Stuart. Screenplay: Sidney Skolsky and Malvin Wald. Music: Elmer Bernstein. Film Editor: Philip R. Rosenberg. Narrator: Gene Kelly.

A feature-length documentary on the silent era, beginning with The Great Train Robbery (1903) and ending with The Jazz Singer (1927). Among the film clips are scenes from Intolerance, The Big Parade, The Son of the Sheik, Wings, Ben-Hur, Flesh and the Devil, Rebecca of Sunnybrook Farm, and The Hunchback of Notre Dame. Personalities featured include Chaplin, Garbo, John Gilbert, Mae Marsh, Robert Harron, D. W. Griffith, Valentino, Renee Adoree, the Keystone Kops, Marie Dressler, Clara Bow, Gloria Swanson, Lon Chaney, Francis X. Bushman, Ramon Novarro, Harold Lloyd, Douglas Fairbanks, Pola Negri, Norma Shearer, Phyllis Haver, Roscoe "Fatty" Arbuckle, and Mabel Normand. Shaw in Variety (August 2, 1961) described Hollywood: The

Golden Years as "a fascinating parade of the greats of yesteryear." Hollywood: The Golden Years was first screened, under the sponsorship of Proctor and Gamble, on the NBC network on November 29, 1961.

Availability (16mm): Budget Films/Kit Parker Films/ Select

HOLLYWOOD: THE GREAT STARS (54 mins/16mm)

U.S. Fountainhead International/David Wolper Productions. 1963. Producer: Jack Haley, Jr. Director and Screenplay: Marshall Flaum. Music: Elmer Bernstein. Narrator: Henry Fonda.

A well-produced, informative survey of some of Hollywood's unique film personalities, including Clark Gable, Humphrey Bogart and Marilyn Monroe, utilizing film clips and newsreel footage.

Availability: None

HOLLYWOOD: THE SELZNICK YEARS (54 mins/16mm)

U.S. Metromedia Producers Corp. 1969. Executive Producers: Bud Rifkin and Alan Landsburg. Producer, Director and Screenplay: Marshall Flaum. Associate Producer: Sascha Schneider. Music Supervisor: Jack Tillar. Film Editor: Graham Mahin. Additional Film Editing: David Blewitt. Sound Editors: Charles Campbell and Roger Sword. Recording Supervisor: David Ronne. Narrator: Henry Fonda.

An entertaining and informative documentary on the career of producer David O. Selznick, including interviews with Ingrid Bergman, Russell Birdwell, Joseph Cotten, George Cukor, Joan Fontaine, Janet Gaynor, Katharine Hepburn (heard, but not seen), Alfred Hitchcock, Rock Hudson, Dorothy McGuire, Gregory Peck, and King Vidor, and film clips from twenty Selznick productions, including A Bill of Divorcement, Dinner at Eight, King Kong, David Copperfield, A Tale of Two Cities, Intermezzo, Rebecca, Duel in the Sun, A Farewell to Arms, and, of course, Gone with the Wind. Highspots of the documentary include screen tests for the Scarlett O'Hara role by Jean Arthur, Joan Bennett, Susan Hayward, Lana Turner, Paulette Goddard, and Frances Dee, plus screen tests of Laurette Taylor, Maude Adams and Tallulah Bankhead. Hollywood: The Selznick Years was

first televised on the Bell Telephone Hour on the NBC network on March 21, 1969.
Availability (Super 8mm): Niles

HOLLYWOOD, U.S.A. see HOLLYWOOD AND THE STARS

HOLLYWOOD WITHOUT MAKEUP (45 mins/16mm)

A selection of "home movies" by Ken Murray, covering the Hollywood scene from the Thirties through the Sixties, and including footage of Cary Grant, Tyrone Power, Mae West, Clark Gable, Dick Powell, Marilyn Monroe, Jackie Cooper, Harpo and Groucho Marx, Charles Laughton, Walt Disney, Douglas Fairbanks, Jr., Victor McLaglen, Tom Mix, Errol Flynn, Mary Astor, Humphrey Bogart, and rare footage of parties at San Simeon with William Randolph Hearst, Charles Chaplin, John Gilbert, and Marion Davies.
Availability: Budget

HOLLYWOOD: YOU MUST REMEMBER THIS (90 mins/16mm)

U.S. NET. 1973. Producer and Director: Victoria Hochberg. Screenplay and Narrator: Richard Schickel.

A sequel to The Movie Crazy Years (q.v.), presenting a study of Warner Bros. in the Forties. The documentary includes interviews with Frank Capra, John Huston, Raoul Walsh, Howard Hawks, Dalton Trumbo, and John Howard Lawson, and clips from a number of films--not always Warner Bros. productions--but including Yankee Doodle Dandy, Roaring Twenties, They Drive by Night, High Sierra, The Maltese Falcon, Sergeant York, Air Force, Objective Burma, Mission to Moscow, Destination Tokyo, Since You Went Away, Treasure of Sierra Madre, and White Heat.
Availability: United Artists 16 (rental and lease)

HOLLYWOOD'S MUSICAL MOODS (50 mins/16mm)

U.S. Blackwood Productions. 1973. Producer and Director: Christian Blackwood. Screenplay and Narrator: Arthur Kleiner.

The art and history of composing for films told

through the use of film clips and interviews with various composers, including David Raksin and Miklos Rozsa. Film historian William K. Everson writes, "Hollywood's Musical Moods is both highly entertaining and extremely informative, one of the most valuable additions to a distressingly short list of good documentaries about movie-making."

Availability (16mm and video cassette): Blackwood Productions (rental and sale)

HOLLYWOOD'S WILD ANGEL (58 mins/16mm)

U.S. A Film by Christian Blackwood. 1978. Producer and Director: Christian Blackwood. Music: Rich Look and Cathy Chamberlain. Narrator: Richard Koszarski.

A documentary portrait of low budget producer-director-distributor Roger Corman, with comments by Allan Arkush, Paul Bartel, David Carradine, Joe Dante, Jonathan Demme, Peter Fonda, Ron Howard, Jonathan Kaplan, Martin Scorsese, and Roger Corman. A popular film with audiences at the Berlin, London, Edinburgh, and Sydney film festivals.

Availability: Blackwood Productions

HOMAGE TO DR. MAREY (6 mins/35mm)

France. 1954. Producers: Lucien Bull and Pierre Nogues, in association with Tadie Cinéma.

A brief study of Dr. Etienne-Jules Marey's Chronophotographic system of photographs, similar in principle to Eadweard Muybridge's photographic technique. In this short, Dr. Marey's series of still photographs are transferred to film and thus take on movement.

Availability (35mm and 16mm): British Film Institute, London (no American distributor)

HOMAGE TO EADWEARD MUYBRIDGE (2 mins/16mm)

A 1965 University of Southern California production in which the photographs of Eadweard Muybridge are animated.

Availability: USC Film Library

HOMETOWN HOLLYWOOD see KEN MURRAY'S HOMETOWN HOLLYWOOD

HOUDINI (105 mins/35mm)

U.S. Paramount. 1953. Producer: George Pal. Associate Producer: Frank Freeman Jr. Director: George Marshall. Screenplay: Philip Yordan. Based on the Biography, Houdini, His Life Story, by Harold Kellock. Photography: Ernest Laszlo. Technicolor Consultant: Richard Mueller. Art Directors: Hal Pereira and Al Nozaki. Music: Roy Webb. Sound: Harry Mills and Gene Garvin. Film Editor: George Tomasini. Assistant Director: Michael D. Moore.

With Tony Curtis (Houdini), Janet Leigh (Bess), Torin Thatcher (Otto), Angela Clarke (Mrs. Weiss), Stefan Schnabel (Prosecuting Attorney), Ian Wolfe (Fante), Sig Ruman (Schultz), Michael Pate (Dooley), Connie Gilchrist (Mrs. Schultz), Malcolm Lee Beggs (Warden), Frank Orth (White-Haired Man), Barry Bernard (Inspector), Douglas Spencer (Simms), and Billy Bletcher (Italian Basso)

Highly fictionalized account of the life of the world-famous escape artist; who appeared in a number of films.

Availability (16mm): Films Incorporated

HOUSE THAT SHADOWS BUILT, THE (5 reels/35mm)

U.S. Paramount. 1931

The House That Shadows Built--also the title of a 1928 book on Adolph Zukor and Paramount--was Paramount's 20th Anniversary Film. Aside from an extraordinary mish-mash of graphics and musical tracks--the dominant theme being the opening bars of the Paramount Newsreel--the film offers tantalizing glimpses of such stars as Marguerite Clark, Olga Petrova and Dorothy Gish, whose Paramount productions have long since gone the way of all nitrate film. The last two-thirds of The House That Shadows Built features a look at Paramount releases of 1931-1932. This section is of more than passing interest for it reveals, among other things, that Eleanor Boardman was originally slated for the role eventually played by Helen Hayes in Borzage's A Farewell to Arms, and presents a lengthy sequence from an unreleased, and presumably uncompleted, Dorothy Arzner feature, Step-daughters of War, starring Ruth Chatterton. There are also extracts, which today, unfortunately, appear somewhat hackneyed, from An American Tragedy, Monkey Business and The Smiling Lieutenant, among others.

Availability: None (This film has been preserved at the Library of Congress, where a 35mm acetate print is available for study)

HOW THE MYTH WAS MADE (60 mins/16mm)

U.S. WBGH-Boston. 1978. Producer and Director: George Stoney. Co-director and Photography: Jim Brown. Sound: Paul Barnes. Film Editor: Trudy Bagdon.

A study of the making of Robert Flaherty's Man of Aran, including interviews with Harry Watt, Arthur Calder-Marshall, Walter Lassally, John Goldman, and Sir Michael Balcon. The documentary questions Flaherty's integrity because of his re-enactment of many of the incidents in Man of Aran. For more information, see Gordon Hitchens' article in Variety (May 31, 1978).

Availability: Films Incorporated

HOW TO SUCCEED AS A GANGSTER see HOLLYWOOD AND THE STARS

I DON'T CARE GIRL, THE (81 mins/35mm)

U.S. Twentieth Century-Fox. 1952. Producer: George Jessel. Director: Lloyd Bacon. Screenplay: Walter Bullock. Photography: Arthur E. Arling. Song, "As Long as You Care," Lyrics by George Jessel and Music by Joe Cooper. Song, "Here Comes Love Again," Words and Music by George Jessel and Eliot Daniel. Music Director: Lionel Newman. Musical Settings: Joseph C. Wright. Technicolor Color Consultant: Leonard Doss. Art Directors: Lyle Wheeler and Richard Irvine. Set Decorators: Thomas Little and Raymond Boltz. Film Editor: Louis Loeffler. Wardrobe Direction: Charles LeMaire. Costumes: Renie. Vocal Direction: Eliot Daniel. Orchestration: Herbert Spencer. Dance Solos Staged by Seymour Felix. Makeup Artist: Ben Nye. Special Photographic Effects: Ray Kellogg. Sound: Winston H. Leverett and Roger Heman. Assistant Director: Ad Schaumer.

With Mitzi Gaynor (Eva Tanguay), David Wayne (Ed McCoy, Oscar Levant (Bennett), Bob Graham (Larry), Craig Hill (Keene), Warren Stevens (Lawrence), Hazel Brooks (Stella Forrest), Marietta Canty (Maid Dolly), Sam Hearn

(Theatre Owner), Wilton Graff (Flo Ziegfeld), Betty Onge (Olive Thomas), Ruth Hall (Jesse Reed), Barbara Carroll (Zitelka Dolores), Dwayne Ratliff, Bill Foster and Gwyneth Verdon (Speciality Dancers), Irving Gibbs (Gibby), William Bouchey (Manager, Keith Theatre), Jimmy Dodd (Will Rogers), Jean Darling (Lilyan Tashman), Harmon Stevens (W. C. Fields), and Claire Hogan (Sophie Tucker).

Screen biography of Eva Tanguay, the "I Don't Care Girl," presented in the somewhat novel format of having George Jessel playing himself, a Hollywood producer, preparing a musical on the life of the great American vaudeville star who made a brief venture into films. Most reviewers at the time of the film's initial release endorsed Eva Tanguay's motto and didn't care.

Availability (16mm): Films Incorporated

I REMEMBER, I REMEMBER (56 mins/16mm)

G.B. Films of Scotland. 1968.

Variety (September 4, 1968) describes I Remember, I Remember as "a retrospective film by [John] Grierson reflecting his 40 years' work for the documentary film movement." It appears to have been first screened at the 1968 Edinburgh Film Festival, and includes clips from many of Grierson's documentaries.

Availability: Films Incorporated (rental and sale)

I'LL CRY TOMORROW (10,678 ft./117 mins/35mm)

U.S. M-G-M. 1955. Producer: Lawrence Weingarten. Director: Daniel Mann. Screenplay: Helen Deutsch and Jay Richard Kennedy. Based on the Book by Lillian Roth, Mike Connolly and Gerold Frank. Photography: Arthur E. Arling. Music: Alex North. Music Supervisor: Johnny Green. Miss Hayward's Song Arranged and Conducted by Charles Henderson. Art Directors: Cedric Gibbons and Malcolm Brown. Set Decorators: Edwin B. Willis and Hugh Hunt. Special Effects: Warren Newcombe. Film Editor: Harold F. Kress. Costumes: Helen Rose. Recording Supervisor: Dr. Wesley C. Miller. Hair Styles: Sydney Guilaroff. Makeup: William Tuttle. Assistant Director: Al Jennings.

With Susan Hayward (Lillian Roth), Richard Conte

(Tony Bardeman), Eddie Albert (Burt McGuire), Jo Van Fleet (Katie Roth), Don Taylor (Wallie), Ray Danton (David Tredman), Margo (Selma), Virginia Gregg (Ellen), Don Barry (Jerry), David Kasday (David as a Child), Carole Ann Campbell (Lillian as a Child), Peter Leeds (Richard), and Tol Avery (Fat Man).

Feature based on the autobiography of singer and early talkies actress Lillian Roth, with a fine performance by Susan Hayward.

Availability (16mm): Films Incorporated

I'M A STRANGER HERE MYSELF (57 mins/16mm)

U.S. October Films. 1974. Producer: James C. Gutman. Director: David M. Halpern. Screenplay: Myron Meisel. Photography: Austin DeBesche. Film Editors: Richard Bock and Frank Gavin. Music: Richard Bock. Narrator: Howard da Silva.

The title of this documentary on the life and career of director Nicholas Ray is taken from a Sterling Hayden line in Johnny Guitar, "I've a great respect for the gun, and besides I'm a stranger here myself." I'm a Stranger Here Myself includes interviews with Ray himself, plus François Truffaut, Natalie Wood and John Houseman, scenes of Ray at work with his students on We Can't Go Home Again, and clips from They Live by Night, In a Lonely Place, Johnny Guitar, Rebel without a Cause, and 55 Days at Peking. British critic Derek Malcolm described I'm a Stranger Here Myself as "a study which builds, in a commendably short time, a touching image of an artist who was perhaps worse affected by being screwed by the Hollywood system than any other potentially major director."

Availability: Films Incorporated (rental and sale)

IMAGINATIVE GEORGES MELIES, THE (1 reel/16mm)

A compilation by Blackhawk Films of three 1903 productions of Georges Mêliès, copied from material in the Paper Print Collection of the Library of Congress: Bob Kick, the Mischievous Kid, The Oracle of Delphi and The Living Statue.

Availability: None (formerly available for sale on 8mm and 16mm from Blackhawk Films)

IMMORTAL JOLSON, THE see HOLLYWOOD AND THE STARS

IMMORTAL SWAN, THE / LE CYGNE IMMORTEL (38 mins/ 35mm)

G. B. Immortal Swan Productions Ltd. 1935. Director and Screenplay: Edward Nakhimoff. Photography: Phil Greenrod and Guy Green. Sets: Dennis Wreford. Sound: A. G. Ambler. Film Editor: Julia Wolf. Music Director: Vladimir Launitz. Assistant Director: Richard Llewellyn. French Commentary: Albert Gréhan.

A somewhat overly artistic documentary on the life and career of Anna Pavlova, including footage of Pavlova dancing, at her home in Golders Green, London, and talking to her pet swans. The documentary was apparently sponsored by Pavlova's husband and manager, Victor Dandré.

Availability (16mm): The Museum of Modern Art (incomplete and with French commentary)

IN MEMORY OF EISENSTEIN (2 reels/35mm)

U. S. S. R. Central Studio for Documentary Films. 1948. Director and Screenplay: Pera Attasheva.

A brief tribute to the Soviet director, including footage of his funeral and Potylika apartment.

Availability: None

IN SEARCH OF KIM NOVAK see HOLLYWOOD AND THE STARS

IN THE BEGINNING (16mm)

A compilation in twenty-three parts by Kemp R. Niver of films from the Paper Print Collection of the Library of Congress, covering the years 1898 through 1912. The works of Edwin S. Porter, D. W. Griffith, George Méliès, the Nordisk Film Company, and others are covered. Each part varies in length from sixteen minutes through fifty-one minutes. See also The First Twenty Years.

Availability: Macmillan

INCENDIARY BLONDE (113 mins/35mm)

U.S. Paramount. 1945. Executive Producer: B. G. DeSylva. Producer: Joseph Sistrom. Director: George Marshall. Screenplay: Claude Binyon and Frank Butler. Photography: Ray Rennahan. Film Editor: Archie Marshek. Music: Robert Emmett Dolan. Vocal Arrangements: Joseph J. Lilloy. Music Associate: Troy Sanders. Dances: Danny Dare. Art Directors: Hans Dreier and William Flannery. Set Decorator: Steve Seymour. Technicolor Color Consultant: Natalie Kalmus. Associate Technicolor Color Consultant: Morgan Padleford. Process Photography: Farciot Edouart. Costumes: Edith Head. Makeup: Wally Westmore. Sound Recording: Gene Merritt and Walter Oberst.

With Betty Hutton (Texas Guinan), Arturo de Cordova (Bill Kilgannon), Charlie Ruggles (Cherokee Jim), Albert Dekker (Cadden), Barry Fitzgerald (Mike Guinan), Mary Phillips (Bessie Guinan), Edward Ciannelli (Nick, the Greek), The Maxellos (Themselves), Maurice Rocco (Himself), Ted Mapes (Waco Smith), Charles C. Wilson (Mr. Ballinger), Maxine Fife (Pearl Guinan at 21), Carlotta Jelm (Pearl Guinan at 17), Ann Carter (Pearl Guinan at 7), Billy Lechner (Tommy Guinan at 19), Eddie Nichols (Tommy Guinan at 15), George Nokes (Tommy Guinan at 5), Robert Winkler (Willie Guinan), Patricia Prest (Texas Guinan at 9), Billy Curtis (Baby Joe), Edmund MacDonald (Charley Rinaldo), and Don Costello (Gus Rinaldo).

A very wholesome, watered-down film biography of nightclub and vaudeville star Texas Guinan, who was featured in a number of silent Westerns. The critic in Time (August 6, 1945) commented, "It is a brassy synthesis of color, song and dance, spattered with laughs, sniffles and melodrama, and brought to life chiefly by vigorous, charming Betty Hutton."

Availability (16mm): Universal 16

INGMAR BERGMAN (55 mins/16mm)

Sweden. Svenska Filminstitutet. 1971. Director, Screenplay and Film Editor: Stig Björkman. Photography: Roland Lundin. Sound: Jan-Olof Andersson. Production Manager: Staffan Hedqvist.

"The film Ingmar Bergman is a film about Ingmar Bergman as a film director. The film was made during the preparation and shooting of Bergman's film The Touch and gives a unique and penetrating portrait of the film artist Ingmar Bergman. The film also contains a long interview with Bergman where he defines and analyses the practical and ethical sides of film direction."--Svenska Filminstitutet publicity handout. Shot in color, this documentary also includes interviews with the director's actors.

Availability: Films Incorporated

INTERVIEW WITH ALFRED HITCHCOCK (1,512 ft./42 mins/16mm)

G.B. Granada Television. 1966. Producer: Graeme MacDonald. Director: Philip Casson. Interviewer: Michael Scott.

Unedited footage of an interview with Alfred Hitchcock shot for the British television program, Cinema. Hitchcock talks chiefly about his career in British films.

Availability: British Film Institute, London (no American distributor)

INTERVIEW WITH NORMAN McLAREN, AN (30 mins/16mm)

Canada. National Film Board of Canada for CBC. 1957.

Norman McLaren discusses his career with Canadian film critic Clyde Gilmour, and shows excerpts from various of his films to illustrate his animation techniques.

Availability: National Film Board of Canada

INVENTION DU DIABLE, L' (17 mins/16mm)

France. Armor Films. Date unknown. Director: Marcel Gibaud.

A history of film and pre-cinema in the Nineteenth Century.

Availability: F.A.C.S.E.A.

IT BEGAN IN BRIGHTON (3 reels/26 mins/16mm)

G.B. BBC Television. 1966. Directors: Tristram

Powell and Gavin Millar. Research by John Huntley.

A documentary in the BBC's "New Release" series, which examines the work of the British film pioneers who have come to be known as the Brighton school of film-makers, and in particular the films of G. A. Smith (1864-1959). The material included in this film dates from between 1896 and 1902.

Availability: British Film Institute, London (no American distributor)

IT'S SHOWTIME (87 mins/35mm)

U.S. A Weintraub-Heller Production, released by United Artists. 1976. Producers: Fred Weintraub and Paul Heller. Associate Producer: Jon Avnet. Screenplay: Alan Myerson. Music: Artie Butler. Film Editors: Alan Holzman and Peter E. Berger.

A compilation of animals in film, including clips of Asta, Cheetah, Rin Tin Tin, Trigger, Daisy, Lassie, Francis, and Flipper. Among the films featured are *The Extra Girl*, *Lassie Come Home*, *National Velvet*, *Flipper's New Adventure*, *Bedtime for Bonzo*, *A Dog's Life*, *Androcles and the Lion*, and the Dogville Comedies, in which canines takeoff early M-G-M talkies. *Har* in *Variety* (April 2, 1976), described *It's Showtime* as "A project worth doing and well done."

Availability (16mm): Roa's Films

JAMES DEAN STORY, THE (7,359 ft./83 mins/35mm)

U.S. Warner Bros. 1957. Producers and Directors: George W. George and Robert Altman. Screenplay: Stewart Stern. Music: Martin Gabel. Theme Song, "Let Me Be Loved," by Jay Livingston and Ray Evans. Sung by Tommy Sands. Sound Designed by Bert Schoenfeld, James Nelson and Jack Kirschner. Sound Editor: Cathey Burrow. Sound by Ryder Sound Services. Production Designer: Louis Clyde Stoumen. Assistant Production Designer: Abram D. Murray. Still Sequences Photographed by Camera Eye Pictures. Assistant to the Producers: Louis Lombardo. Titles Designed by Maurice Binder. Title Illustrations by David Stone Martin. Contributing Photographers: Dennis Stock, Ray Scatt, Frank Worth, Weegee, Edward Martin, Dick Miller, Peter Basch, Carlyle Blackwell, Jr., Tom Caffrey, Jack Delano, Murray Garrett, Paul Gilliam, Globe Photos, Fred Jordan,

Impact Photos, Louis Lombardo, Magnum Photos, Russ Meyer, Don Ornitz, Paul Pospesil, Charles Robinson, Jack Stager, Phil Stern, Louis Clyde Stoumen, William V. Eercamp, Wide World Photos, U.C.L.A. Department of Theater Arts, and the California Highway Patrol. Narrator: Martin Gabel.

A documentary on the life of actor James Dean, which begins with his death on the highway on September 30, 1955 and the words, "James Dean died this day. He had lived with a great hunger." The film utilizes still photographs, filmed interviews with relatives and friends, and various film clips, including a screen test and footage taken at the premiere of Giant. The following people appear in The James Dean Story: Dean's uncle, aunt, cousin, grandmother, and grandfather; Adeline Hall, his dramatic teacher; Bing Traster, a nurseryman in Fairmount; Mr. Carter, owner of the motorcycle shop in Fairmount; Jerry Luce, owner of Jerry's Bar in New York; Louie De Liso, a waiter in Jerry's Bar; Arnie Langer, a taxicab driver; Arline Sax, a girlfriend in New York; Chris White, a girl at the Actors' Studio; George Ross, a New York Theatrical Press Agent; Robert Jewett, President of Sigma Nu at U.C.L.A.; John Kalin, Dean's fraternity brother; Lew Bracker, a Los Angeles friend; Glenn Kramer, who shared Dean's apartment in Los Angeles; Patsy D'Amore, owner of the Villa Capri restaurant; Billy Karen, D'Amore's partner; Lilli Kardell, an actress friend of Dean; and Officer Nelson of the California Highway Patrol. In describing The James Dean Story as "a curious look at an actor," Newsweek commented, "The narrative, delivered much of the time in tones fit for a historical newsreel of globular significance, takes some getting used to."

Availability: None

JAMES DEAN--THE FIRST AMERICAN TEENAGER (7,189 ft./80 mins/35mm)

G.B. Visual Programme Systems. 1975. Producers: David Puttnam and Sandy Lieberson. Director and Screenplay: Ray Connolly. Photography: Mike Mallory and Robert Gersicoff. Film Editor: Peter Hollywood. Assistant Film Editor: Edward Marnier. Music and Songs: Elton John and David Bowie. Song, "James Dean," Composed and Performed by the Eagles. Sound Editor: Bill Lennard. Sound Re-recording: Bill Rowe. Narrator: Stacy Keach.

A documentary on the life and career of James Dean, utilizing interviews with his friends and colleagues, film clips from East of Eden, Rebel without a Cause and Giant and material from The James Dean Story (q. v.). Originally produced for BBC Television, this feature was released theatrically in 1977. The following talk about Dean: Carroll Baker, Natalie Wood, Sal Mineo, Leonard Rosenman, Dennis Hopper, Nicholas Ray, Sammy Davis, Jr., Leslie Caron, Gene Owen, Peter Witt, Christine White, Corey Allen, Jack Larson, Adeline Hall, Maila Nurmi, and Kenneth Kendall. In The Monthly Film Bulletin (April, 1977), Geoff Brown commented, "Connolly's own commentary, narrated in awed tones by Stacy Keach, blankets the portrait in shallow observations, leaving the spectator still without any intelligent explanation of Dean's contemporary and continuing appeal."

Availability: None

JAMES SALTER (30 mins/16mm)

U.S. KRMA-TV. 1971.

A documentary study of director, writer and novelist James Salter, showing how he "struggles to portray the values, temptations, disillusionments, glories and failures of man."

Availability: Indiana University Audio-Visual Center

JAMES WONG HOWE: CINEMATOGRAPHER (23 mins/16mm)

U.S. Davidson Films. 1973.

An interview with James Wong Howe, in which he talks about his fifty-five years as a cinematographer.

Availability: Indiana University Audio-Visual Center

JAZZ AGE IDOL see VALENTINO: IDOL OF THE JAZZ AGE

JEANNE EAGELS (108 mins/35mm)

U.S. Columbia. 1957. Producer and Director: George Sidney. Screenplay: Daniel Fuchs, Sonya Levien and John Fante. Based on a Story by Daniel Fuchs. Photography: Robert Planck. Art Director: Ross Bellah. Set Decorators: William Kiernan and Alfred E. Spencer. Film Editors: Viola Lawrence and Jerome Thoms. Music: George Duning. Music Conducted by Morris Stoloff. Gowns: Jean Louis. Makeup: Ben Lane. Hair Styles: Helen Hunt. Recording Supervisor: John Livadary. Sound: Franklin Hansen, Jr. Orchestrations by Arthur Morton. Assistant Director: Charles S. Gould.

With Kim Novak (Jeanne Eagels), Jeff Chandler (Sal Satori), Agnes Moorehead (Madame Neilson), Charles Drake (John Donahue), Larry Gates (Al Brooks), Virginia Grey (Elsie Desmond), Gene Lockhart (Equity Board President), Joe de Santis (Frank Satori), Murray Hamilton (Chick O'Hara), Will Wright (Marshal), Sheridan Comerate (Actor, Confederate Officer), Lowell Gilmore (Rev. Dr. Davidson), Juney Ellis (Mrs. Davidson), Beulah Archuletta (Mrs. Horn), Jules Davis (Mr. Horn), Florence MacAfee (Mrs. McPhail), Snub Pollard (Quartermaster Bates), and Joseph Novak (Patron).

Film biography of the great stage actress, who made a number of disappointing film appearances.

Availability: None

JESSE L. LASKY (34 mins/16mm)

Jesse L. Lasky talks to students in the department of cinema at the University of Southern California about his career as a major studio producer and the early years of Hollywood. From the Theatrical Film Symposium Series.

Availability: U.S.C. Film Library

JIMMY FIDLER'S PERSONALITY PARADE (2 reels/35mm)

U.S. M-G-M. 1938. Producer: Ralph Staub. With Jimmy Fidler.

Film of seventy-two film stars, living and dead, is included in this short, described by M-G-M's publicity department as "Probably the most complete pictorial record of Hollywood past great that has been produced."

Availability: None

JOHN BARRYMORE (26 mins/16mm)

U.S. Wolper Productions, released by Official Films.

1963. Producer: David L. Wolper. Music: Jack Tillar. Host/Narrator: Mike Wallace.

A documentary on the life and career of the celebrated stage and screen actor. A film in the "Biography" television series.

Availability: Sterling/University of California Extension Media Center

JOLSON SINGS AGAIN (95 mins/35mm)

U.S. Columbia. 1949. Producer and Screenplay: Sidney Buchman. Director: Henry Levin. Photography: William Snyder. Technicolor Director: Natalie Kalmus. Associate Technicolor Director: Francis Cugat. Art Director: Walter Holscher. Set Decorator: William Kiernan. Film Editor: William Lyon. Montage Director: Lawrence W. Butler. Orchestrations: Larry Russell. Music: George Duning. Music Adviser: Saul Chaplin. Songs Staged by Audrene Brier. Recording--Dialogue: George Cooper. Recording--Music: Philip Faulkner. Re-recording: Richard Olson. Music Director: Morris Stoloff. Makeup: Clay Campbell. Hair Styles: Helen Hunt. Gowns: Jean Louis. Assistant Director: Milton Feldman.

With Larry Parks (Al Jolson), Barbara Hale (Ellen Clark), William Demarest (Steve Martin), Ludwig Donath (Cantor Yoelson), Bill Goodwin (Tom Baron), Myron McCormick (Ralph Bryant), Tamara Shayne (Mama Yoelson), Eric Wilton (Henry), Robert Emmett Keane (Charlie), Peter Brocco (Captain of Waiters), Dick Cogan (Soldier), Martin Garralaga (Mr. Estrada), Michael Cisney (Writer), Ben Erway (Writer), Helen Mowery (Script Girl), Morris Stoloff (Orchestra Leader), Philip Faulkner, Jr. (Sound Mixer), Virginia Mullen (Mrs. Bryant), Nelson Leigh (Theatre Manager), Margie Stapp (Nurse), and Frank McLure, Jock O'Mahoney, Betty Hill, Charles Regan, Charles Perry, Richard Gordon, David Newell, Joe Gilbert, David Horsley, Wanda Perry, Louise Illington, Gertrude Astor, Steve Benton, and Eleanor Marvak.

According to Variety's critic, twenty-seven Jolson songs are featured in this sequel to The Jolson Story.

Availability (16mm): Macmillan

JOLSON STORY, THE (126 mins/35mm)

U.S. Columbia. 1946 (reissued 1969). Producer:

Sidney Skolsky. Associate Producer: Gordon S. Griffith. Director: Alfred E. Green. Screenplay: Stephen Longstreet. Adaptation: Harry Chandlee and Andrew Solt. Photography: Joseph Walker. Technicolor Director: Natalie Kalmus. Technicolor Associate Director: Morgan Padelford. Art Directors: Stephen Gooson and Walter Holscher. Set Decorators: William Kiernan and Louis Diage. Film Editor: William Lyon. Music Director: M. W. Stoloff. Vocal Arrangements: Saul Chaplin. Orchestral Arrangements: Martin Fried. Music Recording: Edwin Wetzel. Re-recording: Russell Malmgren. Montage Director: Lawrence W. Butler. Dances Staged by Jack Cole. Production Numbers Directed by Joseph H. Lewis. Gowns: Jean Louis. Makeup: Clay Campbell. Hair Styles: Helen Hunt. Sound Recording: Hugh McDowell. Assistant Director: Wilbur McGaugh.

With Larry Parks (Al Jolson), Evelyn Keyes (Julie Benson), William Demarest (Steve Martin), Bill Goodwin (Tom Baron), Ludwig Donath (Cantor Yoelson), Tamara Shayne (Mrs. Yoelson), John Alexander (Lew Dockstader), Jo-Carroll Dennison (Ann Murray), Ernest Cossart (Father McGee), Scotty Beckett (Al Jolson as a Boy), William Forrest (Dick Glenn), Ann Todd (Ann Murray as a Girl), Edwin Maxwell (Oscar Hammerstein), and Emmett Vogan (Jonsey).

The voice is Jolson's and the body is Larry Park's in this film biography of the great show business figure, Al Jolson. The presence of William Demarest, who played a small part in The Jazz Singer, is worth noting.

Availability (16mm): Macmillan/Budget/Roa's Films/ The Film Center/Select/Modern Sound Pictures

KAMERA FAHRT, DIE *see* CAMERA GOES ALONG, THE

KEN MURRAY SHOOTING STARS (85 mins/35mm)

U.S. Ken Murray Productions. 1978. Producer and Narrator: Ken Murray. With Bob Hope, Jack Lemmon, Gregory Peck, and Rhonda Fleming.

Ken Murray describes his film as "a fifty year personal history of Hollywood with a cast of over seventy-five of the biggest movie stars. The entire story is told not by old film clips, but by personal films from Ken Murray's voluminous collection, for the most part shot by the producer himself."

Availability (16mm): None

KEN MURRAY'S HOLLYWOOD--MY HOME TOWN see HOLLYWOOD--MY HOME TOWN

KEN MURRAY'S HOMETOWN HOLLYWOOD (1 reel/9 mins/ 35mm)

U.S. Ken Murray Productions. 1973. Producer: Ken Murray.

For more than forty years, Ken Murray has been taking home movies of the Hollywood scene. Murray utilized footage from his archives for this planned series of shorts, of which only one appears to have been released. Ken Murray's Hometown Hollywood #1 includes sequences with John Wayne, Dean Martin, Gregory Peck, Tom Mix, Jack Lemmon, Fredric March, Gary Cooper, Dick Powell, and Maurice Chevalier.

Availability: Ken Murray Productions

KEYSTONE COUPLET, A (1 reel/16mm)

Two half-reelers--A Bandit and Peeping Pete--both produced by Mack Sennett in 1913 and both starring Roscoe "Fatty" Arbuckle.

Availability: Em Gee

KEYSTONE TONIGHT (1 reel/16mm)

A compilation by Blackhawk Films of two 1913 split-reelers: Courage of Sorts, produced by American with Ed Coxen and Winifred Greenwood, and Hide and Seek, produced by Keystone with Mabel Normand.

Availability: None (formerly available for sale on 8mm and 16mm from Blackhawk Films)

KILLIAM, PAUL

Paul Killiam and Killiam Shows have become bywords for the best in silent film presentations, not only in terms of print quality but also as far as intelligent, well-researched productions are concerned. From the Silents Please television series, later released non-theatrically as The History of the Motion Picture, through the current Silent Years features on PBS, it is impossible to fault Paul Killiam's work.

Born on September 12, 1916, Paul Killiam's first brush with show business came with appearances in the Hasty Pudding shows at Harvard University. As "Peter Renwick" he made his Broadway debut in New Faces of 1937, in a company which also included Sonny Tufts, Imogene Coca and Van Johnson. Despite a law degree from Harvard, Killiam's interest remained in the entertainment field, and, in 1946, after a stint as News Director for WOR-Mutual Radio in New York, he opened the Old Knick Music Hall on Second Avenue. The Old Knick specialized in nostalgia, presenting classic melodramas of the past, and an occasional silent film, which Killiam would spoof by likening the characters on screen to members of the audience.

At the Old Knick, Killiam's interest in silent films was established. He set up Killiam Shows to purchase the rights to early motion pictures, beginning with the libraries of the American Biograph (first marketed by Killiam as Biograph Television) and Edison Companies, and later acquiring the D. W. Griffith package from the director's estate. Meanwhile, in 1952, he began the Paul Killiam Show on CBS television, which ran for twenty-six episodes and on which he continued to make fun of early films. However, Killiam gradually developed a respect for the productions of the past, and in the mid-Fifties produced Movie Museum (q. v.), perhaps the first television series to treat silent films with any respect. It was followed a few years later by Silents Please (q. v.), which established Paul Killiam as the leading authority in the restoration and presentation of films from the silent era. He worked--and has continued to work--with major film archives such as the Museum of Modern Art and George Eastman House on their film preservation efforts, and must be given credit for the renovation of the Biograph printer, which permitted the preservation and printing of the original negatives of the American Biograph Company.

Aside from the television series, Paul Killiam co-produced, with Saul J. Turell, two important feature-length documentaries: The Great Chase and The Legend of Valentino (both q. v.). Thanks yet again to his fortitude and perseverance, D. W. Griffith's The Birth of a Nation has been declared in the public domain by the courts, and is now available for purchase and rental for the enjoyment of all.

In recent years, Killiam has produced two series of feature-length productions for PBS, titled The Silent Years. Each series comprised twelve feature films with brand new musical scores--many by the distinguished pianist and composer William Perry, Music Director for the Museum of Modern Art's film screenings--with the first group being introduced by Orson Welles and the second by Lillian Gish. All of Killiam's recent presentations have featured silent films of impeccable print quality, with tints and tones closely approximating the tinting of the original prints. At the time of writing a third series is in production. In addition, Paul Killiam plans a new feature titled Star Vehicle, which will examine the car as performer. He also plans to reactivate the Silents Please series with the addition of new titles, possibly to be called Flashback.

Whatever his activities, film scholars and students throughout the world can only wish him well. For it is Paul Killiam that we must herald as the savior of silent films on television, a man of integrity who has fought long and hard--and continues to fight--for what he believes in. Only the best is good enough for Paul Killiam.

KISS AND OTHER 1895 FILMS (6 mins/16mm)

A selection of pre-1900 films, including The Kiss, Old Maid in a Drawing Room and Street Car Chivalry, compiled by Film Classic Exchange.

Availability: University of California Extension Media Center

LANDMARK FILMS FROM THE FIRST DECADE OF MOTION PICTURE HISTORY see THE GREAT PRIMITIVES

LANGLOIS (52 mins/16mm)

U.S. Hershon-Guerra Productions. 1970. Producers, Directors, Screenplay, Photography, and Film Editors: Eila Hershon and Roberto Guerra.

A study of Henri Langlois, founder of France's Cinemathèque Française. Among those who discuss his work are Lillian Gish, Simone Signoret, Jeanne Moreau, Ingrid Bergman, Catherine Deneuve, Viva, and François Truffaut. Langlois, noted Land in Variety (September 23, 1970), "succeeds in spelling out the place in film history of this pioneer archivist, the boy who devoted his life to collecting and preserving films, out of a great love for the medium." See also 75 Years of Cinema Museum.

Availability: None

LANGUAGE OF THE SILENT FILM, THE (Part One: 100 mins and Part Two: 90 mins/16mm)

U.S. The Museum of Modern Art. 1973. Compiler: Vladimir Petric.

A two-part teaching film, definitely for the more esoteric and heavily intellectual film courses, made up of excerpts from a number of silent classics, including The Birth of a Nation, The Golem, Foolish Wives, Metropolis, and The Passion of Joan of Arc. The sequences were chosen to illustrate various points, such as the use of architecture, lighting and camera movement and the recording of reality, or, as the Museum of Modern Art catalog puts it, "Selections have been made to illustrate basic formal concepts central to an understanding of the art of the silent cinema." The film comes with detailed notes, bibliography and teaching suggestions by Professor Petric.

Availability: The Museum of Modern Art

LAUGH WITH MAX LINDER see EN COMPAGNIE DE MAX LINDER

LAUREL AND HARDY'S LAUGHING 20s (90 mins/35mm)

U.S. Metro-Goldwyn-Mayer. 1965. Producer and Screenplay: Robert Youngson. Associate Producers: Herbert Gelbspan, Alfred Dahlem and Hal Roach Studios. Music: Skeets Alquist. Sound: Val Peters. Narrator: Jay Jackson.

"I recommend the picture called Laurel and Hardy's Laughing 20s to children and to those elders who happen to have been children, and laughing, in the twenties," wrote Brendan Gill in The New Yorker (November 27, 1965). Youngson's feature traces the evolution of the comedy team from the years they worked apart through 1930, and contains clips from the following shorts: The Finishing Touch (1928), From Soup to Nuts (1928), Liberty (1929), Putting Pants on Philip (1928), Sugar Daddies (1927), and Wrong Again (1929).

Availability (16mm): Films Incorporated

LEGEND OF BRUCE LEE

Despite its English-language title, this 1975 Hong Kong feature is not a documentary or even a fictionalized account of the popular Kung Fu star Bruce Lee.

LEGEND OF VALENTINO, THE (56 mins/35mm)

U.S. A Wolper-Sterling Production, released by Sterling Films. 1961. Producers: Saul J. Turell and Paul Killiam. Director: Graeme Ferguson. Screenplay and Film Editors: Saul J. Turell, Paul Killiam and Graeme Ferguson. Music: Alexander Semmler. Music Editor: Harry D. Glass. Supervising Film Editor: Raymond F. Angus. Sound Engineer: Albert Gramaglia. Production Staff: Howard Kuperman, Joseph A. Zysman and Alan Smiler. Research: William K. Everson and Arthur Knight. Treatment: Harvey Bullock. Format Coordinated by Herbert J. Strauss. Narrator: Frank Gallop.

An extremely well-made and intelligent documentary on the life and career of Rudolph Valentino, first televised on WPIX (New York) on May 24, 1961. The production compares Valentino with other silent male stars, such as Charles Ray, William S. Hart and Wallace Reid, and includes newsreel footage of the actor, together with clips from the following films: Son of the Sheik, The Eagle, Blood and Sand, Isle of Love, and Cobra.

Availability (16mm): University of California Extension Media Center

LEGENDARY WEST, THE (51 mins/16mm)

U.S. WTOP-TV. 1975. Producer: Ray Hubbard. Directors and Screenplay: Larry Klein and Stephen Zito. Film Editors: Jane Stubbs and Milton Sink. Narrator: Ben Johnson.

An examination of the real West as compared to the West and its hero as depicted in American films, intended to illustrate that the average American's view and knowledge of the West is almost entirely based on the films he has seen. Or, as the Lucerne Films catalogue has it, "The West was not settled and tamed by faceless and anonymous pioneers. It was done by Broncho Billy Anderson and William S. Hart, by Tom Mix and Roy Rogers, by Henry Fonda, James Stewart and, above all, John Wayne. Our vision of the old West comes from John Ford and James Cruze, Sam Peckinpah and William Wyler."

Availability: Lucerne Films/Budget

LET'S GO TO THE MOVIES (1 reel/9 mins/35mm)

U.S. RKO for the Academy of Motion Picture Arts and Sciences. 1950.

The first and introductory film for a series of one-reelers dealing with various aspects of the film industry. Each short was produced by a different major Hollywood studio, and prepared under the guidance of the Academy of Motion Picture Arts and Sciences. Let's Go to the Movies is the only short in the series which concerns itself with the history of the film industry, tracing, as it does, the development of film showmanship and film equipment, considering the various components needed for film-making, and including clips from Easy Street, The Great Train Robbery, The Birth of a Nation, The Jazz Singer, and Show of Shows. There are errors in the short, but it does hold some interest today, and it is particularly appealing to see the number of vintage cinema fronts shown. Others in this series include This Theatre and You (Warner Bros.), History Brought to Life (Paramount), Pictures Are Adventure (Universal), The Art Director (20th Century-Fox), The Soundman (Columbia), The Cinematographer (Paramount), and The Screen Actor (M-G-M). Several of the shorts are of more than passing interest. Karl Struss is the director of photography featured in The Cinematographer, while Cecil B. DeMille narrates History Brought to Life. The whole series was the subject of a lengthy review by Karel Reisz in The Monthly Film Bulletin (October, 1950), pages 160-162.

Availability (16mm and not necessarily all subjects): Reel Images/National Cinema Service/Budget/USC Film Library/Thunderbird/Indiana University Audio-Visual Center/Images

LIFE AND TIMES OF JOHN HUSTON, ESQ., THE (1,620 ft./45 mins/16mm)

G.B./Canada. Allan King Associates for the BBC and CBC. 1972. Executive Producer: Stephen Hearst. Producer and Screenplay: Roger Graef. Photography: Charles Stewart. Film Editor: Peter Moseley. Sound Editor: Mike Billing. Sound Recording: Christian Wangler and Fred Sharp. Narrator: Patrick Allen.

A documentary on the life and work of the director, including footage of him at work on Reflections in a Golden

Eye, at home in Ireland, and directing Richard Rodney Bennett's opera, The Mines of Sulphur, at La Scala, Milan. Stills from various of his films are also utilized. For more information, see David Wilson's review in The Monthly Film Bulletin (January, 1972), page 9.

Availability: Indiana University Audio-Visual Center/ University of California Extension Media Center

LIFE GOES TO THE MOVIES (13,700 ft./153 mins/35mm)

U.S. Time-Life/20th Century-Fox. 1977. Producers: Mel Stuart, Richard Schickel and Malcolm Leo. Director: Jack Haley, Jr. Screenplay: Richard Schickel. Film Editor: Robert K. Lambert. Narrators: Henry Fonda, Shirley MacLaine and Liza Minelli.

A five-part--The Golden Age of Hollywood (35 mins), The War Years (33 mins), The Post War Years (20 mins), The Fifties (25 mins), and The Movies Today, the New Morality (39 mins)--history of the cinema from the year in which Life magazine was created (1935) through its demise (1972). Many of the film clips are familiar, but Life Goes to the Movies could be a useful teaching film. For more information, see James Manilla's review in Film News (March/April, 1978), pages 22 and 23.

Availability (16mm): Time-Life

LIFE GOES TO WAR (12,000 ft./97 mins/35mm)

U.S. Jack Haley, Jr. Productions/20th Century-Fox/ Time-Life. 1977. Producers: Jack Haley, Jr. and Malcolm Leo. Film Editors: David Blewitt and John Wright. Music: Fred Karlin. Archival Music and Recordings Supervised by John Jensen. Narrator: Johnny Carson.

A superb compilation of film footage--war documentaries, newsreels and features--on the Hollywood film industry's contribution to the Second World War effort. Particular attention is paid to the shorts produced by the Walt Disney studios and the documentaries of John Huston, Frank Capra and John Ford. Johnny Carson's narration is both intelligent and restrained.

Availability (16mm): Time-Life

LIFE STORY OF CHARLES CHAPLIN, THE (2,800 ft. /35mm)

Pioneer. 1926. Producer, Director and Screenplay: H. B. Parkinson.

An unauthorized and never-released account of the life and films of Charles Chaplin, with an actor, Chick Wango, in the title role.

Availability: None

LIGHT FANTASTICK, THE (60 mins/16mm)

Canada. National Film Board of Canada. 1976. Directors: Robert Glover and Michel Patenaude.

A documentary on the early days of animation at the National Film Board of Canada.

Availability: National Film Board of Canada/University of California Extension Media Center

LITTLE MARY (1 reel/12 mins/16mm)

A well-produced compilation of extracts from five Mary Pickford American Biograph productions, directed by D. W. Griffith--All on Account of the Milk (1910), An Arcadian Maid (1910), Never Again (1910), The New York Hat (1912), and The Mender of Nets (1912)--with explanatory titles, prepared by Blackhawk Films.

Availability (16mm and 8mm): Blackhawk Films (sale only)

LOOK AT LIV, A (6,030 ft. /67 mins/35mm)

U.S. Win/Kap Productions. 1977. Producers and Screenplay: Jerry Winters and Richard Kaplan. Director and Interviewer: Richard Kaplan.

A feature-length documentary on the career of Liv Ullmann, including clips from Scenes from a Marriage, Cries and Whispers, Persona, and Face to Face, and footage of Ms. Ullmann at work with Bibi Andersson, David Carradine, Peter Finch, Gene Hackman, Sven Nykvist, and Max Von Sydow. Liv Ullmann is also seen working with Ingmar Bergman on The Serpent's Egg, and A Look at Liv features an

exclusive interview with the director.
Availability: Win/Kap Productions

LORENTZ ON FILM (Four 90 mins programs/16mm)

U.S. WGBH-TV for National Educational Television. 1961.

Six films--The River, The Plow That Broke the Plains, Fight for Life, Nuremberg, and two briefing films for Second World War pilots--are screened, and discussed by Pare Lorentz and film-maker Charles Rockwell.
Availability: None

LOVE GODDESSES, THE (87 mins/35mm)

U.S. Walter Reade-Sterling. 1965. Producers and Screenplay: Saul J. Turrell and Graeme Ferguson. Music: Percy Faith. Film Editors: Nat Greene and Howard Kuperman. Technical Supervisor: Ray Angus. Consultants: Willian K. Everson, Paul Killiam and James A. Lebenthal. Research: Georges Labrousse and Gideon Backmann. Assistants to the Producers: Edward Duffield, Janet Jacobson and Francis Morris. Narrator: Carl King.

A highly entertaining compilation documenting the trends in sex during the history of the cinema, from Theda Bara, Fannie Ward, Lillian Gish, Clara Bow, and Gloria Swanson through Marilyn Monroe, Sophia Loren, Rita Hayworth, and Brigitte Bardot. Other players featured include Pola Negri, Lya De Putti, Louise Brooks, Nita Naldi, Jean Harlow, Carole Lombard, Ginger Rogers, Jeanette MacDonald, Mae West, Ruby Keeler, Dorothy Lamour, Lana Turner, and Betty Grable. A surprising amount of rare footage is included, but there is a heavy reliance on Paramount productions, and Metro-Goldwyn-Mayer and Universal films are conscpicuous by their absence. Stanley Kauffman, in the New Republic (March 20, 1965), commented, "The compilation is brightly edited, never tedious, and rarely sexy."
Availability (16mm): Janus Films/The Museum of Modern Art

LOVE ME OR LEAVE ME (122 mins/35mm)

U.S. M-G-M. 1955. Producer: Joe Pasternak.

Director: Charles Vidor. Screenplay: Daniel Fuchs and Isobel Lennart. Story: Daniel Fuchs. Photography: Arthur E. Arling. Song, "I'll Never Stop Loving You," Music by Nicholas Brodszky and Lyrics by Sammy Cahn. Song, "Never Look Back," Music and Lyrics by Chilton Price. Original Ruth Etting Songs Composed by Irving Berlin, DeSylva, Brown and Henderson, Walter Donaldson, Arthur Freed, Gus Kahn, McCarthy and Monaco, Rodgers and Hart, and Turk and Ahlert. Doris Day's Songs Arranged and Conducted by Percy Faith. Music Supervisor: George Stoll. Art Directors: Cedric Gibbons and Urie McCleary. Set Decorators: Edwin B. Willis and Jack D. Moore. Color Consultant: Alvord Eiseman. Assistant Director: Ridgeway Callow. Costumes: Helen Rose. Film Editor: Ralph E. Winters. Recording Supervisor: Wesley C. Miller. Music Advisor: Irving Aaronson. Special Effects: Warren Newcombe. Hair Styles: Sydney Guilaroff. Makeup: William Tuttle. Dances Originated and Supervised by Alex Romero.

With Doris Day (Ruth Etting), James Cagney (Martin Snyder), Cameron Mitchell (Johnny Alderman), Robert Keith (Bernard V. Loomis), Tom Tully (Frobisher), Harry Bellaver (Georgie), Richard Gaines (Paul Hunter), Peter Leeds (Fred Taylor), Claude Stroud (Eddie Fulton), Audrey Young (Jingle Girl), and John Harding (Greg Trent).

The life story of singer Ruth Etting, who made a number of film appearances. According to publicity at the time of the film's release, Love Me or Leave Me was based on the contents of Miss Etting's personal scrapbook, a fifty-pound volume, twelve inches thick, covering the years 1920 through 1938.

Availability (16mm): Films Incorporated

LUBIN PROGRAM (28 mins/16mm)

A package of four films produced by the Philadelphia-based film pioneer, Siegmund Lubin: Bold Bank Robbery (1903), She Would Be an Actress (1909), Drunkard's Child (1909), and An Unexpected Guest (1909).

Availability: Macmillan

LUBIN SHOWMAN'S REEL (1 reel/16mm)

A compilation by Blackhawk Films of Lubin productions from 1904.

Availability (16mm and 8mm): Blackhawk (sale only)

LUMIERE (40 mins/35mm)

France. 1953. Producer: Nicole-Eva Terquem. Director: Ghislain Cloquet. Screenplay and Narrator: Abel Gance.

The history of the French film industry as seen through the eyes of one of the Lumière Brothers.
Availability (16mm): F.A.C.S.E.A.

LUMIERE FILMS (20 mins/16mm)

A package of Lumière films produced during 1895 and 1896, and including Feeding the Baby and Teasing the Gardener, compiled by the Museum of Modern Art.
Availability: The Museum of Modern Art

LUMIERE PROGRAM No. 1 (15 mins/16mm)

A package of films produced during 1895 and 1896 by Auguste and Louis Lumière: Workers Leaving the Lumière Factory, Train Entering a Station, A Game of Cards, Boys Sailing Boats, Tuileries Gardens, Paris, Demolition of a Wall, Baths at Milan, Italy, French Dragoons, Gondola Party, Sack Race, Military Review, Hungary, German Hussars Jumping Fences, Feeding the Swans, and The Boiler.
Availability: Macmillan

LUMIERE PROGRAM No. 2 (15 mins/16mm)

A package of films produced between 1895 and 1898 by Auguste and Louis Lumière: Workers Leaving the Lumière Factory, Demolition of a Wall, Showball Fight, Firemen Answering the Call, Feeding the Baby, Children at Play, Dancing Children, A Game of Cards, Watering the Gardener, Watering the Card Players, Photography, Women Fighting, Train Entering a Station, Farmyard, Quarreling Infants, The Boiler, Children Digging Shrimp, and Swimming in the Sea. A Music track has been added.
Availability: Macmillan

LUMIERE YEARS, THE / LES ANNEES LUMIERE--1895-1900 (87 mins/35mm)

France. Eilmanthrope-Editions/TV-Rencontre-ORTF. 1971. Directors: Jean Chapot and Régis Hanrion. Music: Pierre Dutour. Commentary: Claude Roy.

A compilation of films produced by the Lumière Brothers throughout the world between 1895 and 1900, ending with the 1900 Paris Exposition.

Availability (16mm): University of California Extension Media Center/Films Incorporated

M-G-M's BIG PARADE OF COMEDY see BIG PARADE OF COMEDY, THE

MACABRE MINI SHORTS (1 reel/16mm)

Nine "short films of horror" produced between 1895 and 1905 by Georges Méliès and the Edison Company.

Availability (16mm and 8mm): Thunderbird (sale only)

MACK SENNETT PROGRAM (110 mins/16mm)

A package of six films produced by Mack Sennett, compiled by the Museum of Modern Art: Comrades (1911), Mabel's Dramatic Career (1913), The Surf Girl (1916), His Bread and Butter (1916), The Clever Dummy (1917), and Astray from the Steerage (1920).

Availability: The Museum of Modern Art

MADE FOR LAUGHS (3, 130 ft. /34 mins/35mm)

G.B. Hammer/Exclusive. 1952. Produced and Compiled by James M. Anderson. Narrator: Bryan Michie.

A compilation of early silent footage featuring, among others, John Bunny, Flora Finch, William S. Hart, Mabel Normand, Ford Sterling, Billy Reeves, Charles Chaplin, Syd Chaplin, Mack Swain, Louise Fazenda, Charlie Murray, Roscoe "Fatty" Arbuckle, Helen Gardner, and Mr. and Mrs. Sidney Drew. According to William K. Everson, in a Theodore Huff Memorial Film Society program note, "One of the highlights is a substantial chunk of a particularly good Broncho Billy Anderson western, and there is a fascinating condensation of a 1911 melodrama of piracy, shot in Bermuda. Unfortunately, the film is an excellent example of how not to put this sort of material on the screen. The selections and editing are somewhat slapdash, and crude imitations of old slides and subtitles are put in at intervals for the sake of laughs. The narration doesn't laugh at the films, thank heavens, but it does include a number of singularly unfunny puns and so-called jokes."

Availability: None

MAGIC BOX, THE (118 mins/35mm)

G.B. Festival Film Productions/J. Arthur Rank. 1951. Producer: Ronald Neame. Director: John Boulting. Screenplay: Eric Ambler. Based on Friese-Greene, Close-Up of an Inventor by Ray Allister. Photography: Jack Cardiff. Production Design: John Bryan. Music: William Alwyn. Musical Director: Muir Mathieson. Film Editor: Richard Best. Assistant Director: Cliff Owen.

With Robert Donat (William Friese-Greene), Margaret Johnston (Edith Harrison), Maria Schell (Helen Friese-Greene), John Howard Davies (Maurice Friese-Greene), David Oake (Claude Friese-Greene), Renee Asherson (Miss Tagg), Richard Attenborough (Jack Carter), Robert Beatty (Lord Beaverbrook), Michael Denison (Reporter), Henry Edwards (Butler), Leo Genn (Dacres), Marius Goring (House Agent), Joyce Grenfell (Mrs. Clare), Robertson Hare (Sitter), Kathleen Harrison (Mother), William Hartnell (Sergeant), Stanley Holloway (Broker's Man), Jack Hulbert (Sergeant), Glynis Johns (May Jones), Mervyn Johns (Pawnbroker), Barry Jones (Doctor), Miles Malleson (Conductor), Muir Mathieson (Sir Arthur Sullivan), A. E. Matthews (Colonel), John McCallum (Sitter), Bernard Miles (Alfred), Laurence Olivier (PC 94 B), Cecil Parker (Platform Man), Eric Portman (Arthur Collings), Dennis Price (Assistant), Michael Redgrave (Mr. Lege), Margaret Rutherford (Lady Pond), Ronald Shiner (Fairground Barker), Sheila Sim (Nurse), Basil Sydney (William Fox-Talbot), Sybil Thorndike (Sitter), David Tomlinson (Bob), Cecil Trouncer (John Rudge), Peter Ustinov (Industry Man), Frederick Valk (Guttenberg), Kay Walsh (Receptionist), Emlyn Williams (Bank Manager), Harcourt Williams (Tom), and Googie Withers (Sitter).

A biography of the British film pioneer, William

Friese-Greene (1855-1921), whom film historians generally agree, The Magic Box notwithstanding, was not the inventor of cinematography. Almost every British film actor took part in this production which was intended as the film industry's contribution to the Festival of Britain. The noted American film historian Terry Ramsaye wrote in Motion Picture Herald (April 28, 1951), "Here is perversion of history and a tragedy of confusions for the traditions of the art--along with injustice to the very genuine contributions of eminent British scientists and other persons of high skill and demonstrated attainment on the record." However, most American critics liked the film, and many will agree with Philip K. Scheuer's summation in the Los Angeles Times (October 30, 1952): "It is an affectionate tribute to the motion picture in which all motion picture devotees will share."

Availability (16mm): Budget Films/United Films/Corinth

MAGIC LANTERN MOVIE, THE (9 mins/16mm)

U.S. A Film by Maxine Haleff. 1976. Animation: Bob Fontana. Antique Slides and Projectors from the Collection of Nat C. Myers, Jr. Narrator: Cecile Starr.

A brief study of the magic lantern, its history and development, to the accompaniment of music from antique music boxes. Also included in this short are extracts from George Mêliès' The Magic Lantern (1903).

Availability: Cecile Starr (rental and sale)

MAGIC MEMORIES (1 reel/16mm)

A package of film clips, compiled by Murray Glass, illustrating "movie magic"--use of double exposures, trick films, etc.--from 1901 through 1923, and including Williamson's The Big Swallow, Zecca's Naughty Lulu, Mêliès' The Magic Dice, and It's a Gift with Snub Pollard.

Availability: Em Gee

MAGIC MOVIE MOMENTS (952 ft./10 mins/35mm)

U.S. Warner Bros. 1953. Producer and Screenplay: Robert Youngson. Film Editor: Albert Helmes. Narrator: Dwight Weist.

This short features the spectacular flood sequences from Michael Curtiz' Noah's Ark (1929).
Availability: None

MAGIC OF MELIES, THE (1 reel/10 mins/16mm)

A compilation by Blackhawk Films of three films produced by Georges Mêliès during 1903 and 1904: Jupiter's Thunderbolts (1903), The Magic Lantern (1903) and The Mermaid (1904).
Availability: Blackhawk (sale)/Macmillan/Em Gee

MAN ABOUT TOWN see SILENCE EST D'OR, LE

MAN CALLED BOGART, THE see HOLLYWOOD AND THE STARS

MAN CALLED EDISON, A (28 mins/16mm)

U.S. 1972. Director: Dennis Atkinson.

A study of the contributions of Thomas Edison to the development of the motion picture, utilizing footage from several pre-1900 Edison productions.
Availability: Budget

MAN OF A THOUSAND FACES (10,915 ft./122 mins/35mm)

U.S. Universal-International. 1956. Producer: Robert Arthur. Director: Joseph Pevney. Screenplay: R. Wright Campbell, Ivan Goff and Ben Roberts. Based on a Story by Ralph Wheelwright. Photography: Russell Metty. Art Directors: Alexander Golitzen and Eric Orbom. Set Decorators: Russell A. Gausman and Julia Heron. Sound: Leslie I. Carey and Robert Pritchard. Film Editor: Ted J. Kent. Costumes: Bill Thomas. Mr. Cagney's Wardrobe: Marilyn Sotto. Makeup: Bud Westmore. Special Photography: Clifford Stine. Technical Advisor: Marjorie Ramsey. Music: Frank Skinner. Music Supervision: Joseph Gershenson. Assistant Director: Phil Bowles.
With James Cagney (Lon Chaney), Dorothy Malone (Cleva Creighton Chaney), Jane Greer (Hazel Bennett Chaney),

Marjorie Rambeau (Gert), Jim Backus (Clarence Locan), Robert Evans (Irving Thalberg), Celia Lovsky (Mrs. Chaney), Jeanne Cagney (Carrie Chaney), Jack Albertson (Dr. J. Wilson Shiels), Roger Smith (Creighton Chaney at 21), Robert Lyden (Creighton Chaney at 13), Rickie Sorenson (Creighton Chaney at 8), Dennis Rush (Creighton Chaney at 4), Nolan Leary (Pa Chaney), Simon Scott (Carl Hastings), Clarence Kolb (Himself), Danny Beck (Max Dill), Phil Van Zandt (George Loane Tucker), Hank Mann (Comedy Waiter), and Snub Pollard (Comedy Waiter).

Quite a good and entertaining film biography, but James Cagney, fine actor that he is, is not Lon Chaney. It is interesting to see Robert Evans, who was later to become head of production at Paramount, portraying another famous production head, Irving Thalberg. Man of a Thousand Faces was billed by Universal-International as its "special picture for Hollywood's Golden Jubilee."

Availability (16mm): Universal 16

MARCH OF THE MOVIES (4,140 ft./46 mins/35mm)

G.B. Associated British Pathé. 1938. Conceived by John Argyle. Compiled and Edited by Howard Gaye. Narrator: Kent Stevenson.

A brief history of the cinema, discussing the work of various pioneers and inventors, including George Eastman, Thomas Edison, the Lumière Brothers, and R. W. Paul, and major early stars such as Mary Pickford and Charles Chaplin. For more information, see the review in The Monthly Film Bulletin (Vol. 5, No. 58, 1938), page 236.

Availability: None

MARCH OF THE MOVIES, THE (73 mins/35mm)

G.B. New Realm. 1965. Producer: E. J. Fancey. Screenplay: Lottie Teasdale. Narrator: Ben Lyon.

A compilation history of the cinema. No other information available.

Availability: None

MARCH OF THE MOVIES (J. Stuart Blackton) see FILM PARADE, THE

MARILYN (7,499 ft./83 mins/35mm)

U.S. Twentieth Century-Fox. 1963. Commentary Written by Harold Medford. Director (Rock Hudson sequence): Henry Koster. Film Editor: Pepe Torres. Narrator: Rock Hudson.

A compilation of footage from the following Marilyn Monroe films produced by Twentieth Century-Fox: A Ticket to Tomahawk, All about Eve, Love Nest, We're Not Married, Don't Bother To Knock, O'Henry's Full House, Monkey Business, Niagara, Gentlemen Prefer Blondes, How To Marry a Millionaire, River of No Return, There's No Business Like Show Business, The Seven Year Itch, and Bus Stop. Also included in this film is silent footage from the last, uncompleted Marilyn Monroe feature, Something's Got To Give, which was eventually reshot as Move Over Darling with Rock Hudson and Doris Day. Marilyn does not discuss the star's private life, nor does it include any footage from her non-Twentieth Century-Fox productions. "The movie-going legions who adored her will revel in every frame of this re-exposed footage," wrote Bosley Crowther in the New York Times (July 18, 1963), "But they will look in vain for those definite but elusive inner qualities which, as the commentary has it, made her 'the needle in the haystack that caught the eye.'"

Availability (16mm): Films Incorporated

MARILYN MONROE (26 mins/16mm)

U.S. An Art Lieberman Production, released by Official Films. 1962. Executive Producer: Seymour Reid. Producer and Director: Art Lieberman. Screenplay: Malvin Wald. Film Editor and Associate Producer: Philip R. Rosenberg. Music: Elmer Bernstein. Narrator: Mike Wallace.

A somewhat rushed documentary on the life and career of Marilyn Monroe, told through newsreel footage and still photographs. There are no interviews with her friends or colleagues and only one film clip, from Columbia's 1948 production of Ladies of the Chorus.

Availability: Em Gee/Budget/Swank/Cinema Eight (sale only)

MARX BROTHERS FESTIVAL (30 mins/16mm)

A package of extracts from three Marx Brothers vehicles: Horse Feathers (1932), Duck Soup (1933) and The Incredible Jewel Robbery (1959). Only Harpo and Chico appear in the last item.

Availability: Macmillan/Swank

MARX BROTHERS FESTIVAL: Part Two (18 mins/16mm)

Despite its title, this is, in reality, a series of extracts from Monkey Business (1931).

Availability: Macmillan

MAX LINDER: COMIC GENIUS (17 mins/16mm)

A compilation of three Max Linder comedies, with music tracks: Max Learns to Skate (1906), Troubles of a Grass Widower (1908) and Max and His Dog (1912).

Availability: Kit Parker (rental and sale)

MAX LINDER PROGRAM (25 mins/16mm)

Three films with French comedian Max Linder, compiled by the Museum of Modern Art: Max Learns to Skate (1906), Troubles of a Grass Widower (1908) and Max and His Dog (1912).

Availability: The Museum of Modern Art

MEET DE SICA (4,071 ft./45 mins/35mm)

Italy. Santa Lucia. 1958. Producer: Christopher Lee Smith. Director: Bika De Reisner. Photography: Julian Lugrin. Film Editor: Stanley Smith. Music: Dorita y Pepe.

A study of Vittorio De Sica as actor and director. Included are extracts from Bicycle Thieves, Shoe-Shine and Miracle in Milan. For more information, see The Monthly Film Bulletin (August, 1959), page 113.

Availability: None

MEETING MILOS FORMAN (30 mins/16mm)

An interview with Milos Forman, in which the Czechoslovakian-born director discusses his work. Extracts from Taking Off, Loves of a Blonde and The Fireman's Ball are also included.

Availability: Macmillan

MELIES PROGRAM No. 1 (28 mins/16mm)

A package of films from the Paper Print Collection of the Library of Congress produced by Georges Méliès during 1903 and 1904: The Inn Where No Man Rests (1903), A Spiritualist Photographer (1903), The Kingdom of the Fairies (1903), The Magic Lantern (1903), The Clock Maker's Dream (1904), The Cook in Trouble (1904), and The Mermaid (1904).
Availability: Macmillan

MELIES TALES OF TERROR (1 reel/16mm)

A compilation by Blackhawk Films of three productions by Georges Méliès: The Melomaniac (1903), The Monster (1903) and The Terrible Turkish Executioner (1904).
Availability (16mm and 8mm): Blackhawk (sale only)

MELLOW DRAMAS (1 reel/8 mins/1949)

U.S. RKO Pathe. 1949. Screenliner #10. Producer: Burton Benjamin. Film Editor: Isaac Kleinerman. Narrator: Andre Baruch.

Serious moments from early silent films played for comedy effect.
Availability: Jackson Dube

MELODRAMA RIDES THE RAILS (1 reel/16mm)

A compilation of three early "railroad" films: Railroad Smashup (Edison, 1904), A Railway Tragedy (American Biograph, 1904) and A Mother's Devotion (Vitagraph, 1911).
Availability: Em Gee (formerly available for sale on 8mm and 16mm from Blackhawk Films)

MEMORIAL TO AL JOLSON (786 ft./9 mins/35mm)

U.S. Columbia. 1952. Director: Ralph Staub. Film Editor: Edmund Kimber. Music: Mischa Bakaleinikoff. Narrator: Jack Benny.

A brief tribute to Al Jolson, with newsreel footage of his home life, a meeting with Valentino and Douglas Fairbanks,

Sr., entertaining the troops in Korea, and relaxing with his wife Ruby Keeler. Jolson's voice is not heard. For more information, see The Monthly Film Bulletin (September, 1952), page 131.

Availability: None

MEMORIES OF FAMOUS HOLLYWOOD COMEDIANS (1 reel/ 10 mins/35mm)

U.S. Columbia "Screen Snapshots" Series. 1951 Producer: Ralph Staub. Narrator: Joe E. Brown.

Brief glimpses of Laurel and Hardy, W. C. Fields, Olsen and Johnson, Roscoe "Fatty" Arbuckle, the Marx Brothers and others. One in the Columbia "Screen Snapshots" series, all of which dealt with the Hollywood scene. For more information on the series see The Great Movie Shorts by Leonard Maltin (Crown, 1972). See also Screen Snapshots, 25th Anniversary Issue.

Availability: None

MEMORIES OF THE SILENT STARS #1: THE MIRTHMAKERS (1 reel/16mm)

A compilation by Blackhawk Films of footage of various silent comedians, including Ben Turpin, Charlie Murray, Charles and Syd Chaplin, Lupino Lane, and Walter Hiers.

Availability: Em Gee (for sale for many years through Blackhawk Films)

MEMORIES OF THE SILENT STARS #II: BEHIND THE SCENES WITH THE STARS (1 reel/16mm)

A compilation by Blackhawk Films of newsreel footage of a number of silent stars, including Clara Bow, Mae Murray, Roscoe "Fatty" Arbuckle, Norma Talmadge, Clara Kimball Young, Walter Hiers, and Lon Chaney.

Availability: None (formerly available for sale on 8mm and 16mm from Blackhawk Films)

MEMORIES OF THE SILENT STARS #III: PERSONALITIES ON PARADE (1 reel/16mm)

A compilation by Blackhawk Films of footage of various

silent film personalities, including Marie Dressler, Douglas Fairbanks, Charles Chaplin, Mary Pickford, D. W. Griffith, Erich von Stroheim, Renee Adoree, John Gilbert, and Norma Shearer.

Availability: Em Gee (for sale for many years through Blackhawk Films)

MEMORIES OF THE SILENT STARS #IV: CANDID MOMENTS WITH THE STARS (1 reel/16mm)

A compilation by Blackhawk Films of newsreel footage of a number of silent stars, including Pearl White, Mary Pickford, Lillian Gish, Dorothy Gish, Anna Q. Nilsson, Viola Dana, Shirley Mason, George "Lefty" Flynn, Lewis Stone, Marion Davies, Alice Joyce, Conway Tearle, Alma Rubens, and Lillian Roth.

Availability (16mm and 8mm): Blackhawk (sale only)

MEMORIES OF THE SILENT STARS #V: THE MEN BEHIND THE MEGAPHONE (1 reel/16mm)

A compilation by Blackhawk Films of newsreel footage of the following directors: Sidney Olcott (directing Timothy's Quest, 1922), Alan Crosland (directing The Face in the Fog, 1922), Ray Smallwood (directing When the Desert Calls, 1922), J. Searle Dawley (directing Has the World Gone Mad!, 1923), Hugo Ballin (with his wife Mabel), Frank Lloyd (directing Winds of Chance, 1925), and William Nigh (directing Notoriety, 1922).

Availability: Blackhawk (sale only)

MEMORIES OF THE SILENT STARS #VI: THE STARS IN THE NEWSREELS (1 reel/16mm)

A 1974 compilation by Blackhawk Films of newsreel footage of the following silent film personalities: Mary Pickford and Douglas Fairbanks, Gloria Swanson, Dorothy Gish, Carl Laemmle, the 1924 WAMPAS Baby Stars (including Clara Bow, Dorothy Mackaill, Elinor Fair, and Marian Nixon), Helen Ferguson, William Russell, Phyllis Haver, Bryant Washburn, George M. Cohan, McIntyre and Heath, Fred Stone, David Butler, Bebe Daniels, Clara Kimball Young, Priscilla Dean, and Tom Mix (in a complete Fox newsreel segment of his trip to Washington to meet President Harding).

Availability: None (formerly available for sale on 16mm and 8mm from Blackhawk Films)

MICHEL SIMON (15 mins/16mm)

Denmark. Laterna Films. A Richard Kaplan Presentation. 1964. Director and Screenplay: Ole Roos. Photography: Peter Roos.

A brief look at the career of the well-known French screen actor, including short clips from a number of his films. For more information, see Rohama Lee's review in Film News (September, 1967), pages 13 and 17.
Availability: Contemporary-McGraw Hill/Images (rental and sale)

MICKEY MOUSE ANNIVERSARY SHOW, THE (8,010 ft./89 mins/35mm)

U.S. Walt Disney. 1968. Producer and Screenplay: Ward Kimball. Director: Robert Stevenson. Assistant to Producer: Louis Debney. Film Editor: Ernie Milano. Music: George Bruns. Sound: Robert O. Cook. Assistant Director: Paul L. Cameron. Narrator: Dean Jones.

A compilation of Mickey Mouse cartoons, in celebration of Mickey's fortieth birthday. Extracts from the following films are included: Steamboat Willie (1928), Plane Crazy (1928), Mickey's Gala Premiere (1933), Mickey's Service Station (1935), Mickey's Fire Brigade (1935), Thru the Mirror (1936), Lonesome Ghosts (1937), Hawaiian Holiday (1937), Mickey's Trailer (1938), The Pointer (1939), Beach Picnic (1939), Mickey's Surprise Party (1939), Fantasia (1940), Tugboat Mickey (1940), Symphony Hour (1942), Mickey's Delayed Date (1947), and Mickey and the Seal (1948).
Availability: None

MICKEY MOUSE: THE FIRST FIFTY YEARS (18 mins/Super 8mm)

A 1978 compilation of clips from Mickey Mouse cartoons, in celebration of Mickey's fiftieth birthday. Included are extracts from Steamboat Willie, Fantasia and The Mickey Mouse Club.
Availability: Walt Disney/Blackhawk

MICKEY'S MEMORABLE MOMENTS (400 ft. /8mm)

Excerpts from five Walt Disney/Mickey Mouse cartoons: *Magician Mickey* (1937), *Brave Little Tailor* (1938), *Mickey's Delayed Date* (1947), *Mickey and the Seal* (1948), and *Simple Things* (1953).
Availability: Walt Disney 8mm

MILESTONES FOR MICKEY (41 mins/35mm)

U.S. Walt Disney. 1974.

A compilation of vintage Mickey Mouse cartoons, with no linking commentary: *Plane Crazy* (1928), *Mickey's Service Station* (1935), *The Band Concert* (1935), *Thru the Mirror* (1936), *The Sorcerer's Apprentice* (a shortened version from *Fantasia*, 1940), and the *Mickey Mouse Club* March.
Availability (16mm): Twyman/Select

MILESTONES IN ANIMATION (40 mins/35mm)

U.S. Walt Disney. 1973.

A compilation of vintage Disney cartoons, with no linking commentary: *Steamboat Willie* (1928), *The Skeleton Dance* (1929), *Flowers and Trees* (1932), *The Three Little Pigs* (1933), and *The Old Mill* (1937).
Availability (16mm): Twyman/Select

MILLION DOLLAR MERMAID (10, 381 ft. /115 mins/35mm)

U.S. M-G-M. 1952. Producer: Arthur Hornblow, Jr. Director: Mervyn LeRoy. Screenplay: Everett Freeman. Based on an Unpublished Autobiography by Annette Kellerman. Photography: George Folsey. Music Director: Adolph Deutsch. Fountain and Smoke Numbers Staged by Busby Berkeley. Underwater Choreography: Audrene Brier. Orchestrations: Alexander Courage. Technicolor Color Consultant: Henri Jaffa. Art Directors: Cedric Gibbons and Jack Martin Smith. Film Editor: John McSweeney, Jr. Assistant Director: Howard W. Koch. Recording Supervisor: Douglas Shearer. Set Decorators: Edwin B. Willis and Richard Pefferle. Color Consultant: Alvord Eiseman. Special Effects: A. Arnold Gillespie and Warren Newcombe.

Montage Sequences by Peter Ballbusch. Costumes for Musical Sequences by Helen Rose. Costumes: Walter Plunkett. Hair Styles: Sydney Guilaroff. Makeup Created by William Tuttle.

With Esther Williams (Annette Kellerman), Victor Mature (James Sullivan), Walter Pidgeon (Frederick Kellerman), David Brian (Alfred Harper), Donna Corcoran (Annette at ten), Jesse White (Doc Cronnol), Maria Tallchief (Pavlova), Howard Freeman (Aldrich), Charles Watts (Policeman), Wilton Graff (Garvey), Frank Ferguson (Prosecutor), James Bell (Judge), James Flavin (Conductor), and Willis Bouchey (Director).

A fictionalized biography of the vaudeville and film star, Annette Kellerman, who acted as technical advisor on the production, and who, as a swimming star, was quite definitely the Esther Williams of her day. Former silent star Creighton Hale was an extra in the film.

Availability (16mm): Films Incorporated

MOMENTS IN MUSIC (10 mins/16mm)

A collection of musical excerpts from pre-1951 Hollywood productions, includes Up in Arms, The Great Caruso, A Song to Remember, Neptune's Daughter, Road to Rio, and Anchors Aweigh.

Availability: Indiana University Audio-Visual Center

MONSTERS WE'VE KNOWN AND LOVED see HOLLYWOOD AND THE STARS

MORE FROM THE ENCHANTED STUDIO (2 reels/16mm)

U.S. Blackhawk Films. 1976. Compiled and Annotated by Anthony Slide.

A compilation, with historical notations, of productions by the French Pathé Frères Company: The Yawner (1907), Poor Coat (1907), Whiffles Wins a Beauty Prize (circa 1910), I Fetch the Bread (circa 1906), and Down in the Deep (1906). See also The Enchanted Studio.

Availability (16mm and 8mm): Blackhawk (sale only)/ Images

MOVIE CRAZY YEARS, THE (90 mins/16mm)

U.S. NET. 1972. Producer: David Loxton. Screenplay and Narrator: Richard Schickel.

An introduction to the golden years of Warner Bros., including interviews with Bette Davis, Edward G. Robinson, Olivia de Havilland, Pat O'Brien, Joan Blondell, Mervyn LeRoy, Busby Berkeley, William Wellman, Hal Wallis, Dalton Trumbo, and John Bright, and clips from Wild Boys of the Road, Footlight Parade, Dangerous, Jezebel, Dark Victory, A Midsummer Night's Dream, Captain Blood, Charge of the Light Brigade, 42nd Street, The Jazz Singer, Gold Diggers of 1935, Little Caesar, Public Enemy, and I Am a Fugitive from a Chain Gang. See also Hollywood: You Must Remember This.

Availability: United Artists 16 (rental and lease)

MOVIE-GO-ROUND (4,039 ft./45 mins/35mm)

G.B. A Fama Films Production released by Ambassador Film Productions. A Gilbert Church and J. C. Jones Presentation. 1949. Director: Fred Weiss. Music: Hans May and others.

With Donald Biset (The Old Time Projector) and Rene Goddard (The Modern Projector).

An argument between an old and new projector, in which the silent projector laments its conversion to sound, and recalls the early silent films, newsreels, Keystone comedies and Westerns. For more information, see The Monthly Film Bulletin (March 31, 1949), page 38.

Availability: None

MOVIE MEMORIES (33 mins/35mm)

According to the Cinema Eight catalogue, this 1939 "documentary depicts evolution of motion pictures from the beginning and the many people who contributed so much to its success--plus scenes from some of the early great screen classics." It sounds suspiciously like a shortened version of J. Stuart Blackton's The Film Parade (q.v.).

Availability (16mm): Cinema Eight (sale)/Kit Parker (rental)

MOVIE MEMORIES (1,251 ft./14 mins/35mm)

G.B. Inspiration, released by Twentieth Century-Fox. 1948. Producer, Director and Screenplay: Horace Shepherd. Narrator: Ronald Waldman.

"A miniature history of the development of the cinema, including shots of the first Bioscope theatre in London and scenes from old films starring such legendary figures as Rudolph Valentino and Betty Compson."--The Cinema (February 25, 1948).

Availability: None

MOVIE MEMORIES (1 reel/8 mins)

U.S. RKO Pathé. 1949. Screenliner #5. Producer: Burton Benjamin. Film Editor: Isaac Kleinerman. Narrator: Andre Baruch.

Extracts from silent films of the early 'teens played for comedy effect.

Availability: Jackson Dube

MOVIE MILESTONES (120 mins/35mm)

U.S. American Society of Cinematographers. 1966. Compilers: Arthur Miller and Charles G. Clarke.

Compiled for the 50th anniversary celebration of the Society of Motion Picture and Television Engineers, Movie Milestones consists of clips from motion pictures of the past, including The Birth of a Nation, Intolerance, 7th Heaven, Sunrise, and Gone with the Wind, which illustrate the development of the photographer's art. The compilation closes with shots of Karl Struss at work on a modern Hollywood production.

Availability: None

MOVIE MILESTONES (1 reel/10 mins/35mm)

U.S. Paramount Varieties. 1935. Screenplay: Bert Enis. Narrator: Norman Brokenshire.

Highlights from four Paramount silent features: The

Miracle Man (1919), Blood and Sand (1922), The Covered Wagon (1923), and Beau Geste (1926). The chief interest this short holds today is in the clip from The Miracle Man, now believed to be a "lost" film, in which Chaney first made an impression.

Availability (16mm): Em Gee/Select (This short was available for sale, on 8mm and 16mm, for many years)

MOVIE MILESTONES # 2 (1 reel/10 mins/35mm)

U.S. Paramount Varieties. 1936. Screenplay: H. A. Woodmansee. Narrator: Alois Havrilla.

Highlights from four Paramount silent features: The Ten Commandments (1923), Old Ironsides (1926), Behind the Front (1926), and The Way of All Flesh (1928). The chief interest this short holds today is in the clip from the last film, now believed "lost."

Availability (16mm): Em Gee (This short was available for sale, on 8mm and 16mm, for many years)

MOVIE MUSEUM (10 mins/16mm)

U.S. Sterling Television. 1954/1955. Curator: Paul Killiam. Supervisor: Saul J. Turell. Scripts: June Bundy, Arthur Knight and Gideon Bachman. Research: William K. Everson. Film Editor: W. Campbell Dalzell. Music: Eddie Bernard. Narrator: Paul Killiam.

A popular television series from the Fifties, which preceded Silents Please. It consisted of considerably condensed versions of Edison and American Biograph shorts, plus an occasional feature prefaced by interest shorts or newsreel clips. The following is a complete listing of the 176 programs in the series:

1. A Girl and Her Trust (1912) and The British Royal Family (1896). 2. A Dash through the Clouds (1912) and Fatima's Dance. 3. The Goddess of Sagebrush Gulch (1911) and Easter Parade on Fifth Avenue. 4. 1776 or The Hessian Renegades (1909) and The Vatican (1896). 5. Lily of the Tenements (1909) and Feeding the Chickens (1897). 6. The Drunkard's Reformation (1909) and A (W)ringing Good Joke (1896). 7. A Terrible Discovery (1911) and New York Steam Elevated (1897). 8. Comrades (1911) and The Dreyfus Affair--Emile Zola (1899). 9. The Miser's Heart (1911) and

Boer War (1900). 10. Man's Genesis (1912) and Queen Victoria (1901). 11. The Usurer (1910) and President McKinley's Inauguration (1897). 12. Married for Millions (1906) and The Dam Family (1905). 13. Through the Breakers (1909) and U.S. Cavalry at the Inauguration of the Cuban Republic (1902). 14. The Switch Tower (1911) and Pope Leo XIII (1896). 15. The Kleptomaniac (1905) and Coney Island (1903). 16. The Nihilists (1905) and Jeffries-Corbett Fight (1903). 17. The Two Paths (1911) and The Black Diamond Express (1897). 18. Cartoons on Tour (1912) and Battleship Indiana (1903). 19. The Light That Came (1909) and Washing the Baby (1893). 20. The Last Deal (1909) and The Tailor's Dummy (1898). 21. At Dawn (1913) and The Kiss (1896). 22. As It Might Have Been (1914) and The Battle of Santiago Bay (1898). 23. The Voice of the Violin (1909) and Young Edward VIII (1900). 24. Lena and the Geese (1912) and McKinley at Home (1896). 25. The Musketeers of Pig Alley (1912) and The Burning Stable (1897). 26. Winning Back His Love (1910) and Turning the Tables (1903). 27. The Noise of Bombs (1913) and The First Movie Advertisement (1894). 28. Cupid vs. Cigarettes (1913) and Galveston Disaster (1900). 29. The Message of the Violin (1910) and Gans vs. Nelson Prize Fight (1906). 30. The New York Hat (1912) and Capture of a Roof Burglar (1898). 31. The Lonedale Operator (1911) and San Francisco (1900). 32. A Mother's Influence (1911) and The Barber Shop (1895). 33. The Lonely Villa (1909) and Baseball (1906). 34. Because He Loved Her (1913) and Suffragettes (1905). 35. His Bitter Pill (1913) and Annette Kellerman (1916). 36. Cursed by His Beauty (1913) and Thomas Edison (1895). 37. Wife and Auto Trouble (1913) and The Spanish-American War (1900). 38. Rudolph Valentino Program No. 1. 39. A Natural Born Gambler (1915). 40. The Mission of Mr. Foo (1915) and Dickson/Edison Experimental Sound Short (1900). 41. Fatty Joins the Force (1914) and McKinley's Funeral (1901). 42. The Plumber (1914) and The Election of 1896. 43. Second Fiddle (1923). 44. Hash House Mashers (1913) and The Test of a Man (1913). 45. Valentino Program No. 2 and Mabel's Stratagem (1913). 46. Dr. Jekyll and Mr. Hyde (1920). 47. Clara Bow. 48. His Second Childhood (1915) and Spanish-American War Bond Drive (1898). 49. Valentino Program No. 3 and The Unappreciated Joke and Streetcar Chivalry (both 1900). 50. Dealing for Daisy (1914, incorrect title of a William S. Hart feature) and Rector's to Claremont (1900). 51. A Squaw's Love (1912) and The Movie's First Baby (1893). 52. The Manicure Lady (1911) and William F. Cody (1910). 53. The Revenue Man and His Girl

(1911) and Chicago World's Fair (1893). 54. The Primal Call (1912) and Admiral Dewey's Flagship. 55. At the Crossroads of Life (1908) and How Jones Lost His Roll (1903). 56. The Wrong Track (1914). 57. The Drummer of the Eight (1913). 58. Her Awakening (1912). 59. Ella Cinders (1926). 60. The Heart of a Waif (1915) and Black Maria Magic (1900). 61. The Mad Dancer (1925). 62. Wilful Ambrose (1913) and Lumiere (1900-1905). 63. What Drink Did (1909) and Bathing at Brighton (1910). 64. Gloria Swanson Program No. 1. 65. The Failure (1912) and Early French Police (1912). 66. Blind Love (1912) and Wallace Beery (1914). 67. Makers and Spenders (1912) and Coronation of Edward VII (1902). 68. The Making of Crooks (1914). 69. The Lost World (1925). 70. Her Terrible Ordeal (1912) and The Sisters Bon Bon (1900). 71. The Crooked Way (1911) and Bicycle Race Film Advertisement (1900). 72. The Rocky Road (1909) and Lady of Paris (1905). 73. Gloria Swanson Program No. 2. 74. The Wanderer (1913) and A Vitagraph Romance (1912). 75. The Great Train Robbery (1903) and Pre-Screen Movies (1893). 76. Possibilities of War in the Air (1906) and The Firebug (1905). 77. Through Darkened Vales (1911) and Poor Algy (1905). 78. What a Change of Clothes Did (1912) and New York Politics (1900). 79. The Lesser Evil (1912) and Winter Straw Ride (1906). 80. Resurrection (1909) and Early Censorship. 81. Ambrose's First Falsehood (1913) and Early Newsreel Personalities (1900). 82. Valentino Program No. 4 and Old New York (1900). 83. Lady Windermere's Fan (1925). 84. Saved from Himself (1911) and Koster and Bial's Music Hall (1895-1900). 85. Two Wagons, Both Covered (1923). 86. Confidence (1909) and Fashions (1900). 87. The Drop Kick (1925). 88. Blazing the Trail (1912) and Charles Pathe (1908). 89. A Change of Spirit (1911) and The First Film Actors (1900). 90. Married (1925). 91. Meddling Women (1924). 92. Saved from the Vampire (1915) and Bicycle Police (1903). 93. All That Glitters (1924). 94. Speed Kings (1913) and Rescued from an Eagle's Nest (1905). 95. Beau Brummel (1924). 96-99. Beau Brummel (continued). 100. Grass (1926). 101. Old Heidelberg (1916). 102. Desperate Encounter between Burglar and Police (1900) and Lindbergh (1927). 103. The Hardest Way (1920) and Keystone Bathing Beauties (1914). 104. The Clodhopper (1917). 105-106. The Clodhopper (continued). 107. The Devil Dodger (1916, correct title Hell's Hinges). 108. The Devil Dodger (concluded). 109. De Wolf Hopper (1918). 110. De Wolf Hopper (concluded). 111. With a Kodak (1915) and The Suburbanite (1903). 112.

The Story of Mae Murray. 113. The Woman (1912). 114. Dizzy Heights and Daring Hearts (1916). 115. Her Torpedoed Love (1917). 116. When a Man's a Prince (1918). 117. East Lynne (1913) and Biograph's Bad Boy (1903). 118. Hoodoo Ann (1916). 119-120. Hoodoo Ann (continued). 121. For His Son (1912). 122. Santa Claus vs. Cupid (1915). 123. The Adventure of the Wrong Santa Claus (1914) and A Holiday Pageant at Home (1900). 124. Buster Keaton (1923). 125. Pathways of Life (1915). 126. Captain January (1924). 127. His Trust (1911) and The Burglar and the Bundle (1903). 128. The Black Pirate (1926) and A Joke on the Roundsman (1905). 129. The Arcadian Maid (1909) and Laughing Gas (1905). 130. All Aboard (1918) and Boys after School (1902). 131. Peck's Bad Boy (1921). 132-134. Peck's Bad Boy (continued). 135. The Americano (1919). 136-137. The Americano (continued). 138. Enoch Arden (1911). 139. Enoch Arden (concluded). 140. Conquest of the North Pole (1908) and Carole Lombard. 141. How John Came Home and Otis Skinner (1920). 142. The Phantom of the Opera (1925). 143. Hustlin' Hank (1922). 144. A Temporary Truce (1912) and The Ruffian's Reward (1903). 145. Mr. Robinson Crusoe (1931) and John Bunny (1912). 146. The House with Closed Shutters (1910). 147. Silent Heroes (1913). 148. Pride of Pikeville (1915). 149. Golden Rule Kate (1915). 150. The Love Thief (1914) and The Pickford Family. 151. The Sea Ghost. 152. Don't Park There (1922). 153. Fighting Blood (1911). 154. The Telephone Girl and the Lady (1913). 155. Jubilo Jr. (1924) and The Cherokee Kid. 156. Jubilo Jr. (concluded). 157. The Last Drop of Water (1911) and Fay Templeton. 158. Past Redemption (1914). 159. My Boy (1921). 160-161. My Boy (continued). 162. The Hunchback of Notre Dame (1923). 163-166. The Hunchback of Notre Dame (continued). 167. The Iron Mask (1929) and Model Wanted (1907). The Gaucho (1928) and Nurse Wanted (1906). 170. A Corner in Wheat (1909). 171. The Unwelcome Guest (1913). 172. Boobs in the Wood (1924) and Tom, Tom, the Piper's Son (1905). 173. Boobs in the Wood (concluded). 174. The Serial Queens (1914-1926). 175. Life of an American Policeman (1905) and The Gibson Goddess (1909). 176. Fish (1916) and Dream of a Race Track Fiend (1905). (This information came from the records of Killiam Shows, and in some cases dates may be incorrect and titles may not be originals.)

Availability: Killiam Shows (a number of titles in the Movie Museum series are available for sale on 8mm and 16mm from Blackhawk, but its catalogue does not indicate if the film is the Movie Museum version)

MOVIES, THE (30 mins/16mm)

U.S. WTTW-TV. 1961.

A film in the "American Memoir" series, in which Dr. James Dodds traces the development of the motion picture and the changes in the taste of the American filmgoing public. It "points out that there have been some distinguished films despite a motion picture industry that continues to search for the lowest common denominator of taste."

Availability: Indiana University Audio-Visual Center/ University of California Extension Media Center

MOVIES ARE ADVENTURE <u>see</u> LET'S GO TO THE MOVIES

MOVIES ARE MY LIFE: A PROFILE OF MARTIN SCORSESE (61 mins/35mm)

G.B. A Film by Peter Hayden. 1978. Producers: Peter Hayden and Steven Prince. Associate Producer: Chris Ranger. Director: Peter Hayden. Photography: Joe Marquette. Film Editor: Carl Thompson. Sound: Michael Euje.

A portrait of American film director Martin Scorsese, as seen by his colleagues, including John Cassavetes, Jay Cocks, Robert De Niro, Brian DePalma, Jodie Foster, Liza Minnelli, and Robbie Robertson. Clips from a number of Scorsese's films are also included. Screened at the 1979 Toronto and New York Film Festivals.

Availability (16mm): None

MOVIES GO WEST, THE (1 reel/14 mins/16mm)

U.S. Geoffrey Bell Productions. 1974. Producer and Director: Geoffrey Bell. Screenplay: Jameson Goldner. Photography: Marvin Becker. Film Editor: Lela Smith. Music Consultant: Warner Jepson.

"An important chapter of early film history is documented through the reminiscences of Hal Angus, a member of the original Western Essanay Film Manufacturing Company players. Angus visits the studio site in Niles, near San Francisco Bay, and the nearby location ranch areas where, between 1909 and 1916, 'Broncho Billy' Anderson produced and starred in hundreds of outdoor adventure stories--the first Westerns to be filmed in authentic locales of the Great West. Old photographs, film clips and advertisements show how Anderson created the prototype of the cowboy movie hero and established the format of the classic American Western." --Geoffrey Bell.

Availability: University of California Extension Media Center (rental and sale)/U.S.C. Film Library

MOVIES LEARN TO TALK, THE (26 mins/16mm)

U.S. CBS for "The Twentieth Century" series. 1959. Producer: Burton Benjamin. Screenplay and Research: Don Miller. Film Editor: Aram Boyajian. Story Editor: Marshall Flaum. Host/Narrator: Walter Cronkite.

A very fine history of the development of sound motion pictures, first televised on October 25, 1959. The Movies Learn to Talk includes examples of the various sound experiments, including Edison's Kinetophone, Gaumont's Cyrano de Bergerac with Cocquelin, an extract from a Lee De Forest Phonofilm, and the Theodore W. Case/E. I. Sponable tests. Also included in this documentary are clips from Don Juan, The Jazz Singer, The Lights of New York, Sunrise, In Old Arizona, Steamboat Willie, and George Bernard Shaw's appearance before the Fox Movietone cameras. "Movie History on TV" by Don Miller, published in Films in Review (February, 1960), pages 65-69, is a detailed account of the making of this short. The best introduction to the history of sound available.

Availability: University of California Extension Media Center/Contemporary-McGraw Hill (rental and sale)/U.S.C. Film Library/Images/Em Gee

MOVIES MARCH ON, THE (2 reels/21 mins/35mm)

U.S. RKO release of a "March of Time" subject. Volume 5, Number 12. 1939. Producer: Louis de Rochemont. Director: Alan Brown.

The March of Time's tribute to the Film Library of the Museum of Modern Art, from which all the clips used in this compilation came. Sequences are shown from the following films: the May Irwin-John C. Rice The Kiss, The Great

Train Robbery, The New York Hat, The Fugitive, Tillie's Punctured Romance, A Night Out, The Birth of a Nation, Thais, The Flesh and the Devil, The Jazz Singer, A Fool There Was, Robin Hood, The Four Horsemen of the Apocalypse, The Covered Wagon, The Big Parade, All Quiet on the Western Front, Steamboat Willie, and The Life of Emile Zola, among others. The Movies March On is still of interest, despite the familiarity of most of the clips, and it is particularly fascinating to see John Abbott and Iris Barry, director and curator respectively of the Film Library of the Museum of Modern Art, intently taking notes in their projection room. "It is at once an informative record and excellent entertainment," wrote Paul C. Mooney, Jr. in The Motion Picture Herald (July 8, 1939).

Availability (16mm): The Museum of Modern Art

MOVIES' STORY (25 mins/16mm)

U.S. S-L Film productions. 1970.

A study of the development of the film industry from 1895 through 1915, utilizing film clips from the work of Georges Méliès, Edwin S. Porter, D. W. Griffith, and Charles Chaplin.

Availability: University of California Extension Media Center

MOVING PICTURE BOYS IN THE GREAT WAR, THE (51 mins/16mm)

U.S. Post-Newsweek Productions and Blackhawk Films. 1975. Executive Producer: Ray Hubbard. Producer: David Shepard. Director and Film Editor: Larry Ward. Screenplay: John Abel and Peter Dufour. Business Manager: Robert C. Allen.

An intelligent and entertaining study of the film industry's involvement in the First World War, told through the use of contemporary music and clips from fictional, promotional and news films. Sequences from the following films are utilized: Hoodoo Ann (1916), Civilization (1916), The Mystery of the Double Cross (serial), My Four Years in Germany (1918), The Sinking of the Lusitania (1918), Swat the Spy (1918), The Kingdom of Hope (1917), The Man Who Was Afraid (1917), The Unbeliever (1918), Hearts of the World

(1917), The Heart of Humanity (1918), Yankee Doodle in Berlin (1919), Doing His Bit, Happy Hooligan, AWOL (1919), America's Answer (1918), Pershing's Crusaders (1918), Liberty Loan Drives, The 2nd Liberty Loan Appeal, Banzai (1918), The Bond (1918), Gas and Fire (1918), The Log of the U-35 (1918), Photographic Activities of the Signal Corps A.E.F. (1917-1918), Draft and Mobilization Activities (1917-1918), War Risk Insurance (1918), His Best Gift (1918), Official War Reviews (1918), A Dramatization of the Valorous Deeds of Hunter J. Wickersham (1918), War Bond Rallies (1918-1919), Count Dohna and His Moewe (1918), The Battle of the Somme (1916), Flashes of Action (1925), War As It Really Is (1916), The Great War, and assorted newsreels from Pathé, Mutual and Universal (1916-1919). The Bulk of the footage came from the film collections of Blackhawk Films, the Library of Congress and the National Archives.

Availability (16mm and 8mm): Blackhawk (sale only)

MUSIC FOR THE MOVIES (60 mins/16mm)

U.S. KABC-TV for the "Expedition Los Angeles" series. Date Unknown.

Film composer Elmer Bernstein discusses his work, and explains the conception and construction of the music for a number of films including Summer and Smoke, God's Little Acre, The Magnificent Seven, and Walk on the Wild Side.

Availability: None

MYSTERIOUS MARVELS OF MELIES (1 reel/16mm)

A package of four shorts produced by Georges Méliès during 1903 and 1904, compiled by Murray Glass: The Mad Musician, The Terrible Turkish Executioner, The Magic Well, and The Wizard Alcofrisbas.

Availability: Em Gee

MYSTICAL MAGIC OF MELIES (1 reel/16mm)

A compilation of three Georges Méliès productions from 1903: Jack and Jim, Jack Jaggs and Dum Dum and The Mystical Flame.

Availability: Em Gee

NAISSANCE DU CINEMA (40 mins/35mm)

France. Les Films du Compas. 1947. Producer and Director: Roger Leenhardt. Photography: Pierre Levent. Based on Historical Documentation by Georges Sadoul. Music: Guy Bernard Delapierre. Assistants: Pierre Biro and Louis Raitière. Art Director: Maurice Collasson. Animation: Gabriel Allignet and Robert Raphaël.

A beautifully produced documentary on pre- and early cinema--originally released with color sequences in Agfacolor--using actors to recreate persons and events. Naissance du Cinéma covers the history of the magic lantern, the Thaumatrope, the Zoetrope, and the work of Dr. Etienne-Jules Marey, Thomas Edison and the Lumière Brothers. The highspot is undoubtedly a brilliant recreation of Emile Reynaud's Théâtre Optique. Naissance du Cinéma is also available in two parts with English commentary, titled Biography of the Motion Picture Camera and Animated Cartoons: The Toy That Grew Up.

Availability (35mm and 16mm): The Museum of Modern Art (with French commentary)

NATALIE WOOD, HOLLYWOOD'S CHILD see HOLLYWOOD AND THE STARS

NEGRO IN ENTERTAINMENT, THE (1 reel/10 mins/35mm)

U.S. Presented by Chesterfield Cigarettes. 1950. Producer: E. M. Glucksman. Hosts: Bill Lund and Hedda Motan.

Clips of W. C. Handy, Ethel Waters, Louis Armstrong, Bill Robinson, Duke Ellington, Fats Waller and others, interspersed with shots of the hosts smoking Chesterfield cigarettes.

Availability (16mm): Thunderbird (sale)/Kit Parker (rental)

NEOREALISM (30 mins/16mm)

Italy. RAI-TV. 1972.

The history of the Italian neorealist movement is examined by those who took part in it. Rossellini, De Sica, Pasolini, Bertolucci, and Antonioni discuss their films, and people living in the areas of Rome where Open City was filmed discuss its making. Among the film clips used are extracts from Open City (1945), Paisan (1946) and Umberto D (1952). Booklist described Neorealism as "a marriage between poetic visuals and realistic document."

Availability: Texture Films/University of California Extension Media Center

NEWSFRONT (110 mins/35mm)

Australia. A Palm Beach Pictures Production. 1978. Producer: David Elfick. Director and Screenplay: Phillip Noyce. Based on an original screenplay by Bob Ellis, from an idea by David Elfick. Photography: Vincent Monton. Film Editor: John Scott. Sound: Tim Lloyd. Music: William Motzing. Art Director: Lissa Coote. Costumes: Norma Moriceau.

With Bill Hunter (Len Maguire), Wendy Hughes (Amy), Gerard Kennedy (Frank Maguire), Chris Haywood (Chris), Angela Punch (Fay Maguire), John Ewart (Charlie), Don Crosby (A. C. Marwood), and Bryan Brown (Geoff).

A recreation of the activities of a newsreel company, Cinetone, during the Forties and Fifties. Screened at the 1978 Karlovy Vary and New York Film Festivals, Newsfront was favorably reviewed by Charles Ryweck in The Hollywood Reporter (October 5, 1978).

Availability (16mm): None

NICKELETTE (10 mins/35mm)

"Excerpts of entertainment from the days of soft coal and hard liquor. You'll see Rudolph Valentino cast in the role of gangster--you'll join in singing 'The Curse of an Aching Heart'--and you'll cheer for Little Nell in trouble again. A wonderful page of movie history."--description in the Swank catalogue. No other information available.

Availability (16mm): Swank

NICKELODEON (10,973 ft. /121 mins/35mm)

U.S. Columbia/British Lion/EMI. 1976. Producers:

Irwin Winkler and Robert Chartoff. Associate Producer: Frank Marshall. Director: Peter Bogdanovich. Screenplay: W. D. Richter and Peter Bogdanovich. Photography: Laszlo Kovacs. Music Director and Arrangements: Richard Hazard. Piano Rolls and Cylinders from the Collection of Lennie Marvin. Special Photographic Effects: Howard A. Anderson Company. Art Director: Richard Berger. Set Decorator: Darrell Silvera. Special Effects: Cliff Wenger. Film Editor: William Carruth. Costumes: Theadora Van Runkle. Choreography: Rita Abrams. Sound Editors: Kay Rose, Richard Burrow, Michael Colgan, Vickie Sampson, and Mort Tubor. Sound Recording: Barry Thomas. Sound Re-recording: Arthur Piantadosi, Les Fresholtz and Michael Minkler. Stunt Coordinator: Hal Needham. Stunts: Hal Needham, Julie Ann Johnson, Joe Ansler, Ron Stein, and Charles Tamburro. Head Wrangler: Stevie Myers. Dog Trainer: Robert Weatherwax. Assistant Directors: Jack Sanders, Arne Schmidt and Steve Lim.

With Ryan O'Neal (Leo Harrigan), Burt Reynolds (Buck Greenway), Tatum O'Neal (Alice Forsythe), Brian Keith (H. H. Cobb), Stella Stevens (Marty Reeves), John Ritter (Franklin Frank), Jane Hitchcock (Kathleen Cooke), Jack Perkins (Michael Gilhooley), Brion James (Bailiff), Sidney Armus (Judge), Joe Warfield (Defense Attorney), Tamar Cooper (Edna Mae Gilhooley), Alan Gibbs (Patents Hooligan), Matthew Anden (Hecky), Lorenzo Music and Arnold Soboloff (Cobb's Writers), Jeffrey Byron (Steve), Priscilla Pointer (Mabel), Don Calfa (Waldo), Philip Burns (Duncan), Edward Marshall (Rialto Hotel Clerk), John Blackwell (Louie), E. J. Andre, Christa Lang and Maurice Manson (Stage Performers), Louis Guss (Dinsdale), Frank Marshall (Dinsdale's Assistant), Andrew Winner (Stage Manager), Matilda Calnan (German Bakery Lady), Gustaf and Bertil Unger (German Producers), James O'Connell and Ric Mancini (Patents Thugs), Mark Dennis (Cobb's Cutter), E. Hampton Beagle (Leo's Train Conductor), Hedgemon Lewis (Train Waiter), Bill Riddle (Sally), Dino Judd (Old Timer), Harry Carey Jr. (Dobey), James Best (Jim), Jack Verbois (Jack), John Chappell (John), George Gaynes (Reginald Kingsley), Carleton Rippel (Depot Man), Rita Abrams, Sara Jane Gould and Mary Beth Bell (Duth Damsels), M. Emmet Walsh (Father Logan), Miriam Bird Nethery (Aunt Lula), Rusty Blitz (Nickelodeon Barker), Les Josephson (Nickelodeon Bouncer), Tom Erhart (Nickelodeon Projectionist), Griffin O'Neal (Bicycle Boy), Patricia O'Neal, Morgan Farley, Anna Thea, Elaine Partnow, Joseph G. Medalis, Billy Beck, and Roger Hampton (Movie Fanatics), Gordon Hurst (Policeman), Charles Thomas Murphy (Hollywood

Realtor), Hamilton Camp (Blacker), Ted Gehring (Stoneman), Stanley Brock (Parker), Vincent Milana (Frank's Director), Lee Gordon Moore (Alice's Director), John Finnegan (Kathleen's Director), Christian Grey (Buck's Director), Robert E. Ball (Leo's Actor), Chief Elmer Tugsmith (Elmer), and Rude Frimel (Orchestra Conductor).

A fictionalized account of early film-making in America, which utilizes incidents told to Peter Bogdanovich by veteran director Allan Dwan. Perhaps the best thing in Nickelodeon is a clip from Griffith's The Birth of a Nation. For a very detailed and intelligent study of this feature, see Jonathan Rosenbaum's review in The Monthly Film Bulletin (February, 1977), pages 27-28.

Availability (16mm): Swank

NICKELODEON MEMORIES (circa 32 mins/16mm)

U.S. Academy of Motion Picture Arts and Sciences. 1939.

Subtitled "Scenes from the period when 'Motion Picture Art' was more motion than art." Presumably compiled for a one-shot screening by the Academy, this compilation consists chiefly of newsreel footage with some extracts from early films, which are generally misidentified.

Availability: None (A 16mm print is available for study at the Academy of Motion Picture Arts and Sciences)

NORMAN JEWISON, FILM MAKER (50 mins/16mm)

Canada. National Film Board of Canada. 1971. Producer and Director: Doug Jackson. Photography: Eugene Boyko. Film Editors: Malca Gillson, Eddie Le Lorrain and Les Halman. Produced with the co-operation of United Artists and Mirisch Productions.

A study of Norman Jewison as he directs Fiddler on the Roof in Yugoslavia.

Availability: National Film Board of Canada

ODEON CAVALCADE (1,260 ft./35 mins/16mm)

G.B. Greendow for the Arts Council of Great Britain.

1973. Producer, Screenplay and Narrator: Barry Clayton. Based on an idea by Dennis Sharp. Assistant Director: Malcolm Hignett. Photography: Mike Davis, Stephen Goldblatt and Frank Hardie. Film Editor: Peter Day. Sound: Michael Lax and Tony Anscombe. Research: Dennis Sharp.

A film study of the Odeon Cinema chain in England, featuring the Odeons in Balham, Hendon, Kingstanding, Leicester Square, Muswell Hill, Southgate, Sutton Coldfield, Woolwich, and Warley. The production also includes an interview with Mrs. Oscar Deutsch, the widow of the founder of the chain, and clips from four films: Looking on the Bright Side (1932), 42nd Street (1933), Dance Band (1935), and Keep Fit (1937). For more information, see The Monthly Film Bulletin (December, 1973), pages 256-257.

Availability: Films Incorporated (sale)/American Federation of the Arts (rental)

ODYSSEY OF RITA HAYWORTH, THE see HOLLYWOOD AND THE STARS

OKAY FOR SOUND (2 reels/20 mins/35mm)

U.S. Warner Bros. 1946.

Produced to commemorate the twentieth anniversary of talking pictures, Okay for Sound illustrated the development of the sound motion picture from the experiments of Thomas Edison through the latest productions from the Warner Bros. Burbank studios, and included clips from Don Juan, The Jazz Singer and The Singing Fool together with extracts from contemporary Warner Bros. features. Okay for Sound received its premiere along with Night and Day at 250 theatres on August 4, 1946. Aside from this short, Warner Bros. celebrated the twentieth anniversary of talking pictures with the sponsorship of a book, also titled Okay for Sound, published by Duell, Sloan and Pearce and authored by Professor Frederic M. Thrasher of New York University. In addition, Colonel Jack L. Warner presented a print of The Lights of New York to the Library of Congress and an original Vitaphone turntable to the Smithsonian.

Availability: Em Gee/United Artists 16

OLD TIME CINEMA (8 reels/90 mins/35mm)

U.S. The British Film Institute for the National Film Theatre. 1952.

A reconstruction of a typical cinema program of the early 'teens, including The Road to Ruin (a 1914 Barker Company feature), an extract from The Passions of Men (1914 Clarendon Films feature), The Lovesick Maidens of Cuddleton (1912 John Bunny comedy), Bully Boy No. 1 (a 1914 Lancelot Speed cartoon), Making Christmas Crackers (1910), A Day in the Life of a Rickshaw Boy (1912 travelogue), and Pathé's Animated Gazette (an example of a typical 1913/1914 newsreel).

Availability (35mm and 16mm): British Film Institute, London (no American distributor)

ON LOCATION, THE NIGHT OF THE IGUANA see HOLLYWOOD AND THE STARS

ONE AND ONLY BING, THE see HOLLYWOOD AND THE STARS

THE OPERATOR CRANKED--THE PICTURE MOVED (1 reel/16mm)

Subtitled "Glimpses of Some Pioneer Producers and Their Work," this heavily annotated--six introductory title cards--Blackhawk Films compilation looks at film production in the 1890s. It includes glimpses of Fred Ott (not sneezing); "Layman," an 1897 vaudeville actor, demonstrating why he was billed as "The Man with a Thousand Faces"; female impersonator Gilbert Saroney in Old Maid in a Drawing Room; Kaiser Wilhelm of Germany reviewing his troops; various Lumière subjects, including Workers Leaving the Factory; and closes with an unidentified clip from a 1912 Vitagraph production, A Vitagraph Romance.

Availability (16mm and 8mm): Blackhawk (sale only)

ORIGINS OF THE CINEMA (13 mins/16mm)

A series of clips from early, turn of the century, productions, without linking titles, and including shots of motion picture apparatus and early studios. Some of the footage may possibly be from J. Stuart Blackton's The Film Parade (q. v.).

Availability: Kit Parker

ORIGINS OF THE MOTION PICTURE (2 reels/20 mins/35mm)

U.S. U.S. Naval Photographic Center. 1955. No Technical Credits Published. Produced in collaboration with the Library of Congress, the Smithsonian Institution, the National Archives, Thomas Alva Edison Foundation, and George Eastman House. "Much of the historical source material was derived from the book, Magic Shadows: The Story of the Origin of Motion Pictures by Martin Quigley, Jr."

A solid, informative--and generally dull--documentary describing the events leading to the perfection of motion pictures. In view of its sponsorship, Origins of the Motion Picture opens, appropriately enough, with shots of "the great white fleet of the United States Navy" in the 1890s, and then, thankfully, ignores the Navy until its closing sequences. Among the topics covered are the wall paintings of primitive cavemen, Leonardo da Vinci's camera obscura, Athanasius Kircher and his theatre of mirrors, the development of the magic lantern, Peter Mark Roget and the theory of persistence of vision, Dr. Paris and his Thaumatrope, Joseph Plateau's Phenakistiscope, the Zoetrope, Emile Reynaud's Praxinoscope, the photographic work of Louis Daguerre and the Langenheim Brothers of Philadelphia, the experiments of Eadweard Muybridge and Dr. Marey, George Eastman, and Thomas Edison, who receives the most attention--with hardly a mention of the work of W. K. L. Dickson.

Availability (16mm): The Museum of Modern Art (rental)/Reel Images (sale)/Em Gee (rental)

OSCAR'S FIRST FIFTY YEARS (26 mins/35mm)

U.S. Academy of Motion Picture Arts and Sciences. 1978. Producer and Director: Charles Braverman. Coproducer: Michael Roach. Screenplay: Martin M. Cooper. Photography: Chuy Elizondo. Film Editor: Marshall Harvey. Titles and Montage Sequences: Ken Rudolph. Sound: Mark Krenzien. Gaffer: Hal Trussell. Key Grip. Henry Grattan. Assistant Cameraman: Chuck Minsky. Animation Cameraman: William Coffin. Assistant Film Editor: Greg

McCarty. Grip: Willy Horner. Script Supervisor: Lili Ungar Harary. Still Photographer: Marcia Reed. Make-up: Harry Thomas. Academy Liaison: Rodney Recor. Narrator: Jack Lemmon.

Jack Lemmon takes viewers on a tour of the Academy's premises, talks about its founding and a number of its activities including the Margaret Herrick Library, the National Film Information Service, the Student Film Awards, the Academy Players Directory, and the Visiting Artists Program. The last is discussed by Verna Fields. A clip from a 1977 Student Film Award-winner, The Muse by Paul Demeyer is shown. The last half of Oscar's First Fifty Years is taken up with clips--amusing and emotional--from past Academy Award Shows. A short, eight-minute version of this film was distributed theatrically immediately prior to the 50th Academy Awards Presentation.

Availability (35mm and 16mm): The Academy of Motion Picture Arts and Sciences

OSCARS, MOMENTS OF GREATNESS, THE see HOLLYWOOD AND THE STARS

OTTO MESSMER AND FELIX THE CAT (25 mins/16mm)

U.S. A Film by John Canemaker. 1977. Producer, Director, Screenplay, Film Editor, and Narrator: John Canemaker. Photography: Richard W. Adams. Music: Ross Care.

This is Part Two in John Canemaker's Animation Pioneers series; Part One was titled Remembering Winsor McCay. In this short, Otto Messmer, who created and animated Felix the Cat and directed over 200 Felix the Cat cartoons, talks about his work at the age of eighty-four. Clips from five Felix the Cat cartoons are included in the film. A Study Guide is also available from the distributor.

Availability: John Canemaker (sale and rental)

PAPA'S DELICATE CONDITION

1962 feature based on Corinne Griffith's novel concerning her family life in pre-World War One Texas, which does not deal with the actress' film career.

PASSIONATE INDUSTRY, THE (5,620 ft. /59 mins/35mm)

Australia. Australian Commonwealth Film Unit. 1973. Producer: Frank Bagnall. Director, Screenplay and Research: Joan Long. Photography: Mick Bornemann and Michael Edols. Music: Al Franks. Film Editor: Ian Walker. Sound: Howard Spry and Julian Ellingworth.

A sequel to The Pictures That Moved, this documentary covers the history of Australian cinema from 1920 through 1929. Included is footage from fifty newsreels and sixteen features, together with many still photographs.

Availability: Australian Information Service

PATHE NEWSREEL, THE (20 mins/16mm)

A representative sampling of Pathê newsreel items, compiled by the Museum of Modern Art: Wilson Signs Declaration of War (1917), Suffragettes Riot at White House (1918), Wilson Speaks for Treaty (1919), Battleship Maryland Launched (1920), Destruction of Home Made Stills (1920), San Luis Obispo Oil Fire (1926), Valentino Funeral (1926), Sioux Adopt Coolidge (1926), Joe Powers Sits on Flagpole (1928), Mussolini Reviews Troops (1931), Billy Sunday Cures Depression (1931).

Availability: The Museum of Modern Art

PATHE PRIMITIVES # 1 (1 reel/16mm)

A package of three French films from circa 1905, compiled by Murray Glass: Ten Wives for One Husband, An Exciting Ride and Up in the Tower.

Availability: Em Gee

PATHE PRIMITIVES # 2 (1 reel/16mm)

A package of three French films from circa 1905-1907, compiled by Murray Glass: The Enchanted Palace, Thomas's Inheritance and The End of a Dream.

Availability: Em Gee

PAUL KILLIAM SHOW, THE see KILLIAM, PAUL

PAUL NEWMAN, ACTOR IN A HURRY see HOLLYWOOD AND THE STARS

PAUL ROBESON: THE TALLEST TREE IN THE FOREST (90 mins/16mm)

U.S. A Film by Gil Noble for the ABC Television Series "Like It Is." 1977. Producer and Screenplay: Gil Noble.

A documentary on the life and career of Paul Robeson, which went into production shortly before his death in January of 1976. The film includes interviews with Paul Robeson, Jr., Harry Belafonte and others, together with clips from various films in which Robeson had starring roles, including The Emperor Jones and Song of Freedom. Most of the visual material came from the Paul Robeson Archive. Other sequences include a London production of Othello with Robeson, and various of the entertainer's concerts. "There emerged the story of a man of extraordinary principle who refused to bend even one inch from his convictions. There has unfolded a story of a man of prestigious abilities not just in drama, film, singing, and sports, but also in scholarship."--Phoenix Films.

Availability: Phoenix Films/Budget

PERILS OF PAULINE, THE (98 mins/35mm)

U.S. Paramount. 1947. Producer: Sol C. Siegel. Director: George Marshall. Screenplay: P. J. Wolfson and Frank Butler. Based on an Original Story by P. J. Wolfson. Photography: Ray Rennahan. Art Directors: Hans Dreier and Roland Anderson. Set Decorators: Sam Comer and Ray Moyer. Technicolor Consultant: Natalie Kalmus. Associate Technicolor Consultant: Robert Brower. Songs: Frank Lesser. Music Score: Robert Emmett Dolan. Music Associate: Troy Sanders. Vocal Arrangements: Joseph J. Lilley. Dances: Billy Daniels. Chorus Number: Waldo Angelo. Film Editor: Arthur Schmidt. Sound: Gene Merritt and Walter Oberst. Special Effects: Gordon Jennings. Process Photography: Farciot Edouart. Costumes: Edith Head. Makeup: Wally Westmore. Technical Advisor: Louis Gasnier.

With Betty Hutton (Pearl White), John Lund (Michael Farrington), Billy De Wolfe (Timmy), William Demarest

(Chuck McManus), Constance Collier (Julia Gibbs), Frank Faylen (Joe Gurt), William Farnum (Hero, Western Saloon Set), Chester Conklin (First Chef Comic), Paul Panzer (Gentleman, Interior Drawing Room), Snub Pollard (Propman, Western Saloon), James Finlayson (Second Chef Comic), Creighton Hale (Marcelled Leading Man), Hank Mann (Chef Comic), Francis McDonald (Heavy, Western Saloon Set), Bert Roach (Bartender, Western Saloon Set), Heinie Conklin (Studio Cop), Franklin Farnum (Friar John), Ethel Clayton (Lady Montague), Julia Faye (Nurse), Frank Mayo (Reporter), Rex Lease (Reporter), Bess Flowers (Woman Reporter), and Jean Acker (Switchboard Operator).

A highly fictionalized (i. e., inaccurate) version of the life and career of Pearl White, but who cares with so many former silent players in the cast, Pearl White's director, Louis Gasnier acting as a Technical Advisor, and, as an added bonus, Constance Collier being hit in the face with a custard pie!

Availability: None

PERILS OF PAULINE, THE (1967)

A comedy in the supposed style of early serials, which has absolutely nothing to do with either Pearl White or her serial, The Perils of Pauline.

PERSONALITY PARADE see JIMMY FIDLER'S PERSONALITY PARADE

PICTURE SHOW MAN, THE (99 mins/35mm)

Australia. Limelight Productions. Producer and Screenplay: Joan Long. Director: John Power. Photography: Geoff Burton. Film Editor: Nick Beauman. Art Director: David Copping. Costumes: Judy Dorsman. Production Supervisor: Basil Appleby. Music: Peter Best. Sound: Ken Hammond. Assistant Director: Mark Egerton.

With Rod Taylor (Palmer), John Meillon (Pop), John Ewart (Freddie), Harold Hopkins (Larry), Patrick Cargill (Fitzwilliam), Yelena Zigon (Madame Cavalli), Garry McDonald (Lou), Sally Conabere (Lucy), Judy Morris (Miss Lockhart), and Jeannie Drynan (Mrs. Duncan).

A fictionalized account of a traveling film showman in the Australian outback of the 1920s. For more information, see William K. Everson's highly favorable review in Films in Review (November, 1977), pages 565-566.

Availability: None

PICTURES ARE ADVENTURE see LET'S GO TO THE MOVIES

PICTURES THAT MOVED, THE (45 mins/35mm)

Australia. Australian Commonwealth Film Unit. 1968. Producer: Frank Bagnall. Director: Alan Anderson. Screenplay: Joan Long. Music: Al Franks.

A documentary on Australian film production from 1896 through 1920, utilizing interviews, film clips and photographic stills. The Pictures That Moved studies The Story of the Kelly Gang (1906), and includes newsreel footage of 1901 aboriginal ceremonies and Frank Hurley's film record of Mawson's 1911 South Pole expedition. The highspot of the documentary is a lengthy extract from Raymond Longford's 1920 production of The Sentimental Bloke, the best-known of all Australian silent films. See also The Passionate Industry.

Availability: Australian Information Service

PIER PAOLO PASOLINI (30 mins/35mm)

Italy. 1970. Producers: Frederick Hayman-Chaffey and Anthony J. Ciccolini, Jr. Director: Carlo Hayman-Chaffey. Photography: Gordon Gardner. Music: Andro Cecovini.

A documentary on the work of the late Italian film director, utilizing interviews with several of his colleagues and co-workers, including Alberto Moravia, Cesare Zavattini, Sergio Citti, Ninetto Davoli, and Franco Citti. The film is in Italian with English voice-overs.

Availability (16mm): Macmillan/Indiana University Audio-Visual Center

PIONEERS IN CELLULOID (90 mins/16mm)

Subtitled Beginning of the Silent Feature Film, this compilation was inspired by Albert E. Smith's autobiography, Two Reels and a Crank, and features a number of Vitagraph shorts together with that company's 1912 production of Vanity Fair. It was produced by Jack Lewis of the Lewis Film Service, Wichita, Kansas, and reviewed in Film News (Volume 14, Number 2, 1954), page 13.

Availability: None

POPEYE FOLLIES: HIS LIFE AND TIMES, THE (85 mins/35mm)

U.S. United Artists. 1974.

A compilation of Popeye cartoons, interspersed with clips of celebrities of the Thirties, such as Will Rogers, Al Jolson and James Cagney. Among the Popeye cartoons included are Goonland and A Dream Walking.

Availability (16mm): United Artists 16

PORTER/EDISON PROGRAM No. 1 (22 mins/16mm)

A package of twelve Edison shorts produced by Edwin S. Porter between 1898 and 1902: Elopement on Horseback (1898), Strange Adventure of a New York Drummer (1899), Uncle Josh's Nightmare (1900), Terrible Teddy, the Grizzly King (1901), Love by the Light of the Moon (1901), Circular Panorama of Electric Tower (1901), Panorama of Esplanade by Night (1901), Martyred Presidents (1901), Uncle Josh at the Moving Picture Show (1902), The Twentieth Century Tramp (1902), Fun in a Bakery Shop (1902), and Jack and the Beanstalk (1902).

Availability: Macmillan

PORTER/EDISON PROGRAM No. 2 (29 mins/16mm)

A package of four Edison shorts produced by Edwin S. Porter during 1903 and 1904: Uncle Tom's Cabin (1903), The Gay Shoe Clerk (1903), A Romance of the Rail (1903), and Rounding Up of the "Yeggmen."

Availability: Macmillan

PORTER/EDISON PROGRAM No. 3 (28 mins/16mm)

A package of three Edison shorts produced by Edwin S. Porter during 1904 and 1905: European Rest Cure (1904), The Ex-Convict (1904) and The Kleptomaniac (1905).
Availability: Macmillan

PORTER/EDISON PROGRAM No. 4 (16 mins/16mm)

A package of three Edison shorts produced by Edwin S. Porter during 1905: The Seven Ages, How Jones Lost His Roll and The Whole Dam Family and the Dam Dog.
Availability: Macmillan

PROPAGANDA FILMS I (105 mins/16mm)

A package of extracts from German propaganda films, compiled by the Museum of Modern Art: The Triumph of the Will (1936), Pilots, Gunners, Radio Operators (1937), Baptism of Fire (1940), and sequences from various 1940 German newsreels.
Availability: The Museum of Modern Art

PROPAGANDA FILMS II (27 mins/16mm)

A package of three films concerning the Nazi German martyr Horst Wessel, compiled by the Museum of Modern Art: Blutendes Deutschland extract (1933), Hans Westmar, Einer von Vielen extract (1934) and Für Uns (1937).
Availability: The Museum of Modern Art

RAMBLIN' AROUND HOLLYWOOD (1 reel/35mm)

Ken Murray wanders into a vault piled high with "old" films--what better excuse for ten minutes of nostalgia-filled film clips?
Availability (16mm): Em Gee

REMEMBERING WINSOR McCAY (20 mins/16mm)

U.S. A Film by John Canemaker. 1976. Producer, Director, Screenplay and Film Editor: John Canemaker.

Photography: Chirine. Piano Score: William Perry.

This is Part One in John Canemaker's Animation Pioneers series; Part Two was titled Otto Messmer and Felix the Cat. Eighty-four year old John A. Fitzsimmons, who assisted Winsor McCay on two of his ten films, recalls McCay's career as a comic strip artist, vaudeville performer and animation film pioneer. Excerpts from three of McCay's films--Gertie the Dinosaur (1914), The Sinking of the Lusitania (1918) and a hand-colored version of Little Nemo (1911)--are included. A Study Guide is also available from the distributor.

Availability: John Canemaker (sale and rental)

REMINISCENCES OF 1915 (circa 60 mins/35mm)

U.S. Blackton Productions. 1926. Producer: J. Stuart Blackton.

A compilation of clips from almost one hundred early Vitagraph productions, presented at the Hollywood Writers Club on January 21, 1926, as a preview to J. Stuart Blackton's latest feature Bride of the Storm. For more information, see "Memories of Yesteryear" by Bernard A. Holway in The Motion Picture Director (February, 1926), page 52.

Availability: None

RETURN FARE TO LAUGHTER (3,492 ft./38 mins/35mm)

G.B. Butcher's Film Service. 1950. Producer: Henry E. Fisher. Written and Compiled by James M. Anderson. Music: De Wolfe. Piano Improvisation: Rose Treacher. Narrator: Frederick Grisewood.

An "animated scrapbook" of clips of films from the Edwardian era, with the emphasis, as always in these James M. Anderson/Henry E. Fisher compilations, on comedy.

Availability: None

RICHARD TAUBER STORY, THE see YOU ARE THE WORLD FOR ME

RICHARD WILLIAMS (30 mins/16mm)

U.S. NET. 1968. Producer: J. C. Sheers. Director and Film Editor: Robert Morgan.

A documentary study of animator Richard Williams at work in his London studio, together with clips from a number of his shorts. For more information, see John Canemaker's review in Film News (March/April, 1978), page 12.
Availability: Indiana University Audio-Visual Center

RICHTER ON FILM (13 mins/16mm)

U.S. A Film by Cecile Starr. 1972.

Cecile Starr interviews avant-garde painter and filmmaker Hans Richter on his career. Clips from some of Richter's early German experimental films are included in the short.
Availability: Cecile Starr (rental and sale)

ROAD TO HOLLYWOOD (70 mins/35mm)

U.S. Astor Pictures. 1948.

A compilation of shorts from the early Thirties, produced by Mack Sennett and featuring Bing Crosby.
Availability (16mm): Select

SAD CLOWNS, THE (The History of the Motion Picture/ Silents Please series)

Chaplin, Keaton and Langdon demonstrate their own individual methods of inducing laughter and tears, co-produced and written by Paul Killiam and Saul J. Turell. For more information, see The History of the Motion Picture series.
Availability (16mm): Blackhawk (sale)/Killiam Shows (rental)/Select (rental)

SAGA OF WILLIAM S. HART, THE (4 reels/43 mins/16mm)

A compilation of scenes from ten William S. Hart

films produced between 1914 and 1925: On the Night Stage, Hell's Hinges, The Aryan, The Square Deal Man, The Desert Man, Wolf Lowry, The Toll Gate, The Testing Block, O'Malley of the Mounted, and Three Word Brand.

Availability: Macmillan/Blackhawk (8mm sale only)/ Em Gee

SATYAJIT RAY (1 reel/13 mins/16mm)

India. 1967. Producer and Director: B. D. Garga. Photography: Dilip Mukherjee.

Indian director Satyajit Ray explains his views on cinema and is seen directing his 1954 production of Pather Panchali.

Availability: Macmillan/Indiana University Audio-Visual Center

SCRAPBOOK FOR 1933 (5,189 ft. /57 mins/35mm)

G.B. Associated British-Pathé. 1949. In Charge of Production: Howard Thomas. Producer: Peter Baylis. Screenplay: Jack Howells. Based on the BBC Radio series. Film Editor: A. Milner-Gardner. Settings: Joy Thomas. Music: Alan Paul. Sound: W. S. Bland and George Newberry. Narrator: Stephen Murray. Voices: Joyce Grenfell, Maurice Denham, James Hayter, Howard Marion-Crawford, Hugh Griffith, Michael Balfour, Robert Ayres, and Cedric Connor.

A compilation of newsreel footage from the early Thirties, including personalities of the period, and clips from features--The Sign of the Cross, The Private Life of Henry VIII and 42nd Street--playing in London during 1933. For more information, see The Monthly Film Bulletin (January-February, 1950), page 14.

Availability: None

THE SCREEN ACTOR see LET'S GO TO THE MOVIES

SCREEN DIRECTOR, THE see LET'S GO TO THE MOVIES

SCREEN SNAPSHOTS, 25th ANNIVERSARY ISSUE (1 reel/10 mins/35mm)

U.S. Columbia "Screen Snapshots" Series. 1946. Producer: Ralph Staub.

An entertaining tribute to an entertaining series, with tributes from Walt Disney, Rosalind Russell, Cecil B. DeMille, and Louella Parsons, and a moving salute to Hollywood stars who were by then deceased. For more information on the "Screen Snapshots" series, all of which dealt with the Hollywood scene, see The Great Movie Shorts by Leonard Maltin (Crown, 1972). See also Memories of Famous Hollywood Comedians.

Availability (16mm): Em Gee

SCREEN WRITER, THE see LET'S GO TO THE MOVIES

SCREENING ROOM, THE

A sequel to Shadows on the Wall (q. v.). James Limbacher hosted and developed this advanced, more generic survey of film history, told through a series of thirty programs.

Availability (videotape): Wayne State University

SECRETS OF HOLLYWOOD (3 reels/35mm)

U.S. 1933.

Silent screen actress Mae Busch turns over the pages of a scrapbook of scene stills from silent films, and as she does a clip from the film is shown. Most of the footage is taken from Thomas H. Ince productions.

Availability (16mm): Thunderbird (sale only)

SELECTION OF EARLY FILMS (3 reels/35 mins/35mm)

A package of films intended to illustrate the main stages in the development of the cinema in England, although not all the shorts included are British, compiled by the British Film Institute: Train Entering a Station (1895), The India-rubber Head (1902), Queen Victoria's Funeral (1901), The

Revolving Table (1903), Answering a Call (1901), The Burning Stable (1900), The Great Train Robbery--extract (1903), The Well-Washed House (circa 1907), Drama among the Puppets (1908), Dante's Inferno--extract (1909), Simple Charity--extract (1910), and East Lynne--extract (1913).

Availability (35mm and 16mm): British Film Institute, London (no American distributor)

SELZNICK YEARS, THE *see* HOLLYWOOD: THE SELZNICK YEARS

SERGEI EISENSTEIN (4,500 ft./50 mins/35mm)

U.S.S.R. Central Studio of Documentary Films, Moscow. 1958. Producer: V. Katanyan. Screenplay: R. Yureneva. Photography: M. Glider.

A biographical documentary on the life and work of Russia's most famous and influential film director, with clips from various of his films, shots of him instructing his students at the State School of Cinematography, and tributes by Sergei Prokofiev, Gregori Alexandrov and Giuseppe de Santis. For more information, see *The Monthly Film Bulletin* (July, 1960), page 103.

Availability (16mm): Macmillan/University of California Extension Media Center/Cinema Eight (sale only)/Images (rental and sale)

THE SERIALS (The History of the Motion Picture/Silents Please series)

An absorbing and highly entertaining look at the silent serials from 1914 through 1929, their heroines--Pearl White, Ruth Roland and Helen Holmes--and their villains--Boris Karloff and Warner Oland. Co-produced and written by Paul Killiam and Saul J. Turell. For more information, see *The History of the Motion Picture* series.

Availability (16mm): Blackhawk (sale)/Killiam Shows (rental)/Budget (rental)

75 YEARS OF CINEMA MUSEUM (70 mins/16mm)

U.S. Hershon-Guerra Productions. 1972. Producers,

Directors, Screenplay, Photography, and Film Editors: Eila Hershon and Roberto Guerra. Narrator: Lindsay Anderson.

The second of two documentaries devoted to the work of Henri Langlois, founder of the Cinemathèque Française. This film is chiefly concerned with the creation of Langlois' film museum at the Palais de Chaillot, at which he is visited by King Vidor, Colleen Moore, Raoul Walsh, Henry Hathaway, and Akira Kurosawa. "Langlois is well caught in his ways and ideas," commented Mosk in Variety (December 6, 1972). See also Langlois.

Availability: None

SHADOWS ON THE WALL

A series of fifty-five thirty-minute programs tracing the history of the motion picture from 1896 through the Second World War, with clips from more than 130 films, developed and hosted by James Limbacher. See also The Screening Room.

Availability (videotape): Wayne State University

SHIP'S REPORTER (Each Part: approx. 25 mins/16mm)

A series of compilations by Leonard Maltin for Select of various interviews from the Fifties television series, Ship's Reporter. Most of the interviews are very poorly handled, but the series does present a fascinating, candid look at film and other personalities. Part One (Stars) features interviews with Paul Muni, Robert Cummings, Buster Keaton, Laurence Olivier and Vivien Leigh, Bela Lugosi, and Buster Crabbe. Part Two (The Opera World) features Lily Pons, Mary Garden, Bruno Walter, Rudolph Bing, Jan Kiepura, and Maria Jeritza. Part Three (British Stars) includes Glynis Johns, Flora Robson, Francis L. Sullivan, Michael Wilding, and Anna Neagle and Herbert Wilcox. Part Four (Hollywood Favorites) features Roland Young, Van Heflin, Sabu, Donald O'Connor, and Nat Pendleton. Part Five (The Theatre and Literary World) includes Carson McCullers, Will Durant, Bella Spewack, Monica Dickens, John P. Marquand, Robert Sherwood, and Richard Rodgers. Part Six (Celebrities and Personalities) features Al Capp, Josephine Baker, Noel Coward, Moss Hart and Kitty Carlisle, Gaylord Hauser, Hope Hampton, Admiral Halsey, and Nat King Cole.

Availability: Select

SHIRLEY TEMPLE: THE BIGGEST LITTLE STAR OF THE THIRTIES (1 reel/9 mins/16mm)

U.S. Blackhawk. 1976.

Culled from the archives of Fox Movietone News, this documentary includes footage of Shirley Temple walking the beach at Waikiki, roasting hotdogs with Eleanor Roosevelt, appearing at the Hollywood premiere of her film Wee Willie Winkie, driving her own car on the Twentieth Century-Fox backlot, and receiving a Special Academy Award in 1934.

Availability (16mm and 8mm): Blackhawk (sale only)

SHOOTING STARS see KEN MURRAY SHOOTING STARS

SHORT HISTORY OF ANIMATION, A (60 mins/16mm)

A package of animated films, compiled by the Museum of Modern Art: Skladanowsky's Animated Pictures (circa 1879), Cohl's Drame chez les fantoches (1907), Winsor McCay's Gertie the Dinosaur (1914), Bud Fisher's Mutt and Jeff (circa 1918), Disney's Newman's Laugh-o-Gram (1920), Pat Sullivan and Otto Messmer's Felix the Cat (1924), Disney's Steamboat Willie (1928), Disney's Mad Dog (1932), and Lotte Reiniger's Carmen (1933).

Availability: The Museum of Modern Art

SHOWMAN (52 mins/16mm)

U.S. A Film by the Maysles Brothers. 1963. Producers and Directors: Albert and David Maysles. Film Editors: Dan Williams and David Maysles.

A cinéma vérité study of veteran showman, promoter and distributor Joseph E. Levine, as he conducts business in his unique manner, argues about the art of the film with David Susskind, reminisces with boyhood friends from Boston's West End, and presents an Oscar to Sophia Loren in Cannes. For more information, see Arthur Schlesinger, Jr.'s review in Show (December, 1963) and Sibyl March's review in The Seventh Art (Winter, 1963).

Availability: Maysles Films

SILENCE EST D'OR, LE / MAN ABOUT TOWN / GOLDEN SILENCE / SILENCE IS GOLDEN (8, 906 ft. /99 mins/35mm)

France. Pathé-RKO Radio. 1947. Director and Screenplay: René Clair. Photography: Armand Thirard. Music: Georges van Parys. Art Director: Léon Barsacq. Costumes: Christian Dior.

With Maurice Chevalier (M. Emile), François Perier (Jacques), Marcelle Derrien (Madeleine), Dany Robin (Lucette), Paul Oliver (Le Comptable), Gaston Modot (L'Opérateur), Robert Pizani (Duperrier), Raymond Cordy (Le Frisé), Paul Demange (Le Sultan), and Bernard Lajarrige (Paulo).

A charming fictionalized account of film-making in the Paris of 1906, when a comedian becomes a producer. For more information, see The Monthly Film Bulletin (August 31, 1948), pages 119-120.

Availability (16mm): Film Classic Exchange/United Films

SILENCE IS GOLDEN see SILENCE EST D'OR, LE

SILENTS PLEASE see HISTORY OF THE MOTION PICTURE series

SILVER SHADOWS (20 mins/16mm)

U.S. Bell and Howell. Circa 1948.

A shortened version of J. Stuart Blackton's The Film Parade (q. v.).

Availability (16mm and 8mm): Thunderbird (sale only)

SINGIN' IN THE RAIN (9, 238 ft. /103 mins/35mm)

U.S. M-G-M. 1952. Producer: Arthur Freed. Directors: Gene Kelly and Stanley Donen. Story and Screenplay: Adolph Green and Betty Comden. Lyrics: Arthur Freed. Music: Nacio Herb Brown. Photography: Harold Rosson. Technicolor Color Consultants: Henri Jaffa and James Gooch. Art Directors: Cedric Gibbons and Randall Duell. Set Decorators: Edwin B. Willis and Jacque Mapes. Film Editor: Adrienne Fazan. Recording Supervisor: Douglas Shearer. Orchestrations: Conrad Salinger Wally Heglin and Skip Martin. Vocal Arrangements By Jeff Alexander. Special Effects: Warren Newcombe and Irving G. Ries. Costumes: Walter Plunkett. Hair Styles: Sydney Guilaroff. Makeup: William Tuttle. Assistant Director: Marvin Stuart.

With Gene Kelly (Don Lockwood), Donald O'Connor (Cosmo Brown), Debbie Reynolds (Kathy Selden), Jean Hagen (Lina Lamont), Millard Mitchell (R. F. Simpson), Cyd Charisse (Dancer), Douglas Fowley (Roscoe Dexter), and Rita Moreno (Zelda Zanders).

Entertaining cult musical dealing with the film industry at the transition to sound. Most of the songs--such as "Broadway Melody," "You Were Meant for Me" and "Singin' in the Rain"--date from the right period in film history, but the production as a whole has more of a feel of the Fifties than the late Twenties. Watch for early talkies star Mae Clarke in the small role of a hairdresser.

Availability (16mm): Films Incorporated

SIRENS, SYMBOLS AND GLAMOUR GIRLS _see_ HOLLYWOOD AND THE STARS

SLAPPIEST DAYS OF OUR LIVES, THE (5,520 ft./61 mins/35mm)

G.B. Adelphi. 1953. Screenplay: R. A. Bradford. Film Editor: Hillary Long.

Intended as a tribute to Mack Sennett, this compilation includes clips from the comedies of Harold Lloyd, Buster Keaton, Laurel and Hardy, Moran and Mack, and Billy Bevan, among others. "No more disagreeable and vulgar tribute to Sennett could be conceived," wrote Gavin Lambert in _The Monthly Film Bulletin_ (March, 1953).

Availability: None

SLAPSTICK (The History of the Motion Picture/Silents Please series)

"A cavalcade of the best from the great age of visual humor," featuring the work of Monty Banks, Charley Chase, Roscoe "Fatty" Arbuckle, the Keystone Kops, Charles Chaplin, and others, co-produced by Paul Killiam and Saul J.

Turell and written by Paul Killiam. For more information see *The History of the Motion Picture* series.

Availability (16mm): Blackhawk (sale)/Killiam Shows (rental)

SO THIS IS LOVE

A 1953 fictionalized account of the life and career of opera singer Grace Moore from 1917 through 1928, which does not deal with her film career.

SOME OF THE GREATEST (975 ft. /11 mins/35mm)

U.S. Warner Bros. 1955. Producer and Screenplay: Robert Youngson. Film Editor: Albert Helmes. Narrator: Dwight Weist.

This short features extracts from Alan Crosland's *Don Juan* (1926).

Availability: Reel Images

SOUND OF LAUGHTER, THE (75 mins/35mm)

U.S. Union Films. 1963. Producers: Barry B. Yellen and Irvin S. Dorfman. Director: John O Shaughnessy. Narration and Continuity Written by Fred Saidy. Narrator: Ed Wynn.

A compilation of clips from Educational Comedies produced between 1931 and 1938, introduced by Ed Wynn in the guise of a college professor. Among the performers--seen largely at a disadvantage in such obviously second-rate films --are Bing Crosby, Bob Hope, Danny Kaye, Buster Keaton, Bert Lahr, Harry Langdon, The Ritz Brothers, Shirley Temple, Milton Berle, Andy Clyde, Imogene Coca, Joan Davis, Billy Gilbert, Charlotte Greenwood, Edgar Kennedy, Joe Cook, and Lillian Roth. As Bosley Crowther wrote in the *New York Times* (December 18, 1963), the funniest thing about the feature "is to see how ridiculously unfunny most of its comedy is."

Availability (16mm): Macmillan/Modern Sound Pictures/Select/Roa's Films

THE SOUNDMAN see LET'S GO TO THE MOVIES

SPILLS FOR THRILLS (18 mins/35mm)

U.S. Warner Bros. "Broadway Brevities" series. 1940. Producer and Director: DeLeon Anthony. Narrator: Knox Manning.

The work of the Hollywood stuntmen is illustrated through a series of clips from silent and sound Warner Bros. productions.

Availability (16mm): Kit Parker/United Artists 16

STAR (720 ft. /20 mins/16mm)

G.B. Alan Lovell Production with the Assistance of the British Film Institute Education Department. 1966. Producers: Rick Witcombe, Michael Dibb and Michael Philps. Director and Screenplay: Alan Lovell. Film Editors: Michael Dibb and Michael Philps. Graphics: Mario Lippa. Made with the Technical Assistance of Nick Hales, John Fletcher, David Muir, Norman Roundell, Owen McCann, John Ponsford, Peter Theobald, Howard Billingham, Dateline Productions, and David Naden Associates. Narrator: John Arden.

A study of actress Julie Christie through interviews and film clips from Dr. Zhivago, Billy Liar, Darling, and Fahrenheit 451, together with a sequence from the British television serial, A for Andromeda.

Availability: Contemporary-McGraw Hill Films

STAR! / THOSE WERE THE HAPPY TIMES (120 mins/35mm)

U.S. Twentieth Century Fox/Robert Wise Productions. 1968. Producer: Saul Chaplin. Director: Robert Wise. Screenplay: William Fairchild. Photography: Ernest Laszlo. Dances and Musical Numbers Staged by Michael Kidd. Music Supervised and Conducted by Lennie Hayton. Title Song, "Star!," by Sammy Cahn and Jimmy Van Heusen. Song, "In My Garden of Joy," by Saul Chaplin. Production Designer: Boris Leven. Set Decorators: Walter M. Scott and Howard Bristol. Costumes: Donald Brooks. Production Associate: Maurice Zuberano. Film Editor: William Reynolds. Sound:

Murray Spivack, Douglas O. Williams and Bernard Freericks. Dance Assistant: Sheilah Hackett. Unit Production Manager: Saul Wurtzel. Music Editor: Robert Tracy. Special Photographic Effects: L. B. Abbott, Art Cruickshank and Emil Kosa Jr. Hair Styles for Miss Andrews: Hal Saunders. Makeup: William Buell and William Turner. Wardrobe: Ed Wynigear and Adele Balkan. Jewelry: Cartier, Inc. Wigs: Cal-East, Inc. Furs: Somper Furs. Assistant Director: Ridgeway Callow.

With Julie Andrews (Gertrude Lawrence), Richard Crenna (Richard Aldrich), Michael Craig (Sir Anthony Spencer), Daniel Massey (Noel Coward), Robert Reed (Charles Fraser), Bruce Forsyth (Arthur Lawrence), Beryl Reid (Rose), John Collin (Jack Roper), Alan Oppenheimer (Andre Charlot), Richard Karlan (David Holtzman), Lynley Laurence (Billie Carleton), Garrett Lewis (Jack Buchanan), Elizabeth St. Clair (Jeannie Banks), Jenny Agutter (Pamela), Anthony Eisley (Ben Mitchell), Jock Livingston (Alexander Woollcott), J. Pat O'Malley (Dan), Harvey Jason (Bert), Damian London (Jerry Paul), Richard Angarola (Cesare), Matilda Calnan (Dorothy), Lester Matthews (Lord Chamberlain), Bernard Fox (Assistant to Lord Chamberlain), Murray Matheson (Bankruptcy Judge), Robin Hughes (Hyde Park Speaker), and Jeannette Landis, Dinah Ann Rogers, Barbara Sandland, Ellen Plasschaert, and Ann Hubbell (The Daffodil Girls).

Fictionalized account of the life of the stage and occasional screen star Gertrude Lawrence.

Availability (16mm): Films Incorporated

STAR FOR MAX, A (7 mins/16mm)

As a star is dedicated to Max Steiner on Hollywood Boulevard's Walk of Fame, his wife, Elmer Bernstein and others talk about his work. Also included are clips from some of the composer's films.

Availability: Budget

STARS OF YESTERDAY (914 ft. /35mm)

U.S. Warner Bros. /Vitaphone Corporation. 1931. Director: Burnet Hershey. Film Editor: Bert Frank.

A compilation of short clips from early silent films, featuring the following personalities: Helen Holmes,

Mary Fuller, Theda Bara, Mabel Normand, Ford Sterling, Mack Sennett, Mildred Harris, Rudolph Valentino, Mary Miles Minter, Clara Kimball Young, Betty Blythe, Sarah Bernhardt, G. M. Anderson, Marguerite Clayton, Roscoe "Fatty" Arbuckle, Al St. John, William S. Hart, Charles Ray, Louise Glaum, Texas Guinan, and the Keystone Kops.

Availability: None (This short is preserved in Britain's National Film Archive)

STARS THAT MADE THE CINEMA, THE (4 reels/40 mins/35mm)

G.B. The National Film Theatre/British Film Institute. 1952. Compiler: Karel Reisz. Musical Accompaniment Arranged by John Huntley.

Compiled for the opening of Britain's National Film Theatre, most major stars from the silent era, both American and European, are represented in this well-edited production. Among the sequences included are Lillian Gish and Robert Harron in _Hearts of the World_, Betty Balfour in _Squibs Wins the Calcutta Sweep_, Mary Pickford in _The Hoodlum_, Douglas Fairbanks in _Robin Hood_, and Harold Lloyd in _Safety Last_.

Availability (35mm and 16mm): British Film Institute, London (no American distributor)

STOP! LOOK! AND LAUGH! (78 mins/35mm)

U.S. Columbia. 1960. Producer: Harry Romm. Associate Producer: Martha Vera Romm. Director: Jules White. Song, "Stop! Look! and Laugh!," Lyrics by Stanley Styne and Music by George Duning. Music Conductor: Mischa Bakaleinikoff. Film Editor: Jerome Thoms. Assistant Director: Milton Feldman. _Cinderella_ Sequence: Producer and Screenplay: Sid Kuller. Director: Lou Brandt. Art Director: Robert Bryer. _Paul Winchell_ Sequences: Director: Paul Appell. Photography: William Steiner. Assistant to the Producer: Marty Roth.

A series of episodes from ten 3 Stooges comedies produced between 1944 and 1956, linked together by ventriloquist Paul Winchell with Jerry Mahoney and Knucklehead Smiff, plus an episode with the Marquis Chimps and Joe Bolton acting the story of _Cinderella_. As one critic commented,

the only criticism must be on intellectual and artistic levels.
Availability (16mm): Twyman

STORY OF THE ANIMATED DRAWING, THE (47 mins/35mm)

U.S. Walt Disney Productions. 1955. Producer: Walt Disney. Director (Animation): Wilfred Jackson. Director (Live Action): William Beaudine. Screenplay: Dick Huemer and McLaren Stewart. Photography: Charles Boyle. Music: Joseph S. Dubin. Production Supervisor: Harry Tytle. Animation Art Work: McLaren Stewart and Jay J. Gould. Film Editor: Everett Dodd. Film Research: Robert Sunderland. Special Processes: Ub Iwerks. Sound: Robert O. Cook. Assistant Director: Gordon McLean. Narrator: Walt Disney.

A history of animation, from the drawings of the primitive caveman through the sophisticated work of the Disney craftsmen, first televised in the "Disneyland" television series over the ABC network on November 30, 1955. A superbly-produced documentary, with some excellent footage devoted to pre-cinema and optical toys.

Availability: None (a twenty-one-minute version titled History of Animation, q.v., is available for rental from Walt Disney)

STORY OF THOMAS ALVA EDISON, THE

According to a news item in Variety (August 30, 1954), a film with this title, produced by Jules Levey, received its premiere in the newly reconstructed Black Maria at the Edison Museum in West Orange. No other information has been found concerning the production.

STORY OF VERNON AND IRENE CASTLE, THE (90 mins/35mm)

U.S. RKO. 1939. Executive Producer: Pandro S. Berman. Producer: George Haight. Director: H. C. Potter. Screenplay: Richard Sherman. Adaptation: Oscar Hammerstein II and Dorothy Yost. Based on "My Husband" and "My Memories of Vernon Castle," by Irene Castle. Photography: Robert de Grasse. Special Effects: Vernon L. Walker. Montages: Douglas Travers. Music Director:

Victor Baravelle. Ensembles: Hermes Pan. Art Director: Van Nest Polglase. Associate Art Director: Perry Ferguson. Set Decorator: Darrell Silvera. Costumes: Walter Plunkett and Edward Stevenson. Ginger Rogers Gowns: Irene Castle. Film Editor: William Hamilton. Sound: Richard Van Hessen. Assistant Director: Argyle Nelson.

With Fred Astaire (Vernon Castle), Ginger Rogers (Irene Castle), Edna May Oliver (Maggie Sutton), Walter Brennan (Walter Ash), Lew Fields (Himself), Etienne Girardot (Papa Aubel), Rolfe Sedan (Emile Aubel), Janet Beecher (Mrs. Foote), Robert Strange (Dr. Foote), Leonid Kinsky (Artist), Clarence Derwent (Papa Louis), Victor Varconi (The Grand Duke), Frances Mercer (Claire Ford), Donald MacBride (Hotel Manager), Douglas Walton (Student Pilot), and Sonny Lamont (Charlie).

Biography of the famous dancing team, the female half of which was a popular film star in the 'teens. For more information, see The Fred Astaire and Ginger Rogers Book by Arlene Croce (Outerbridge and Lazard, 1972).

Availability (16mm): Films Incorporated

STORY OF WILL ROGERS, THE (9,782 ft./110 mins/35mm)

U.S. Warner Bros. 1952. Producer: Robert Arthur. Director: Michael Curtiz. Screenplay: Frank Davis and Stanley Roberts. Adaptation: John C. Moffitt. Based on The Saturday Evening Post story, "Uncle Clem's Boy," by Mrs. Will Rogers. Photography: Wilfrid M. Cline. Technicolor Color Consultant: Mitchell G. Kovaleski. Art Director: Edward Carrere. Sound: Charles Lang. Film Editor: Folmar Blangsted. Dialogue Director: Norman Stuart. Technical Adviser: Montie Montana. Set Decorator: George James Hopkins. Wardrobe: Milo Anderson. Original Music: Victor Young. Orchestrations: Leo Shuken and Sid Cutner. Makeup: Gordon Bau. Assistant Director: Sherry Shourds.

With Will Rogers, Jr. (Will Rogers), Jane Wyman (Mrs. Will Rogers), Carl Benton Reid (Clem Rogers), Eve Miller (Cora Marshall), James Gleason (Bert Lynn), Slim Pickens (Dusty Donovan), Noah Beery, Jr. (Wiley Post), Mary Wickes (Mrs. Foster), Steve Brodie (Dave Marshall). Pinky Tomlin (Orville James), Margaret Field (Sally Rogers), Virgil S. Taylor (Art Frazer), Richard Kean (Mr. Cavendish), Jay Silverheels (Joe Arrow), William Forrest (Flo Ziegfeld), Earl Lee (President Wilson), Brian Daly (Tom McSpadden), and Eddie Cantor (Himself).

"A warm, tender tale of an unpretentious man," is how The Hollywood Reporter (July 11, 1952) described this film biography of Will Rogers.

Availability (16mm): Warner Bros.

SUNSET BOULEVARD (111 mins/35mm)

U.S. Paramount. 1950. Producer: Charles Brackett. Director: Billy Wilder. Screenplay: Charles Brackett, Billy Wilder and D. M. Marshman, Jr. Photography: John F. Seitz. Process Photography: Farciot Edouart. Special Photographic Effects: Gordon Jennings. Art Directors: Hans Dreier and John Meehan. Set Decorators: Sam Comer and Ray Moyer. Editorial Supervisor: Doane Harrison. Film Editor: Arthur Schmidt. Music: Franz Waxman. "Salome's Dance of the Seven Veils" by Richard Strauss. Song, "The Paramount Don't-Want-Me Blues," by Jay Livingston and Ray Evans. Sound: Harry Lindgren and John Cope. Assistant Director: C. C. Coleman, Jr.

With Gloria Swanson (Norma Desmond), William Holden (Joe Gillis), Erich von Stroheim (Max von Mayerling), Nancy Olson (Betty Schaefer), Fred Clark (Sheldrake), Jack Webb (Artie Green), Lloyd Gough (Morino), Franklin Farnum (Undertaker), Larry Blake (First Finance Man), Charles Dayton (Second Finance Man), and Cecil B. DeMille, Hedda Hopper, Buster Keaton, H. B. Warner, Ray Evans, Jay Livingston, and Anna Q. Nilsson (Themselves).

It is hard to define Sunset Boulevard as a film on film history, but it does contain a lot of truth, and many involuntarily retired silent stars did and do resemble Norma Desmond. Sunset Boulevard also deserves mention because of the number of silent stars appearing in the production, and aside from those listed in the credits above, viewers may catch glimpses of Gertrude Astor, Creighton Hale and Eva Novak.

Availability (16mm): Films Incorporated

SUPERNATURAL OF MELIES, THE (1 reel/16mm)

A compilation of two Georges Méliès productions from 1903: The Infernal Cauldron and The Damnation of Faust.

Availability: Em Gee/Blackhawk (8mm sale only)

SURREALISM OF MELIES, THE (1 reel/16mm)

A compilation of two Georges Méliès productions from 1903: The Ballet Master's Dream and Fairy Kingdom.
Availability: Em Gee/Blackhawk (sale only)

SWASHBUCKLERS, THE see HOLLYWOOD AND THE STARS

SWEDISH CINEMA CLASSICS (34 mins/16mm)

Sweden. Svensk Filmindustri in cooperation with the Swedish Film Institute. 1959. Compiler: Gardar Sahlberg.

A representative sampling of Swedish films from the early 'teens through the mid-Twenties. Extracts from the following productions are included: Ingeborg Holm (1913), Terje Vigen (1916), The Outlaw and His Wife (1917), Jerusalem (1925), The Phantom Chariot (1920), Erotikon (1920), The Treasure of Arne (1919), and The Story of Gosta Berling (1924). A good introduction to the work of Victor Sjöström, Gustaf Molander and Mauritz Stiller.
Availability: The Museum of Modern Art

SWEET MEMORIES

This seven-minute short features clips from The Plastic Age (1925), with Clark Gable, Clara Bow and Gilbert Roland, and Millard Webb on the set of The Sea Beast (1926), directing a love scene between John Barrymore and Dolores Costello.
Availability (16mm): Budget

TALK WITH CARMEN D'AVINO, A (8 mins/16mm)

U.S. A Film by Cecile Starr. 1972. Producer and Director: Cecile Starr.

Carmen D'Avino discusses his work in the animation field.
Availability: Cecile Starr

TEENAGE IDOLS see HOLLYWOOD AND THE STARS

THAT'S ACTION (? /35mm)

U.S. Schine Productions. 1977. Producer and Director: G. David Schine. Screenplay: G. David Schine and James R. Silke. Film Design: James R. Silke. Film Editor: Jack Holmes. Music Supervision: Nelson Riddle. Narrator: Art Linkletter.

In an interview with the Los Angeles Times (May 2, 1977), G. David Schine described That's Action as "the story of the action hero in the '30s, '40s and '50s as he ventures into the world in a quest for romance and adventure, seeking to prove himself as a man, getting into trouble, meeting adversaries either one-on-one or on the battlefield, falling in love, being beguiled, always doing his duty, fighting for what he believes in." Among the players featured in this compilation, which was apparently chiefly drawn from the films of Republic Pictures, are John Wayne, Victor McLaglen, Maureen O'Hara, Douglas Fairbanks, Ernest Borgnine, Joan Crawford, Marlene Dietrich, Barry Fitzgerald, Cary Grant, Sterling Hayden, Rita Hayworth, Sam Jaffe, Ben Johnson, Katy Jurado, Charles Laughton, Walter Pidgeon, Barbara Stanwyck, and Claire Trevor.

Availability: None

THAT'S CARRY ON (8,524 ft. /95 mins/35mm)

G.B. Peter Rogers Productions. 1977. Producer: Peter Rogers. Director: Gerald Thomas. Screenplay: Tony Church. Photography: Tony Imi. Production Manager: Roy Goddard. Film Editor: Jack Gardner. Music: Eric Rogers. Sound Editor: Christopher Lancaster. Sound Recording: Denny Daniel and Ken Barker.

Barbara Windsor and Kenneth Williams are in a projection booth and introduce extracts from the twenty-eight films in the popular "Carry On" comedy series, from Carry On Sergeant (1958) through Carry On England (1976). For more information, see John Pym's review in The Monthly Film Bulletin (March, 1978), page 55.

Availability: None

THAT'S DEGREDATION

A compilation by Roninfilm of extracts from exploitation films of the Thirties, including Inside Forgotten Women, The White Slave Trade, Gambling with Souls, Assassin of Youth, Forbidden Dreams, The Devil's Root, Reefer Madness, Damaged Lives, and Lunacy.

Availability (16mm): Roninfilm

THAT'S ENTERTAINMENT! (133 mins/35mm)

U.S. M-G-M. 1974. Executive Producer: Daniel Melnick. Producer, Director and Screenplay: Jack Haley, Jr. Additional Music Adapted by Henry Mancini. Film Editors: Bud Friedgen and David E. Blewitt. Assistant Film Editors: Ana Luisa Corley Perez, Todd C. Ramsay, Ramon G. Caballero, and Abe Lincoln, Jr. Apprentice Film Editors: Michael J. Sheridan and George Y. Nakama. M-G-M Head Film Librarian: Mort Feinstein. Musical Supervisor: Jesse Kaye. Additional Music Edited by William Saracino. Sound Re-recording Mixers: Hal Watkins, Aaron Rochin, Lyle Burbridge, Harry W. Tetrick, and William L. McCaughey. Optical Supervision: Robert Hoag and Jim Liles. Additional Photography: Gene Polito, Ernest Laszlo, Russell Metty, Ennio Guarnieri, and Allan Green. Unit Production Managers: Wally Samson and William Poole. Assistant Directors: Richard Bremerkamp, David Silver and Claude Binyon, Jr. Narrators: Fred Astaire, Bing Crosby, Gene Kelly, Peter Lawford, Liza Minnelli, Donald O'Connor, Debbie Reynolds, Mickey Rooney, Frank Sinatra, James Stewart, and Elizabeth Taylor.

Memorable moments from great M-G-M film musicals, produced between 1929 and 1958. Included are clips from five shorts--Starlite Days at the Lido, See If, Pirate Party on Catalina, Every Sunday, and La Fiesta Santa Barbara--and sequences from the following features: An American in Paris (1951), Anchors Aweigh (1945), Babes in Arms (1939), Babes on Broadway (1942), The Band Wagon (1953), The Barkleys of Broadway (1949), Bathing Beauty (1944), Boom Town (1940), Born to Dance (1936), The Broadway Melody (1929), Broadway Melody of 1936 (1935), Broadway Melody of 1938 (1937), Broadway Melody of 1940 (1940), Broadway to Hollywood (1933), Chained (1934), Cynthia (1947), The Dancing Lady (1933), Dangerous When Wet (1953), A Date with Judy (1948), Free and Easy (1930), Gigi (1958), Girl Crazy

(1943), Going Hollywood (1933), Gone with the Wind (1939), Good News (1947), The Great Ziegfeld (1936), The Harvey Girls (1946), High Society (1956), Hit the Deck (1955), The Hollywood Review (1929), Honky Tonk (1941), Idiot's Delight (1939), I Love Melvin (1953), In the Good Old Summertime (1949), It Happened in Brooklyn (1947), Little Nellie Kelly (1940), Living in a Big Way (1947), Love Finds Andy Hardy (1938), Meet Me in St. Louis (1944), Million Dollar Mermaid (1952), Mutiny on the Bounty (1935), Neptune's Daughter (1949), On an Island with You (1948), On the Town (1949), Pagan Love Song (1950), The Pirate (1948), Reckless (1935), Rosalie (1937), Rose Marie (1936), Royal Wedding (1951), San Francisco (1936), Seven Brides for Seven Brothers (1954), Show Boat (1951), Singin' in the Rain (1952), Small Town Girl (1953), Speak Easily (1932), Strike Up the Band (1940), Summer Stock (1950), Suzy (1936), Take Me Out to the Ball Game (1949), Test Pilot (1938), This Time for Keeps (1942), Thousands Cheer (1944), Three Little Words (1950), Thrill of a Romance (1945), Toast of New Orleans (1950), Two Weeks with Love (1950), The Wizard of Oz (1939), Words and Music (1948), Ziegfeld Follies of 1946, and Ziegfeld Girl (1941).

Availability (16mm): Films Incorporated

THAT'S ENTERTAINMENT Part Two (125 mins/35mm)

U.S. M-G-M. 1976. Producers: Saul Chaplin and Daniel Melnick. Director (New Sequences): Gene Kelly. Narration Written by Leonard Gershe. Main Credit Titles: Saul Bass. Music Arranged and Conducted by Nelson Riddle. Special Lyrics: Howard Dietz and Saul Chaplin. Photography: George Folsey. Film Editors: Bud Friedgen and David Blewitt. Contributing Film Editors: David Bretherton and Peter C. Johnson. Assistant Film Editors: Michael J. Sheridan, Ana Luisa Perez, Ramon G. Caballero, and Dennis Lee Galling. Production Designer: John De Cuir. Special Appearance by Sammy Cahn. Animation: Hanna-Barbera Productions. Production Manager: Maurice Vaccarino. Assistant Director: William R. Poole. Wardrobe for Mr. Astaire and Mr. Kelly: Filipo. Makeup: Charles Schram and John Inzerella. Sound: Bill Edmondson. Script Supervisor: Dorothy Aldrin. Property Master: Anthony Bavero. Music Editor: William Saracino. Music Supervisor: Harry J. Lojewski. Sound Re-recording Mixers: Hal Watkins and Aaron Rochin. Optical Supervision: Jim Liles. Narrators: Fred Astaire and Gene Kelly.

Highlights from the following M-G-M productions are interspersed with new musical numbers by Fred Astaire and Gene Kelly: Abbott and Costello in Hollywood (1945), Adam's Rib (1949), An American in Paris (1951), Anchors Aweigh (1945), Annie Get Your Gun (1950), The Band Wagon (1953), The Barkleys of Broadway (1949), The Belle of New York (1952), Bombshell (1933), Boom Town (1940), Born To Dance (1936), Boys Town (1938), The Broadway Melody (1929), Broadway Melody of 1936 (1935), Broadway Serenade (1939), Cabin in the Sky (1943), China Seas (1935), Dancing Lady (1933), David Copperfield (1935), A Day at the Races (1937), Dinner at Eight (1934), Easter Parade (1948), Easy To Love (1953), For Me and My Gal (1942), Gigi (1958), Girl Crazy (1943), Going Hollywood (1933), Gone with the Wind (1939), Goodbye Mr. Chips (1939), Grand Hotel (1932), The Great Waltz (1938), High Society (1956), Hollywood Party (1934), Invitation to the Dance (1957), It Happened in Brooklyn (1947), It's Always Fair Weather (1955), Jumbo (1962), Kiss Me Kate (1953), Lady Be Good (1941), Lassie Come Home (1943), Laurel and Hardy's Laughing Twenties (1965), Lili (1953), Listen Darling (1938), Lovely To Look At (1952), Love Me or Leave Me (1955), Meet Me in St. Louis (1945), The Merry Widow (1934), The Merry Widow (1952), New Moon (1940), A Night at the Opera (1935), Ninotchka (1939), Pat and Mike (1952), The Philadelphia Story (1941), The Pirate (1948), Private Lives (1931), Saratoga (1937), Silk Stockings (1957), Singin' in the Rain (1952), Small Town Girl (1953), Songwriters Revue (1930), Strange Cargo (1940), A Tale of Two Cities (1935), Tarzan the Ape-Man (1932), The Tender Trap (1955), The Thin Man (1934), Three Little Words (1950), Till the Clouds Roll By (1946), Two-Faced Woman (1941), Two Girls and a Sailor (1944), White Cargo (1942), Without Love (1945), Words and Music (1948), and Ziegfeld Girl (1941). Also included are clips from thirteen Fitzpatrick "Traveltalks," produced between 1934 and 1953.

Availability (16mm): Films Incorporated

THAT'S EROTICA! (120 mins/16mm)

U.S. Mitchell Brothers Film Group. 1975.

Described in an advertisement in the Los Angeles Times as "a salute to the Blue Age of eroticism, to the featurette, to live sound, to fantasy, to early stars like George S. McDonald, Kim Pope, Greg and Bobbi, and Mary David. I've viewed over 100 Mitchell Brothers sound fea-

turettes and have snipped some of the hottest footage."
Availability: None

THEN AND NOW (1 reel/9 mins/35mm)

U.S. Universal-International. 1952.

A capsule history of forty years of Universal Pictures told through extracts from its features through The World in His Arms (1952). The short was apparently distributed, without charge, to theatres screening the last named film.
Availability: None

THEY WENT THAT-A-WAY *see* HOLLYWOOD AND THE STARS

35mm MOTION PICTURE PROJECTOR, THE (3 reels/16mm)

A tour of the impressive collection of projection apparatus held by Don Malkames.
Availability: None (formerly available for sale on 8mm from Blackhawk)

30 YEARS OF FUN (7,620 ft./85 mins/35mm)

U.S. Twentieth Century-Fox. 1963. Producer and Screenplay: Robert Youngson. Associate Producers: Alfred Dahlem and John E. Allen. Music: Bernard Green and Jack Shaindlin. Orchestration: Bernard Green and Milton Weinstein. Music Supervision: Jack Shaindlin. Song, "Bring Back the Laughter": Music by Bernard Green and Lyrics by Robert Youngson. Production Manager: I. Hill Youngson. Sound: Dick Vorisek. Film Quality Control: Paul Guffanti. Narrator: Jay Jackson.

A typical Robert Youngson comedy compilation, similar in content and appeal to his earlier features. As Tube in Variety (February 11, 1963) noted, "As in all compilations, there are ups and downs in 30 Years of Fun, but audiences young and old should find the total experience hearty and fascinating." Featured comedians include Charlie Chaplin, Buster Keaton, Laurel and Hardy, Harry Langdon, Syd Chaplin, Charlie Chase, Snub Pollard, Billy Bevan, Phyllis Haver,

Vernon Dent, Carter De Haven, Edna Purviance, Eric Campbell, and Andy Clyde. There are also glimpses of a number of other film personalities, including Mary Pickford, Douglas Fairbanks, Greta Garbo, and John Gilbert. The highspot of the production consists of a series of Chaplin clips from The Floorwalker, The Pawnshop, Easy Street, and The Rink. For more information, see The Monthly Film Bulletin (August, 1963), page 123.

Availability (16mm): Films Incorporated/Twyman/ Macmillan

THIS THEATRE AND YOU see LET'S GO TO THE MOVIES

THOMAS EDISON (26 mins/16mm)

U.S. Wolper Productions, released by Official Films. 1962. Producer: David L. Wolper. Music: Jack Tillar. Host/Narrator: Mike Wallace.

A documentary on the life and career of the great American inventor. A film in the "Biography" television series.

Availability: U.S.C. Film Library/Indiana University Audio-Visual Center/Sterling

THOSE DARING YOUNG FILM MAKERS BY THE GOLDEN GATE (23 mins/910 ft./16mm)

U.S. A Film by Geoffrey Bell. 1979. Director: Geoffrey Bell. Screenplay: E. G. Valens. Photography: Joe Winters. Music: Warner Jepson. Film Editor: Lela Smith.

"This instructional documentary film tells the story of an early movie company, the California Motion Picture Corporation, whose ambition was to unite the glory of the theatre with all the verve and mass appeal of the movies. It is set at a time when San Francisco was the theatrical center of the Pacific Coast and was host to the gorgeous 1915 International Exposition. Interwoven with the story line are such themes as the interchange between the stage and early movies (particuarly 19th-century melodrama and the stock company format), the importance of distribution and promotion in film, and the advantages and disadvantages of the independent film maker. Many of the visuals are from glass plate photographic originals. Included is some rare film footage, circa 1915, as well as color sequences made on location and animation graphics in color. The score is specially arranged from music of the period."--Geoffrey Bell.

Availability: University of California Extension Media Center

THOSE EXCITING DAYS (949 ft. /11 mins/35mm)

U.S. Warner Bros. 1955. Producer and Screenplay: Robert Youngson. Film Editor: Albert Helmes. Narrator: Dwight Weist.

A compilation of newsreel footage of the First World War. The film offers the somewhat biased opinion that the only outcome of the Russian Revolution was that "the evil of Communism was loosed upon the earth."

Availability: None

THOSE WERE THE DAYS (3,300 ft. /35mm)

G.B. Butcher's Film Service. 1946. Producer: Bishu Sen. Associate Producer: Henry E. Fisher. Film Editor: Philip Wrestler. Music: De Wolfe. At the Piano: Terence Casey. Recording: Harry Sheridan. Narrator: Kenneth Horne.

Clips from early silent films played for their comedy value, including a Max Linder short and Georges Méliès' _A Trip to the Moon._

Availability: None

THOSE WERE THE HAPPY TIMES _see_ STAR!

THREE EARLY AMERICAN PRODUCERS (24 mins/16mm)

A package of five films from the Library of Congress Paper Print Collection: _Love and War_ (1899, James H. White), _The Girl from Montana_, _His First Ride_ and _The Bandit King_ (all 1907, William N. Selig), and _The Bank Robbery_ (1908, Oklahoma Natural Mutoscene Company).

Availability: Macmillan

THREE ITALIAN COMEDIES (29 mins/16mm)

A package of three early Italian comedies, compiled by the Museum of Modern Art: Trouble with a Rocket (1911), Polidor's Wedding (1912) and Amor pedestre (1914).
Availability: The Museum of Modern Art

THREE RAILWAY CRASHES (1 reel/9 mins/16mm)

Three railroad crashes staged for silent films, excerpted by the British Film Institute: The Wreck (1914), The Juggernaut (1915) and The Wreckers (1928).
Availability: British Film Institute, London (no American distributor)

3 STOOGES FOLLIES, THE (106 mins/35mm)

U.S. Columbia. 1974.

Despite its title, this compilation offers more than just the 3 Stooges. It is, in fact, a selection of Columbia shorts, complete with main titles and credits, from the Thirties and Forties. The 3 Stooges are represented by Violent Is the Word for Curly (1938), Yes, We Have No Bonanza (1939) and You Nazty Spy! (1940). In the last, Curly impersonates Mussolini, while Moe appears as Hitler. Other shorts included in The 3 Stooges Follies are The Crystal Gazebo (1932), a Krazy Kat cartoon; Nothing But Pleasure (1939), with Buster Keaton; Chapter One of the Batman Serial (1943), with J. Carroll Naish; Strife of the Party (1944), with Vera Vague; and the highlight of the program, America Sings with Kate Smith (1942).
Availability (16mm): Twyman

THREE VITAGRAPH COMEDIES (53 mins/16mm)

A package of three Vitagraph comedies, compiled by the Museum of Modern Art: Stenographer Wanted (1912) with Flora Finch and John Bunny, Goodness Gracious (1914) with Clara Kimball Young and Sidney Drew, and The Professional Patient (1917) with Mr. and Mrs. Sidney Drew.
Availability: The Museum of Modern Art

THRILLS FROM THE PAST (971 ft. /11 mins/35mm)

U.S. Warner Bros. 1953. Producer and Screenplay: Robert Youngson. Film Editor: Albert Helmes. Narrator: Dwight Weist.

This short features a highly truncated version of Alan Crosland's Old San Francisco (1927).
Availability: None

TO HELL AND BACK

1955 feature on the war career as a soldier of Audie Murphy (1924-1971), a career which was to lead to a new one, as an actor in Hollywood. However, To Hell and Back does not concern itself with Audie Murphy, the film star.

TOM MIX EARLY FILMS (30 mins/16mm)

A compilation of three early Selig Company films starring Tom Mix: Cactus Jim's Shop Girl (1915), Local Color (1916) and Tom's Strategy (1916).
Availability: Macmillan

TOMMY STEELE STORY, THE (7, 371 ft. /82 mins/35mm)

G.B. Anglo Amalgamated/Nat Cohen and Stuart Levy. 1957. Producer: Herbert Smith. Director: Gerard Bryant. Screenplay: Norman Hudis. Photography: Peter Hennessy. Film Editor: Ann Chegwidden. Art Director: Eric Saw. Songs: Tommy Steele, Lionel Bart, Michael Pratt, Humphrey Littleton, Paul James, Fred Williams, Roger Paul, and Russell Henderson.
With Tommy Steele (Himself), Patrick Westwood (Brushes), Hilda Fenemore (Mrs. Steele), Charles Lamb (Mr. Steele), Peter Lewiston (John Kennedy), John Boxer (Paul Lincoln), Mark Daly (Junkshop Man), and The Steelmen, Humphrey Littleton and His Band, Chas. McDevitt and His Skiffle Group, Nancy Whiskey, the Tommy Eytle Calypso Band, and Chris O'Brien's Caribbeans.

The life story of the popular British singer, who has appeared in both American and British films. For more information, see The Monthly Film Bulletin (July, 1957), pages 90-91.
Availability: None

TOY THAT GREW UP, THE see ANIMATED CARTOONS: THE TOY THAT GREW UP

TRAIN ROLLS ON, THE (33 mins/16mm)

U.S. New Yorker Films. 1974. Director: Chris Marker.

Russian film director Alexander Medvedkin talks about the Cine-Train, a film studio on wheels, which toured the Soviet Union in the early Thirties, and there is footage of the train itself in action.

Availability: New Yorker

TRIO OF EDISON COMEDIES FROM STORE SHOW DAYS, A (1 reel/16mm)

A compilation of three Edison Company productions from 1905 and 1906: Laughing Gas, How Jones Lost His Roll and How the Office Boy Saw the Ball Game.

Availability (16mm and 8mm): Blackhawk (sale only)

TURN OF THE CENTURY (3 reels/16mm)

"A large selection of primitives produced by the different pioneer companies of the period" (1898-1906).

Availability (16mm and 8mm): Thunderbird (sale only)

TURN OF THE CENTURY MACABRE (1 reel/16mm)

A compilation of Edison and American Mutoscope and Biograph productions from the Paper Print Collection of the Library of Congress: Skeleton Dance (1898), Another Job for the Undertaker (1901), Execution of a Spy (1902), The Monster (1903), Electrocuting an Elephant (1903), Reading the Death Sentence (1905), An Execution by Hanging (1905), and In the Tombs (1906).

Availability: Kit Parker

25 YEARS (6,917 ft./77 mins/35mm)

G.B. EMI. Presented by the London Celebrations

Committee for the Queen's Silver Jubilee. 1977. Producer, Director and Screenplay: Peter Morley. Production Coordinator: Anne Boyle. Production Manager: Terry Gould. Photography: Tony Coggins, Eric Van Haren Norman, Mike Delaney, and Harvey Harrison. Film Editor: Jeff Harvey. Titles: Alison Inglis. Sound Recording: Colin Charles, Bernard Childs, Clive Winter, and Laurie Clarkson. Sound Re-recording: Trevor Pyke. Historical Consultant: John Terraine. Film Research: Elizabeth Sussex. Research: Martha Higgins. Production Assistant: Jean Clarkson.

A collection of newsreel footage, with contemporary commentary, covering the reign of England's Queen Elizabeth II, from 1952 through 1977. Most of the footage came from the archives of British Movietone News and Associated British-Pathé. For more information, see Geoff Brown's review in The Monthly Film Bulletin (April, 1977), page 81.

Availability: None

TWENTY YEARS OF ACADEMY AWARDS (20 mins/35mm)

U.S. Academy of Motion Picture Arts and Sciences for RKO release. 1948. Compiler and Narrator: Carey Wilson.

Brief clips, without sound, from Academy Award-winning films in the categories of "Best Picture" and "Best Actor" and "Best Actress" from the first Awards year, 1927-1928 through 1947. The clips from the 1947 Awards year are longer, and do include sound. Carey Wilson narrates the short as if it were "Oscar" speaking. The following personalities are seen receiving their Awards, but yet there is no sound, only Wilson telling you what they said: Shirley Temple, Ronald Colman, Loretta Young, Darryl F. Zanuck, Albert E. Smith, Col. William N. Selig, and James Baskett.

Availability: None (A 16mm print is available for study at the Academy of Motion Picture Arts and Sciences)

TWO BRONCHO BILLY WESTERNS (48 mins/16mm)

A package of two "Broncho Billy" Anderson Westerns, compiled by the Museum of Modern Art: Broncho Billy's Capture (1913) and Shootin' Mad (1918).

Availability: The Museum of Modern Art

TWO EDUCATIONAL FILMS OF 1910 (2 reels/15 mins/35mm)

A package, compiled by the British Film Institute, of two early hand-colored films: the Pathé version of The Eruption of Mount Vesuvius and F. Percy Smith's Birth of a Flower.

Availability (35mm and 16mm): British Film Institute, London (no American distributor)

TWO ITALIAN MELODRAMAS (39 mins/16mm)

Two typical productions from the early years of Italian cinema--Lydia (1912) and an excerpt from La Donna nuda (1914)--compiled by the Museum of Modern Art.

Availability: The Museum of Modern Art

UNDERGROUND FILM (23 mins/16mm)

U.S. KEBS-TV. 1971. Director: Peter Marshall. Photography: Richard Moore. Narrator: Chick Strand.

A study of the underground film movement, told through the work of Chick Strand, who discusses her films and introduces an extract from her award-winning production of Anselmo.

Availability: None

UNSINKABLE BETTE DAVIS, THE see HOLLYWOOD AND THE STARS

VALENTINO (9, 450 ft. /105 mins/35mm)

U.S. Edward Small Productions-Columbia. 1951. Producer: Edward Small. Director: Lewis Allen. Screenplay: George Bruce. Photography: Harry Stradling. Technicolor Color Consultant: Robert Brower. Associate Producer: Jan Grippo. Music: Heinz Roemheld. Music Supervisor: David Chudnow. Film Editor: Daniel Mandell. Art Director: William Flannery. Set Decorator: Howard Bristol. Assistant Director: Emmett Emerson. Special Photographic Effects: John Fulton. Makeup: Ern Westmore. Hair Styles: Marie Clark. Sound: Fred Lau. Gowns: Gwen Wakeling. Additional Gowns: Travis Banton. Dance Director: Larry Ceballos.

With Eleanor Parker (Joan Carlisle), Anthony Dexter (Rudolph Valentino), Richard Carlson (William King), Patricia Medina (Lila Reyes), Joseph Calleia (Luigi Verducci), Dona Drake (Maria Torres), Lloyd Gough (Eddie Morgan), Otto Kruger (Mark Towers), Marietta Canty (Tillie), Paul Bruar (Photographer), and Eric Wilton (Butler).

Highly romanticized version of the story of Rudolph Valentino, with little attempt to recapture the Twenties era when Valentino was at the height of his fame. Alice Terry, Valentino's leading lady in two features, and relatives of Valentino filed suits for damages after the release of Valentino; both suits were settled out of court.

Availability: None

VALENTINO (132 mins/35mm)

G.B. United Artists/A Robert Chartoff, Irwin Winkler Production. 1977. Executive Producer: Robert Chartoff. Director and Screenplay: Ken Russell. Photography: Peter Suschitsky. Associate Producer: Harry Benn. Production Manager: Peter Price. Art Director: Philip Harrison. Set Dresser: Ian Whittaker. Film Editor: Stuart Baird. Costume Designer: Shirley Russell. Continuity: Zelda Barron. Sound Mixer: John Mitchell. Location Manager: Richard Green. Wardrobe Master: Richard Pointing. Wardrobe Mistress: Rebecca Breed. Chief Make-up: Peter Robb-King. Chief Hardresser: Colin Jamison. Production Accountant: Len Cave. Production Secretary: Pat Pennelegion. Casting Director: Maude Spector. Choreography: Gillian Gregory. Property Master: Ray Traynor. Construction Manager: Jeffrey Woodbridge. Dialogue Coach: Marcella Markham. Stills Photographer: Barry Peake. Publicist: Brian Doyle. Camera Operator: Ronnie Taylor. Assistant Director: Jonathan Benson.

With Rudolf Nureyev (Rudolph Valentino), Leslie Caron (Alla Nazimova), Michelle Phillips (Natasha Rambova), Carol Kane (Starlet), Felicity Kendall (June Mathis), Seymour Cassell (George Ullman), Huntz Hall (Jesse Lasky), Alfred Marks (Richard Rowland), David De Keyser (Joseph Schenck), Linda Thorson (Billie Streeter), Leland Palmer (Marjorie Tain), Lindsay Kemp (Angus McBride), Peter Vaughan (Rory O'Neil), Anthony Dowell (Nijinsky), Penelope Milford (Lorna Sinclair), June Bolton (Bianca de Saulles), Robin Clark (Jack de Saulles), William Hootkins (Fatty), John Justin (Sidney Olcott), Anton Diffring (Baron Long), Nicolette Marvin (Marsha Lee), Jennie

Linden (Agnes Ayres), Percy Herbert (Studio Guard), Dudley Sutton (Willie), Christine Carlson (Girl in Tango Sequence), Don Fellows (George Melford), Bill McKinney (Policeman), Marcella Markham (Hooker), John Alderson (Cop), Elizabeth Bagley (Pretty Girl), Charles Farrell (Drunk), Hal Galili (Harry Fischbeck), Richard Le Parmentier (The Sheik), Scott Miller (Ray C. Smallwood), Burnell Tucker (Assistant Director), Diana Von Fossen (Makeup Girl), Ray Jewers (Electrician), Murray Salem (Vagrant), Mildred Shay (Lady at Maxim's), Deirdre Costello (First Whore), Diana Weston (Second Whore), Mark Baker (Assistant Director), and Army Farber (Girl Friend).

A highly romanticized and fictionalized account of the life of Rudolph Valentino, in the Ken Russell manner. For more information, see The Nureyev Valentino: Portrait of a Film by Alexander Bland (Dell, 1977).

Availability (16mm): United Artists 16

VALENTINO: IDOL OF THE JAZZ AGE (1 reel/35mm)

A 1930 tribute to Rudolph Valentino, chiefly utilizing newsreel footage and including extensive coverage of his funeral. An entertaining short for all Valentino fans, and a useful ten-minute introduction to his career for film students.

Availability (16mm): Swank/Thunderbird (sale)/Reel Images (sale)

VALENTINO MYSTIQUE, THE (2, 340 ft. /26 mins/35mm)

U.S. Killiam Shows. 1973. Producer, Screenplay and Narrator: Paul Killiam. Film Editors: Paul Killiam and Jim Seering. Music: Lee Erwin.

A condensed version of The Legend of Valentino (q.v.), similar in format to The Eagle episode in The History of the Motion Picture series, but in color. Originally released in England by Vaughan Films. For more information, see John Gillett's review in The Monthly Film Bulletin (June, 1973), page 137.

Availability (35mm and 16mm): Killiam Shows (rental)/ Blackhawk (sale)

VARIETY TIME (58 mins/35mm)

U.S. RKO. 1948. Producer: George Bilson. Leon Errol and Edgar Kennedy Sequences Directed by Hal Yates. Jack Paar Material Written by Lee Solomon and Joseph Quillan. Leon Errol Screenplay: Hal Law. Edgar Kennedy Screenplay: Hal Yates. Music Director: C. Bakaleinikoff. Art Director: Charles Pyke. Film Editors: Les Millbrook and Edward Williams. Sound: Clem Portman. Special Effects: Vernon L. Walker and Russell A. Cully.

With Edgar Kennedy, Leon Errol, Frankie Carle and His Orchestra, Pat Rooney, Miguelito Valdes, Harold and Lola, Jesse and James, Lynn, Royce and Vanya, Hans Conreid, Dorothy Granger, Jack Norton, Minerva Urecal, Florence Lake, Jack Rice, Dot Farley, and Jack Paar.

Although intended as a film version of a vaudeville bill, Variety Time does include clips from old RKO comedies and extracts from silent films, first used in the RKO "Flicker Flashback" series (q.v.). Jack Paar acts as master of ceremonies for the short.

Availability (16mm): Films Incorporated

VOICE THAT THRILLED THE WORLD, THE (2 reels/20 mins/35mm)

U.S. Warner Bros. 1943. Director: Jean Negulesco. Narrator: Art Gilmore.

A documentary on the rise of the talking picture, beginning with Thomas Edison's recording of "Mary Had a Little Lamb," and including clips from a number of Warner Bros. productions, such as Don Juan, The Jazz Singer, The Singing Fool, Disraeli, The Life of Emile Zola, Sergeant York, and Yankee Doodle Dandy.

Availability (16mm): United Artists 16

WEDDING YELLS (20 mins/35mm)

U.S. Warner Bros. "Broadway Brevities" series. 1942. Narrator: Knox Manning.

One of a series of Warner Bros. compilations utilizing Mack Sennett film clips.

Availability: United Artists 16

WESTERN HERO, THE (30 mins/16mm)

U.S. CBS News "The Twentieth Century" series. 1963. Producer: Isaac Kleinerman. Screenplay: Don Miller. Music: Lawrence Rosenthal. Film Editor: Walter Katz. Narrator: Walter Cronkite.

A documentary on the evolution of the Western hero from The Great Train Robbery (1903) through the television series Gunsmoke. Included are clips from the films of William S. Hart, Tom Mix, Gene Autry, John Wayne, Gary Cooper, and others. For more information see Mimi Ritti's review in Film Library Quarterly (Winter, 1969-70), page 41.

Availability: University of California Extension Media Center

WHEN COMEDY WAS KING (90 mins/35mm)

U.S. Twentieth Century-Fox. 1960. Producer and Screenplay: Robert Youngson. Associate Producers: Herbert Goldspan, John E. Allen and Al Dahlem. Music: Ted Royal. Music Conducted by Sylvan Levin. Musical Supervision: Herman Fuchs and Louis Turchen. Narrator: Dwight Weist.

A brilliant compilation of the best sight comedy routines in the cinema from 1917 through 1928. This second comedy compilation by Robert Youngson is arguably his best work, and a perfect introduction to the history of silent film comedy. Represented in When Comedy Was King are The Keystone Kops, Harry Langdon, Laurel and Hardy, Charlie Chase, Buster Keaton, Edgar Kennedy, Roscoe "Fatty" Arbuckle, Wallace Beery, Charlie Chaplin, Billy Bevan, Andy Clyde, Chester Conklin, Vernon Dent, Gloria Swanson, Ben Turpin, Mabel Normand, The Mack Sennett Bathing Beauties, Snub Pollard, Al St. John, Mack Swain, Teddy the Keystone Dog, Bobby Vernon, Stuart Erwin, Jimmy Finlayson, Madeline Hurlock, Charlie Murray, and Daphne Pollard.

Availability (16mm): Films Incorporated/Macmillan/Kit Parker Films/Budget Films/Swank/Twyman

WHEN TALKIES WERE YOUNG (1,800 ft./18 mins/35mm)

U.S. Warner Bros. 1954. Producer and Screenplay:

Robert Youngson. Music Director: Kenneth Upton. Narrator: Dwight Weist.

This short features clips from five early sound releases of Warner Bros.: Sinner's Holiday (1930), 20,000 Years in Sing Sing (1933), Five Star Final (1931), Night Nurse (1931), and Svengali (1931).

Availability (16mm): Em Gee

WILD AND WONDERFUL THIRTIES, THE see HOLLYWOOD AND THE STARS

WILD PARTY, THE (90 mins/35mm)

U.S. Samuel Z. Arkoff/American International. 1976. Executive Producers: Edgar Lansbury and Joseph Beruh. Producer: Ismail Merchant. Director: James Ivory. Screenplay: Walter Marks. Based on the Narrative Poem by Joseph Moncure March. Photography: Walter Lassally. Original Songs: Walter Marks. Art Director: David Nichols. Film Editor: Kent McKinney. Sound: Gary Alper. Music: Larry Rosenthal. Music Sequences Staged by Patricia Birch. Associate Producer: George Manasse. Dance Music Composed by Louis St. Louis. Costumes: Ron Talsky. Costumes for James Coco, Perry King and David Dukes: Ralph Lauren. Costumes for Jennifer Lee, Dena Dietrich and Tiffany Bolling: Ronald Kolodgie. Jewels: Van Cleef and Arpels. Casting: Lynn Stalmaster and Otto and Windsor. Assistant Director: Edward Folger. Camera Operator: Marcel Shayne. Sound Editor: Mary Brown. Assistant Film Editor: Courtney V. Hazell. Script Supervisor: Marilyn Ciardino. Production Secretary: Janet Sonenberg. Stills: Morgan Renard. Unit Publicist: Allan Ingersoll Segal. Mixer: Richard Vorisek. Music Consultant: Music Maximus. Key Makeup: Louis Lane. Key Hair: John Malone. Key Wardrobe: Eric Kjemvik. Special Effects: Edward Bash. Stunt Coordinator: Terry McComas.

With James Coco (Jolly Grimm), Raquel Welch (Queenie), Perry King (Dale Sword), Tiffany Bolling (Kate), Royal Dano (Tex), David Dukes (James Morrison), Dena Dietrich (Mrs. Murchison), Regis Cordic (Mr. Murchison), Jennifer Lee (Madeline True), Marya Small (Bertha), Bobo Lewis (Wilma), Annette Ferra (Nadine), Eddie Laurence (Kreutzer), Tony Paxton (Sergeant), Waldo K. Berns (Policeman), Nina Faso (The Nurse), Baruch Lumet (Tailor), Martin Kove (Editor), Ralph Manza (Fruit Dealer), Lark Geib (Rosa), Fredric Franklyn (Sam), J. S. Johnson (Morris), Skipper (Phil D'Armano), and Don De Natale (Jackie the Dancer).

Filmed on location at the Mission Inn, Riverside, The Wild Party--despite negative critical and poor boxoffice response--is a well-produced film with a genuine period feel. It is concerned with a fat, silent comedian, obviously based on "Fatty" Arbuckle, facing the destruction of his career through the coming of sound. The reconstruction of a silent comedy is particularly well done.

Availability: None

WILL ROGERS (26 mins/16mm)

U.S. Wolper Productions, released by Official Films. 1962. Producer: David L. Wolper. Music: Jack Tillar. Host/Narrator: Mike Wallace.

A documentary on the life and career of the well-known American humorist, vaudeville, radio, and screen star. A film in the "Biography" television series.

Availability: Sterling/Indiana University Audio-Visual Center

WILL ROGERS (The History of the Motion Picture/Silents Please series)

A study of the popular entertainer and personality, including lengthy clips from Big Moments from Little Pictures (1923) and Don't Park There (1924), co-produced by Paul Killiam and Saul J. Turell and written by Paul Killiam. For more information, see The History of the Motion Picture series.

Availability (16mm): Blackhawk (sale)/Killiam Shows (rental)/Budget (rental)

WILL ROGERS, COWBOY HUMORIST (12 mins/16mm)

U.S. Fox Movietone News. 1953. Producer: Mike Sklar.

A collection of newsreel footage of Will Rogers entertaining at concerts and benefits during the Depression.

Availability (8mm and 16mm): Blackhawk (sale only)

WILL ROGERS STORY, THE see THE STORY OF WILL ROGERS

WILLIAM S. HART (The History of the Motion Picture/Silents Please series)

A superb tribute to the great silent cowboy star William S. Hart, including a truncated version of Hell's Hinges, the landrush sequences from Tumbleweeds and the moving farewell to the screen filmed by Hart for the sound reissue of the latter film in 1939, co-produced and written by Paul Killiam and Saul J. Turell. For more information see The History of the Motion Picture series.

Availability (16mm): Blackhawk (sale)/Killiam Shows (rental)/Budget (rental)

WITH A SONG IN MY HEART

1952 fictionalized account of the career of singer Jane Froman, which does not deal with her minor venture into films.

WIZARD WHO SPAT ON THE FLOOR, THE (41 mins and 60 mins/16mm)

G.B. BBC. 1974. Producer: Robert Vas. Photography: Ernest Vinaze. Film Editor: Jack Dennis.

A study of the life and work of the inventor, Thomas Alva Edison, utilizing rare interviews and documentary footage to illustrate Edison's impact on American life and world culture. Available in two versions.

Availability: Time-Life

WON TON TON, THE DOG WHO SAVED HOLLYWOOD (92 mins/35mm)

U.S. Paramount. 1975. Producers: David V. Picker, Arnold Schulman and Michael Winner. Director: Michael Winner. Screenplay: Arnold Schulman and Cy Howard. Photography: Richard H. Kline. Music: Neal Hefti. Associated Producer and Unit Production Manager: Tim Zinnemann. Art Director: Ward Preston. Set Decorator: Ned

Parsons. Film Editor: Bernard Gribble. Assistant Director: Charles Okun. Second Assistant Director: Arne Schmidt. Sound Editor: Terence Rawlings. Sound Recording: Bob Post. Re-recording Mixer: Hugh Strain. Auditor: Gene Levy. Transportation Captain: James Brubaker. Makeup: Philip Rhodes. Hair Stylist: Billie Laughridge. Assistant to Mr. Picker: Laurence Mark. Assistant to Mr. Winner: John Smallcombe. Dogs Furnished by Lou Schumacher. Dogs Trained by Karl Miller.

With Dennis Morgan (Tour Guide), Shecky Greene (Tourist), Phil Leeds and Cliff Norton (Dog Catchers), Madeline Kahn (Estie Del Ruth), Teri Garr (Fluffy Peters), Romo Vincent (Short Order Cook), Bruce Dern (Grayson Potchuck), Sterling Holloway (Old Man on Bus), William Benedict (Man on Bus), Dorothy Gulliver (Old Woman on Bus), William Demarest (Studio Gatekeeper), Art Carney (J. J. Fromberg), Virginia Mayo (Miss Battley), Henny Youngman (Manny Farber), Rory Calhoun (Philip Hart), Billy Barty (Assistant Director), Henry Wilcoxon (Silent Film Director), Ricardo Montalban (Silent Film Star), Jackie Coogan (Stagehand I), Aldo Ray (Stubby Stebbins), Ethel Merman (Hedda Parsons), Yvonne De Carlo (Cleaning Woman), Joan Blondell (Landlady), Andy Devine (Priest in Dog Pound), Broderick Crawford (Special Effects Man), Richard Arlen (Silent Film Star 2), Jack La Rue (Silent Film Villain), Dorothy Lamour (Visiting Film Star), Phil Silvers (Murray Fromberg), Nancy Walker (Mrs. Fromberg), Gloria De Haven (President's Girl I), Louis Nye (Radio Interviewer), Johnny Weissmuller (Stagehand 2), Stepin' Fetchit (Dancing Butler), Ken Murray (Souvenir Salesman), Rudy Vallee (Autograph Hound), George Jessel (Awards Announcer), Rhonda Fleming (Rhoda Flaming), Ann Miller (President's Girl 2), Dean Stockwell (Paul Lavell), Dick Haymes (James Crawford), Tab Hunter (David Hamilton), Robert Alda (Richard Entwhistle), Eli Mintz (Tailor), Ron Leibman (Rudy Montague), Fritz Feld (Rudy's Butler), Edward Ashley (Second Butler), Kres Mersky (Girl in Arab Film), Jane Connell (Waitress), Janet Blair (President's Girl 3), Dennis Day (Singing Telegraph Man), Mike Mazurki (Studio Guard), The Ritz Brothers (Cleaning Women), Jesse White (Rudy's Agent), Carmel Myers (Woman Journalist), Jack Carter (Male Journalist), Jack Bernardi (Fluff's Escort), Victor Mature (Nick), Barbara Nichols (Nick's Girl), Army Archerd (Premiere MC), Fernando Lamas (Premiere Male Star), Zsa Zsa Gabor (Premiere Female Star), Cyd Charisse (President's Girl 4), Huntz Hall (Moving Man), Doodles Weaver (Man in Mexican Film), Pedro Gonzales-Gonzales (Mexican Projectionist), Eddie Le Veque (Prostitute Customer), Edgar Bergen (Professor

Quicksand), Ronny Graham (Mark Bennett), Morey Amsterdam and Eddie Foy Jr. (Custard Pie Stars), Peter Lawford (Slapstick Star), Patricia Morison and Guy Madison (Stars at Screening), Regis Toomey (Burlesque Stagehand), Alice Faye (Secretary at Gate), Ann Rutherford (Grayson's Studio Secretary), Milton Berle (Blind Man), James E. Brodhead (Priest), John Carradine (Drunk), Keye Luke (Cook in Kitchen), Walter Pidgeon (Grayson's Butler), and Augustus von Schumacher (Won Ton Ton).

A comedy about Hollywood in the Twenties and a German shepherd modelled after Rin-Tin-Tin, Won Ton Ton is a film more interesting for its guest stars than for its plot.

Availability: None

WONDERFUL WORLD OF THOSE CUCKOO CRAZY ANIMALS, THE see IT'S SHOWTIME

WOODY ALLEN: AN AMERICAN COMEDY (1,074 ft./30 mins/16mm)

U.S. Films for the Humanities. 1977. Producer and Director: Harold Mantell. Photography: Peter Sova. Film Editor: Colin Hill.

Comedy genius Woody Allen discusses the influences upon his personality and the sources of his comic art. Also included are film clips from Take the Money and Run, Sleeper, Love and Death, and Annie Hall. For more information, see Judith Trojan's review in Take One (May, 1978), page 8.

Availability: Films for the Humanities (rental and sale)

WORLD OF ABBOTT AND COSTELLO, THE (75 mins/35mm)

U.S. Vanguard Productions/Universal. 1965. Producers: Max J. Rosenberg and Milton Subotsky. Associate Producer: Norman E. Gluck. Narration Written by Gene Wood. Editorial Direction: Sidney Meyer. Assistant Editorial Direction: Nina Feinberg. Music Supervisor: Joseph Gershenson. Title Design: Gil Merit. Narrator: Jack E. Leonard.

A selection of comedy routines from the following Bud Abbott and Lou Costello features: Buck Privates (1941), In the Navy (1941), Ride 'Em Cowboy (1942), Who Done It? (1942), Hit the Ice (1943), In Society (1944), The Naughty Nineties (1945), Little Giant (1946), Buck Privates Come Home (1947), The Wistful Widow of Wagon Gap (1948), Mexican Hayride (1949), Abbott and Costello Meet Frankenstein (1949), Abbott and Costello in the Foreign Legion (1950), Comin' round the Mountain (1951) Lost in Alaska (1952), Abbott and Costello Go to Mars (1953), Abbott and Costello Meet the Keystone Kops (1954), and Abbott and Costello Meet the Mummy (1955). Abbott and Costello are best in small doses, and this compilation probably provides the least painful way of experiencing their humor. For more information, see Allen Eyles review in Films and Filming (May, 1966).

Availability (16mm): Universal 16

WORLD OF DARRYL F. ZANUCK, THE (51 mins/16mm)

U.S. NBC. 1963. Producer and Director: Eugene S. Jones. Screenplay: Joseph Liss. Music: Robert Emmett Dolan. Film Editor: John Christophel. Narrator: Alexander Scourby.

A documentary on the life and work of the well-known producer, describing his early years in Hollywood, his rise to success, his problems with Marilyn Monroe and Elizabeth Taylor, his difficulties with Cleopatra, and his control of Twentieth Century-Fox.

Availability: Indiana University Audio-Visual Center

WORLD OF MAURICE CHEVALIER, THE (58 mins/16mm)

U.S. NBC. 1963. Producer and Director: Eugene S. Jones. Screenplay: Joseph Liss. Photography: Christopher Callery, Bernard Dresner and Cy Avnet. Music: Robert Emmett Dolan. Film Editor: John Christophel. Narrator: Alexander Scourby.

A documentary on the career of the French entertainer, from his early appearances in Paris of the Twenties through his American career, utilizing clips from Chevalier's early Hollywood films and newsreel footage.

Availability: None

WORLD OF SOPHIA LOREN, THE (59 mins/16mm)

U.S. NBC. 1963. Producer and Director: Eugene S. Jones.

The Italian actress discusses her life and her film career.
Availability: None

YANKEE DOODLE DANDY

1942 fictionalized account of the life and career of George M. Cohan, which does not deal with his film career.

YESTERDAY AND TODAY (57 mins/35mm)

U.S. Greshler-United Artists. 1953. Producer and Director: Abner J. Greshler. Screenplay and Narrator: George Jessel. Associate Producer and Editorial Supervisor: Paul Weatherwax. Photography: Stanley Cortez. Music: Eliot Daniel. Sound: William Randall.

Despite its title, this production chiefly features films from the early and pre-teens, together with George Jessel, who appears in person between clips. Perhaps the highspot of _Yesterday and Today_ occurs because the producers were unable to obtain a clip of Al Jolson, and so Jessel produces a photograph of the entertainer and then proceeds to impersonate him singing "Toot, Toot Tootsie." "If the point of the picture was to prove that movies today are better than ever, it makes its point," commented _The Hollywood Reporter_ (November 9, 1953).
Availability: None

YESTERDAY'S WITNESS (52 mins/16mm)

U.S. Blackwood Productions. 1975. Producer and Director: Christian Blackwood. Screenplay: Raymond Fielding. Narrator: Lowell Thomas.

A history of the American newsreel from the silent era through the mid-Fifties. Among those who take part are newsreel commentators Ed Herlihy, Lowell Thomas and Harry Von Zell; newsreel cameramen Norman Alley, Joe Gibson and Max Markman; newsreel editor Bertram Kalisch; and newsreel musical director Jack Shaindlin.

Availability (16mm and video cassette): Blackwood Productions (rental and sale)

YOU ARE THE WORLD FOR ME / THE RICHARD TAUBER STORY / DU BIST DIE WELT FUR MICH (107 mins/35mm)

Germany. Released in the U.S. by Ring Film Corporation. 1965. Director and Screenplay: Ernst Marischka.

With Rudolf Schock (Richard Tauber), Annemarie Dueringer (Christine), Richard Romanowsky, Fritz Imhoff, Dagny Servaes.

A musical biography of the life and career of the popular stage and screen star, Richard Tauber.

Availability: None

YOUNG TOM EDISON (82 mins/35mm)

U.S. M-G-M. 1940. Producer: John W. Considine Jr. Associate Producer: Orville O. Dull. Director: Norman Taurog. Screenplay: Bradbury Foote, Dore Schary and Hugo Butler. Based on Material by H. Alan Dunn. Photography: Sidney Wagner. Music: Edward Ward. Recording Director: Douglas Shearer. Art Directors: Cedric Gibbons and Harry McAfee. Set Decorator: Edwin B. Willis. Men's Costumes: Gile Steele. Women's Costumes: Dolly Tree. Film Editor: Elmo Veron. Makeup Created by Jack Dawn. Assistant Director: William Ryan.

With Mickey Rooney (Tom Edison), Fay Bainter (Mrs. Samuel Edison), George Bancroft (Samuel Edison), Virginia Weidler (Tannie Edison), Eugene Pallette (Mr. Nelson), Victor Kilian (Mr. Dingle), Bobbie Jordan (Joe Dingle), J. M. Kerrigan (Mr. McCarney), Lloyd Corrigan (Dr. Pender), John Kellog (Bill Edison), Clem Bevans (Mr. Waddell), Eily Malyon (School Teacher), Harry Shannon (Captain Brackett), Mitchell Lewis (McGuire), Marvin Stephens (Frank Allen), and Emory Parnell (Bob).

Young Tom Edison was billed as the first biography of a real-life boy that the screen had ever attempted, the boy in question being the person, perhaps erroneously, most associated with the invention of the cinema, Thomas Alva Edison. See also Edison, the Man.

Availability (16mm): Films Incorporated

YOUNGSON, ROBERT

There can be little doubt that Robert Youngson was the father of the compilation film on the history of the cinema. With features such as 30 Years of Fun, Days of Thrills and Laughter, Laurel and Hardy's Laughing 20s, and 4 Clowns, he brought to the public films which were intelligently produced, informative, and, above all, entertaining. It is obvious from his work that here was a man who genuinely loved silent films, and who loved bringing their art before a wider public.

Born in Brooklyn on November 27, 1917, Youngson was educated at New York University and at Harvard University's Graduate School of Business Administration. He entered the film industry with Pathé News in 1941, and during the War produced a number of training films for the U.S. Navy. In 1948, Robert Youngson became a writer, director and producer of shorts for Warner Bros., and among those shorts were a number which used as their basis clips from Warner Bros. features from the late silent and early sound eras.

His features, released through Twentieth Century-Fox and M-G-M, were highly successful, as a news report in Variety of October 19, 1960, indicates. When Comedy Was King cost $100,000 to produce, and during its first six months of release through Twentieth Century-Fox, it grossed $218,393 in domestic rentals. In the same news story, Youngson explained that he would go through half-a-million feet of film before arriving at a final 8,000 ft. of finished film.

Although Youngson never received an Academy Award for his feature compilations, he was the recipient of a number of nominations and awards for his Warner Bros. shorts. Blaze Busters (1950), Gadgets Galore (1955) and I Never Forget a Face (1956) were all nominated for Academy Awards, and he received Best Short Subject Oscars for World of Kids (1951) and This Mechanical Age (1954).

Robert Youngson died in New York on April 8, 1974. Since his death, many others have tried to emulate his work in the field of feature-length comedy compilations, but none has succeeded. It is not too much of an exaggeration to say that M-G-M's That's Entertainment! and That's Entertainment Part Two had their origins in Robert Youngson's 1964 feature, M-G-M's Big Parade of Comedy. Youngson was a unique talent, and all lovers of silent comedy have much for which to thank him. He took one art form, silent screen comedy, and from it created a new art form, the compilation film.

SUBJECT INDEX

This subject index is intended to provide a reference guide to films on individuals, genres, countries, and periods of film history where such items are the chief subject(s) of the production. Documentaries and compilations which contain only a brief clip of a particular performer or director, or from a specific film, have not been subject indexed under that person or film. An asterisk indicates that a film is currently in non-theatrical distribution.

ADDRESSES OF FILM COMPANIES AND DISTRIBUTORS

Academy of Motion Picture
 Arts and Sciences
8949 Wilshire Boulevard
Beverly Hills, Cal. 90211
(213) 278-8990

American Federation of the
 Arts
41 East 65th Street
New York, N.Y. 10021
(212) 988-7700

Australian Information Service
636 Fifth Avenue
New York, N.Y. 10020
(212) 245-4000

Berkeley Films
P. O. Box 4239
Sather Gate Station
Berkeley, Cal. 94704

Blackhawk Films
1235 West 5th Street
Davenport, Iowa 52808
(319) 323-9735

Blackwood Productions
58 West 58th Street
New York, N.Y. 10019
(212) 688-0930

Breakspear Films
66 Derby Street
Leek, Staffs. ST13 5AJ
England

British Film Institute
81 Dean Street
London W1V 6AA
England

Budget Films
4590 Santa Monica Blvd.
Los Angeles, Cal. 90029
(213) 660-0187 /660-0800

John Canemaker
120 West 70th Street
New York, N.Y. 10023
(212) 874-7462/586-6300

Cinema Eight
91 Main Street
Chester, Conn. 06412
(203) 526-9513

Cinema 5
595 Madison Avenue
New York, N.Y. 10022
(212) 421-5555

Contemporary-McGraw Hill
1221 Avenue of the Americas
New York, N.Y. 10020
(609) 448-1700

Corinth Films
410 East 62nd Street
New York, N.Y. 10021
(212) 421-4770

Creative Film Society
7237 Canby Avenue
Reseda, Cal. 91335
(213) 881-3887

Walt Disney Productions
500 South Buena Vista St.
Burbank, Cal. 91521
(213) 845-3141

Jackson Dube
140 East 56th Street
New York, N.Y.
(212) 751-5758

Em Gee Film Library
16024 Ventura Boulevard
Suite 211
Encino, Cal. 91436
(213) 981-5506

F.A.C.S.E.A.
972 Fifth Avenue
New York, N.Y. 10021
(212) 737-9700

The Film Center
908 12th Street N.W.
Washington, D.C. 20005
(202) 393-1205

Film-makers' Cooperative
175 Lexington Avenue
New York, N.Y. 10016

Films for the Humanities
P. O. Box 2053
Princeton, N.J. 08540
(201) 329-6912

Films Incorporated
1144 Wilmette Avenue
Wilmette, Ill. 60091
(312) 256-4730

Good Films
814 Broadway
New York, N.Y. 10003

Grove Press
196 Houston Street
New York, N.Y. 10014
(212) 242-4900

Hurlock Cine-World
13 Arcadia Road
Old Greenwich, Conn. 06870
(203) 637-4319

Images Motion Picture Rental Library
2 Purdy Avenue
Rye, N.Y. 10580
(914) 967-1102

Indiana University Audio-Visual Center
Bloomington, Ind. 47405
(812) 332-0211

Information Service of India
215 Market Street
San Francisco, Cal. 94105
(415) 982-7036

International Film Bureau
332 South Michigan Ave.
Chicago, Ill. 60604
(312) 427-4545

Ivy Films
165 West 46th Street
New York, N.Y. 10036
(212) 765-3940

Janus Films
745 Fifth Avenue
New York, N.Y. 10022
(212) 753-7100

Killiam Shows
6 East 39th Street
New York, N.Y. 10016
(212) 679-8230

Kit Parker Films
P. O. Box 227
Carmel Valley, Cal. 93924
(408) 659-4131/659-3474

Learning Corporation of America
1350 Avenue of the Americas
New York, N.Y. 10019
(212) 397-9330

Lucerne Films
7 Bahama Road
Morris Plains, N.J. 07950
(201) 538-1401

McGraw Hill see Contemporary-McGraw Hill

Macmillan/Audio Brandon
34 MacQuesten Parkway South
Mount Vernon, N.Y. 10550
(914) 664-5051

Maysles Films
250 West 54th Street
New York, N.Y. 10019
(212) 582-6050

Metro-Goldwyn-Mayer
10202 West Washington Blvd.
Culver City, Cal. 90230
(213) 836-3000

Modern Sound Pictures
1402 Howard Street
Omaha, Neb. 68102
(402) 341-8476

Ken Murray Productions
2370 Bowmont Drive
Beverly Hills, Cal. 90210

Museum of Modern Art
11 West 53rd Street
New York, N.Y. 10019
(212) 245-8900

National Cinema Service
333 West 57th Street
New York, N.Y. 10019
(212) 247-4343

National Film Board of Canada
1251 Avenue of the Americas
New York, N.Y. 10020
(212) 586-2400

National Telefilm Associates
12636 Beatrice Avenue
Los Angeles, Cal. 90066
(213) 390-3663

New Yorker Films
16 West 61st Street
New York, N.Y. 10023
(212) 247-6110

Niles Film Products
1141 Mishawaka Avenue
South Bend, Ind. 46615
(800) 348-2462

Perspective Films
369 West Erie Street
Chicago, Ill. 60610
(312) 977-4000

Phoenix Films
470 Park Avenue South
New York, N.Y. 10016
(212) 684-5910

Mary Pickford Company
9350 Wilshire Boulevard
Beverly Hills, Cal. 90212
(213) 272-9035

Pyramid Films
P. O. Box 1048
Santa Monica, Cal. 90406
(213) 828-7577

rbc films
933 North La Brea Avenue
Los Angeles, Cal. 90038
(213) 874-7330

Radim Films
17 West 60th Street
New York, N.Y. 10023
(212) 279-6653

Reel Images
456 Monroe Turnpike
Monroe, Conn. 06468
(203) 261-5022
and
10523 Burbank Boulevard
Suite 104
North Hollywood, Cal. 91601
(213) 762-0653

Roa's Films
1696 North Astor Street
Milwaukee, Wis. 53202
(414) 271-0861

Roninfilm
43 West 61st Street
New York, N.Y. 10023
(212) 757-5715

S-L Film Productions
P. O. Box 41108
Los Angeles, Cal. 90041
(213) 254-8528

Select Film Library
115 West 31st Street
New York, N.Y. 10001
(212) 594-4457

Cecile Starr
50 West 96th Street
New York, N.Y. 10025
(212) 749-1250

Sterling Educational Films
241 East 34th Street
New York, N.Y. 10016
(212) 683-6300

Swank Motion Pictures
201 South Jefferson Avenue
St. Louis, Mo. 63166
(314) 534-6300

Texture Films
1600 Broadway
New York, N.Y. 10019
(212) 586-6960

Thunderbird Films
P. O. Box 65157
Los Angeles, Cal. 90065
(213) 256-1034

Time-Life Films
Time and Life Building
New York, N.Y. 10020
(212) 586-1212

Twyman Films
329 Salem Avenue
Dayton, Ohio 45401
(513) 222-4014

U.S.C. Film Library
University of Southern
California
Division of Cinema
Film Distribution Center
University Park
Los Angeles, Cal. 90007
(213) 741-2235

United Artists 16
729 Seventh Avenue
New York, N.Y. 10019
(212) 575-4715

United Artists Television
729 Seventh Avenue
New York, N.Y. 10019
(212) 575-3000

United Films
1425 South Main Street
Tulsa, Okla. 74119
(918) 583-2681

Universal 16
445 Park Avenue
New York, N.Y. 10022
(212) 759-7500

University of California
Extension Media Center
2223 Fulton Street
Berkeley, Cal. 94720
(415) 642-0460/642-5578/
642-1340

University of Iowa
Audio-Visual Center
Iowa City, Iowa 52242
(319) 353-4717

Warner Bros.
Non-Theatrical Division
4000 Warner Boulevard
Burbank, Cal. 91505
(213) 843-6000

Wayne State University
Instructional Services Dept.
College of Lifelong Learning
2978 West Grand Boulevard
Detroit, Mich. 48202

Peter Werner
c/o 220 North Barrington
Los Angeles, Cal. 90049

Win/Kap Productions
400 West 43rd Street
New York, N.Y. 10036
(212) 279-2794